THE STRANGE DEATH OF EDMUND GODFREY

THE STRANGE
DEATH OF
EDMUND
GODFREY

PLOTS AND POLITICS IN
RESTORATION LONDON

ALAN MARSHALL

SUTTON PUBLISHING

First published in 1999 by
Sutton Publishing Limited · Phoenix Mill
Thrupp · Stroud · Gloucestershire · GL5 2BU

British Library Cataloguing in Publication Data
A catalogue record for this book is available from the British Library

ISBN 0 7509 2100 5

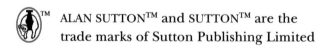 ALAN SUTTON™ and SUTTON™ are the
trade marks of Sutton Publishing Limited

Typeset in 10.5/14 pt Baskerville.
Typesetting and origination by
Sutton Publishing Limited.
Printed in Great Britain by
MPG, Bodmin, Cornwall.

Contents

List of Illustrations

Acknowledgements

As is usual with any historical work, this one has benefited from discussions with a number of friends and colleagues. Particular thanks must go to Erica Fudge and Dominic Aidan Bellenger, who took time out from their own work to read a version of the whole manuscript. I am also grateful for the help and interest of William Hughes, who offered his own insights into some of the medical matters. I would like to acknowledge the advice and encouragement given by Clyve Jones, Denis Judd, Bobby Anderson, Stuart Handley, Mark Knights, John Miller, Janet Clare, John Newsinger, Paul Hyland, Mark Annand, Kimberly Luke and Mark and Emily Smith. I also wish to acknowledge the advice and assistance given by Christopher Feeney and Sarah Moore of Sutton Publishing. The staffs of a number of libraries and institutions also gave their time and assistance, in particular the Guildhall Library, London; the British Museum, London; the British Library, London; the Bodleian Library, Oxford; the Institute of Historical Research, London; the Public Records Office at Kew; the National Library of Ireland, Dublin; the National Portrait Gallery, London; the Greater London Records Office; the BBC Written Archives Centre; the University of Bristol Library; the Senate House Library, University of London; the Wellcome Institute Library; and the Warburg Institute, London.

I should also like to acknowledge the following for permission to reproduce the portraits and images in their care: the British Museum; the National Portrait Gallery, London; the Guildhall Library, London; the Worshipful Company of Makers of Playing Cards, City of London; the British Library and Sotheby's.

Every book should have a dedicatee and in this case it is Claire Tylee, for her patience in enduring many discussions on the life of Edmund Godfrey and for her ingenious solution (which, unfortunately, I had to omit) to Godfrey and his troublesome sword.

'How often have I said to you that when you have eliminated the impossible, whatever remains, however improbable, must be the truth'

Arthur Conan Doyle, *The Sign of Four* (1890)

Good people I pray you give ear unto me,
A story so strange you have never been told.
How the Jesuit, Devil and Pope did agree
Our State to destroy and religion so old
To Murder our King
A Most Horrible Thing!
But first of Sir Godfrey his death I must sing;
Who Murder'd that knight no good Christian could be.
The truth of my story if any man doubt
W'have witnesses ready to swear it all out.

A True Narrative of the Horrid Hellish Popish Plot: The First Part (1680)

Introduction:
A Death in the Family

Primrose Hill near Hampstead was a noted beauty spot on the outskirts of London. On Thursday 17 October 1678, at around 6 o'clock in the evening, a group of fourteen men, led by the local constable of the parish of Marylebone, John Brown, approached the south side of the hill where a dead body had been reported lying among the brambles in a drainage ditch. They were uneasy with the task at hand, as various rumours had already circulated around London in the course of that week. The well-known magistrate Sir Edmund Berry Godfrey was missing, arrests were being made and talk of a new popish scandal was in the air. An informer by the name of Titus Oates had apparently revealed a deeply laid popish conspiracy that threatened the king's life. It was said that even the normally unflappable Charles II was disturbed by these events.

It was soon apparent to the men now standing next to the ditch that whatever the rumours, the man lying face down and run through with a sword really was dead and this was no trick of the light or courtier's ruse. In the gathering gloom the local parish constable and his neighbour William Lock descended into the ditch for a closer look. 'Pray God it be not Sir Edmund Berry Godfrey,' said one of them, 'for he hath been missing for sometime.' With some difficulty Brown and Lock turned over the body and pulled back the coat that had been thrown up over the head. At first both men were unable to recognise the ruddy face of the magistrate who was a well-known figure about the City. With nightfall beginning to close in and the weather turning blustery, Brown, who seems to have been a man of some intelligence and who took his office seriously, finally made his decision. It was no use leaving the body lying there and none of the men with him wished to spend the night on the Hill. With no higher authority readily available, the constable drew out the sword that had pierced the body from chest to back and he, together with his assistants, heaved the corpse of the magistrate out of the ditch. The men then laid the corpse on two staves and raised them up. One of the group gingerly picked up the hat, scabbard, belt, stick and gloves of the dead man, which were lying nearby. They then carried the body over the fields to a somewhat disreputable public house nearby, where further inquiries could be made and a coroner's inquest would sit on the strange death of Edmund Godfrey.[1]

In the seventeenth century death was a familiar matter, so what made this death so singular? In the first place the death of Edmund Godfrey had an air of mystery that could never quite be dispelled. As we shall see, it is a historical puzzle of great complexity and so it had a longevity not usually given to other contemporary deaths. The nature of Godfrey's demise, the sword through the body and the marks on the neck, the fact of his death in the course of that crisis known to contemporaries and to history as the Popish Plot, have all puzzled investigators since 1678. To his contemporaries the death of Edmund Godfrey was naturally attributed to Roman Catholics; the 'villainous papists' had murdered the Protestant magistrate as part of a wider Popish Plot and were intent upon other malicious actions if they were given the chance. Indeed, because of this apparent Catholic involvement three innocent men, Robert Green, Henry Berry and Lawrence Hill, were to die upon the scaffold.

Yet historical mysteries require more than obvious solutions to fascinate and to be sustained. In an era troubled by plots and crimes of one sort or another, this affair stood out. In fact, although the evidence first pointed to murder, then to the possibility of suicide, then again to murder, this political *cause célèbre* was muddied by a number of interested parties over the following years and was frequently re-examined and reinterpreted thereafter. The basic facts of the case appeared clear enough. Sir Edmund Berry Godfrey, a melancholy fifty-six-year-old bachelor and businessman, was also a justice of the peace of good standing in his local community. He left his home early on the morning of Saturday 12 October 1678, having recently become embroiled in the beginnings of a series of lies and exaggerations known as the Popish Plot. He disappeared at some point before 3 o'clock that day and was found five days later, on Thursday 17 October, some miles from his home and dead in a ditch at the foot of Primrose Hill. The question of who killed Godfrey or how he died was of some importance to contemporaries for, as we shall see, the magistrate's death appeared, at least in part, to confirm the truth of the Popish Plot, whose ramifications were daily becoming ever more sinister. Plans to murder the King, raise armies of Roman Catholics and return the nation to popery could all apparently be proven by the death of this one magistrate.

With regard to the case itself, however, it is arguable that most previous investigators have in fact begun at the wrong end of the problem. There is a natural tendency when examining the Godfrey affair to look for a killer, obvious or not, create a profile that fits the suspect and thus 'solve' the mystery. In reality the solution, if any can now really be found as to how Edmund Godfrey met his death, might arguably lie by looking in another direction – namely, Godfrey's background, life and personality. It is through an examination of his life that we may find clues as to his death, and subsequently gauge the impact of his death on Restoration London. In other words we need to know *who* Godfrey was before we can say *why* he had to die.

By adopting this approach, we will be recreating more than just a murder mystery. Edmund Godfrey was a real man, not a fictional character, and although he died in brutal circumstances, he was also someone with a past. His life of nearly fifty-seven years had taken him from his native Kent to Oxford in his early career, and then to London and Westminster in the Restoration period. He had his own thoughts, feelings, friends, enemies and acquaintances who knew him and his doings long before his life ended in so mysterious a fashion. Naturally, as with most men and women of that period, the evidence of Godfrey's life is often sparse and towards its conclusion can be plainly contradictory. Nevertheless, the recent discovery of a series of personal letters between the magistrate and his great friend, the Irish healer Valentine Greatrakes, has done much to place some flesh on the bare bones of the Godfrey story, and with this in mind a re-examination of the mystery of his death now seems in order.[2]

This book will attempt to place Edmund Godfrey, the man at the centre of the story, before examining the circumstances of his death. Consequently, chapters one and two are taken up with exploring Godfrey's early life, his background, family, character and business interests. The context of the Popish Plot and the momentous events in which he became embroiled form the subject of chapter three. Godfrey's last days and his part in the Popish Plot, as well as the reaction to his death, are dealt with in chapters four and five. In the case of Godfrey's last days, I have tried to stay as close as possible to the contemporary evidence, rather than rely upon modern theories, and thus to build up an image of the man as he moved towards his eventual fate. Finally, a review of the evidence relating to his demise, as well as a re-examination of the hunt for a solution to the mystery, are left to chapter six.

As one contemporary put it, for those of 'liquorish fancies, who delight in hearing strange stories', this affair is one of the strangest of the seventeenth century.[3] It is to be hoped that in this most mysterious of mysteries

the art of the reasoner should be used . . . for the sifting of details [rather] than for the acquiring of fresh evidence. The tragedy has been so uncommon, so complete, and of such personal importance to so many people, that we are suffering from a plethora of surmise, conjecture, and hypothesis. The difficulty is to detach the framework of fact – of absolute, undeniable fact – from the embellishments of theorists and reporters. Then, having established ourselves upon this sound basis, it is our duty to see what inferences may be drawn, and which are the special points upon which the whole mystery turns.[4]

CHAPTER ONE

Family and Early Life

I was by birth a gentleman living neither in any considerable height
nor yet in obscurity

Oliver Cromwell

My wife was delivered of another son the 23 Decemb[er] 1621,
between the 3 and 4 of the clock in the morning, being Sunday . . .
They named my son Edmund Berrie.

Thomas Godfrey, Domestic Chronicle

THE GODFREYS OF KENT

Edmund Berry Godfrey was born on Sunday 23 December 1621 into
the prosperous and growing family of Thomas and Sarah Godfrey. He
was the fifth son of his father's second marriage. The Godfreys
themselves were a family of ancient Kentish lineage, who had been
quietly rising among the gentry of Kent for many years.[1] Indeed, it was
said that the Godfrey family tree stretched back, with some
distinction, to one Godfrey le Falconer, himself a son of William
FitzBalderic who had been granted land in Kent by King Henry II in
the twelfth century. Like many another enterprising county family, the
Godfreys had evidently taken to Kent, settling in Lydd where a
Thomas Godfrey, a direct ancestor of our Edmund Godfrey, was
buried in 1430. The family flourished there for over two hundred
years, with many of the Godfreys becoming mayors of the local
community until at least the eighteenth century. They were held in
'good Esteem and Reputation' by most of their neighbours, and they
were also part of an existing sense of Kentish community common to
those days.[2] Indeed, Kent was a 'community of blood and feeling' in

the seventeenth century and the inhabitants Lydd personified Kentish folk.[3] A small town of fewer than 350 people, it had seen better days.[4] Nevertheless, the Godfreys retained a native pride in the county and high on the list of any Kentish family's agenda was a willingness to serve their community. So it seems to have been Edmund's grandfather, imbued with such feelings and also called Thomas, who instilled in the family a desire to make a name for itself in the seventeenth century, and under his guidance the Godfreys became conspicuous among the lesser gentry of the county and sought links with the aristocracy.[5]

His second son, and Edmund's father, who was also given the family Christian name of Thomas, was not the least conspicuous of the Godfrey family, if only because of his ability to sire enormous numbers of offspring by his two marriages.[6] It was said of Thomas, as it had been said of his father, that he was a man who served his 'generation eminently and faithfully', and he was particularly noted as a 'good lover of learning and all ingenuity'. He was certainly generous to all of his children in respect of their education, seeming to see in it the root of success in public life. Indeed, with an inbuilt family pride in all of his doings Thomas even set about keeping a record of the family, and in 1608 he began to write a domestic chronicle of his affairs that he kept, on and off, for the next forty-seven years. It is because of his labours that we are able to perceive the type of family into which the young Edmund Godfrey was born.[7]

In a number of ways, Thomas Godfrey represented many of the unusual features in the Godfrey family. Born on 3 January 1585, he was baptized six days later at Lydd church. He proved to be a man long-lived like much of his family; he was eventually to die in 1664, and was buried at Sellinge in his native Kent after a busy seventy-nine years.[8] In a crowded family home Thomas's upbringing was typical of that of a man from his social background. His father being apparently too busy to look after his second son, Thomas was farmed out to his aunt Berrie, until, aged eight, he was installed in 1593 in Challock Grammar School. This was common at the time. Many children found themselves brought up in a relative's home rather than their own during their minority. While at Challock, Thomas boarded out with yet another of the innumerable Godfrey clan and in 1599, aged fourteen, he was finally sent up to St John's College, Cambridge. There he underwent the standard education of an English gentleman of his day. Thomas Godfrey's tutors were to be Robert Spalding and Peter Benlos. Neither man was particularly prominent in college affairs, but Benlos ultimately proved to be the more interesting, not the least because he was shortly to leave England to become a Jesuit priest. He was certainly enough of an influence upon Thomas Godfrey for his former pupil to want to visit him much later at Louvaine (modern-day Leuven) in 1615. After Cambridge Thomas went on to the Middle Temple of the Inns of Court and there he spent the next three years gaining the legal training thought necessary for a gentleman to survive in the world.[9]

At this point Thomas Godfrey was rescued from the law or a legal career, or, like most of his fellow Kentish gentry, from a swift return to Kent. As the second son he could not inherit his father's estate, so as recompense he was given an introduction by his father to the patronage of Henry Howard, Earl of Northampton, Lord Warden of the Cinque Ports, Lord Privy Seal and an important figure in the political life of the state.[10] It was in the Earl of Northampton's household that Thomas Godfrey found a position as a gentleman in ordinary, where he remained for some two years. Northampton's religion had been Roman Catholic. Although he had adopted the state religion of the day under King James I, he was to return to the beliefs of his youth towards the end of his life. Thomas Godfrey's clientage to Northampton was to prove yet another of his connections with the old religion. Nonetheless in May 1609, aged twenty-four, Thomas Godfrey decided to leave his patron's immediate service and he married for the first time. His new wife was Margaret Lambarde, daughter of William Lambarde of Greenwich.[11] Thomas and his wife retired into the country, although not from an active life. Indeed, he soon purchased the manor of Hodiford in the parish of Sellinge in the Weald of Kent.

By the next year the couple had the beginnings of a young family to support and Thomas was already deep into local politics. As a Northampton client he had become a freeman and jurat of

Winchelsea in 1609, and together with one Thomas Greene, he was sent up to London to deliver a petition to his patron the Lord Warden of the Cinque Ports (Northampton) concerning the election of the mayor of the town. It must have seemed to the citizens of the town that with Thomas Godfrey as their representative their relationship with the Lord Warden would prosper accordingly, and Thomas subsequently held various other offices there. Naturally he gained some social distinction from these professional connections.[12]

Thomas's first wife Margaret died, muttering of angels, in 1611, apparently from complications during childbirth. By the following May the somewhat sentimental, but still business-like Thomas had tired of being a widower and like so many of his contemporaries he remarried, aged twenty-seven. His new wife was Sarah Isles, a young daughter of Thomas Isles of Leeds who had recently relocated to London from Yorkshire.[13] Now living in Hammersmith and Fulham, Thomas Godfrey's new father-in-law was one of the Procurators of the Arches, a high-sounding title masking a minor functionary's position, but the match was another good one for Godfrey. He took his new wife to live in Halling. There in October 1612 Thomas and Sarah set up home in a house located next to the ferry and soon began to create a prolific family. On 23 July 1613 the couple produced twins, who unfortunately died the same day. Sarah also endured a series of miscarriages in 1613 and 1614, but thereafter she continued to produce children for the rest of her life. All told, eighteen children were born to Thomas and Sarah Godfrey.[14]

In his public life, Thomas was successful enough. In April 1614, he was chosen as Member of Parliament for Winchelsea, with his patron Northampton as Lord Warden of the Cinque Ports, using his influence to find his client a seat. Thomas was apparently moderate in his politics and, being of an old country family, his clientage won him some local recognition. In fact, this was the last favour Northampton would do for Thomas because the earl died a few months later, and the parliament itself proved to be a rather abortive affair. Indeed, it went down in history as the 'Addled Parliament', although Thomas Godfrey was not a very prominent figure during its existence and his influence on national events was negligible. In the meantime, however, Thomas had acquired a taste for London life and after a year in Paternoster Row, he and his family finally settled in Grub Street in July 1614.[15]

In March 1615 a break in the routine of the family's social climbing occurred. Thomas Godfrey, with his half-brother Richard, his cousin William Epps and one Adrian Reade (to whom after some discussion, Thomas and Richard lent money in order that he could join the party) organized a visit to northern France and the Netherlands. They obtained their pass from Lord Zouch, the new Lord Warden of the Cinque Ports, and set off for France. They landed at Calais on 16 March 1615 and toured various sites. In particular, they stopped off at St Omers, where they spent Easter day at the Jesuit college and then moved on to Flanders and Douai; the latter was a noted English recusant haunt. They also visited 'Nôtre Dame de Hale', a pilgrimage site, and finally Louvaine, where Thomas Godfrey reacquainted himself with his former tutor Peter Benlos, now a Jesuit priest going by the name of Father Benson. The party then moved through Flanders and into the United Provinces, before returning home to England on 25 April 1616.[16]

Why Thomas and his friends undertook such a visit is not very clear from his 'Domestic Chronicle'. It may have been in part a holiday, or in part a business trip. Perhaps significantly, he does not say. The peculiar aspect of the trip, especially given his son's future history, was, of course, the visit to the Jesuits and Benlos. Naturally, Thomas Godfrey was neither the first nor the last Protestant to be entertained by Jesuits in these parts, but it is clear that none of the Godfreys were particularly hostile to Roman Catholicism, which, given most Englishmen's attitudes to Roman Catholics (as we shall see), at least marked them out as atypical.[17] Thomas Godfrey, Lambarde (his eldest son by his first marriage) and his most troubled offspring, Edmund, all had fairly amicable relations with Catholics both at home and abroad. We might also reflect that Thomas had served in a Catholic household, his former tutor at Cambridge had converted to Catholicism, and his patron was also a Catholic nobleman, albeit one who kept his Catholicism private. Lambarde Godfrey went on to become a lawyer, recorder of Maidstone, served on the county committee for Kent and was a member of parliament for the county in the 1650s. He went so far as to openly defend the rights of Roman Catholics in one of the Cromwellian parliaments. It may well be that some of Thomas Godfrey's apparent liberalism in religion and his religious tolerance were passed on his sons; if so, his views were taken to heart. Thomas also seems to have been something of a compromiser in his politics, coming down neither on one side nor the other in the great debates of the day, but his generous attitudes do not appear to have prevented his further election to parliament in 1627.[18]

Not that Thomas was above acquiring minor court office. Ten years earlier, in 1617, he had become a 'Sewer' of the Chamber Extraordinary. In July 1618, however, he again went abroad, this time taking his wife, her friend Mrs Anne Whetenhall and his friend Edmund Harrison with him. Again they visited St Omers, returning to England in August. Thomas then started to busy himself with land speculation. This mainly consisted of the purchase of marsh and woodland in the districts of West Hith, Hopton and Standford, as well as a house and land at Braband Lees. In December 1621 Edmund Bury Godfrey was born and in the same year his grandfather, being decayed in memory and body, finally left Lydd and went to his son Richard's home to live out his last years. As the eldest son, Peter Godfrey took much of the estate, but the three half-brothers (Peter, Richard and Thomas) agreed to split some of their father's estate in return for his maintenance.

As the round of births and deaths in Thomas and Sarah Godfrey's family continued unabated, the young Edmund Godfrey witnessed what appeared to be an endless succession of family celebrations followed by family funerals, as each child was born and more often than not died. The psychological effects of this upon the young child are difficult to assess. Social historians have argued for years over the nature of the early modern English family.[19] The growth of affective individualism (an interest in the self with a recognition of individuality and a growth in affectionate relations within the nuclear family), the pattern of child rearing and the nature of relationships within it have all been pursued with equal vigour, as we learn ever more about the internal workings of the family structure of the day. In reality, there seems little doubt that despite its share of tragedies and Thomas's travels, the Godfrey family was a relatively stable unit. Thomas would on occasion have appeared a harsh and authoritarian figure to his children, a patriarch, but he did his best for them in terms of affection, setting them up for life with as good an education and patrimony as possible. Edmund's mother, however, remains a shadowy figure, even, one suspects, to her husband, and she must unfortunately remain so, for we know little about her other than that she suffered through the birth and death of her children on a regular basis. In short, in many ways the Godfreys were a fairly typical gentry family.[20]

In 1627 Thomas once more found himself in parliament, this time for the New Romney constituency.[21] As before, although he did not excel as a parliamentarian his presence in the House eventually led to other gains. In May 1632 he was made Scout Master throughout the lath of Shepway and he was also sworn in as a justice of the peace in 1630. His last attendance in parliament was to be in April 1640. In the Short Parliament (lasting three weeks) of that year Thomas once again sat for New Romney until parliament itself was hastily dissolved in May 1640 by Charles I. Thereafter Thomas Godfrey did not seek or was not given a chance to sit in the Long Parliament that was to shape England's destiny for the next ten years.[22]

What then can we make of Edmund Godfrey's family background? It is clear that the family was apparently solid and respectable, albeit with what at the time would be seen as some slightly dubious religious leanings. Led by the enterprising Thomas, his sons made their own way in the world and chose their offices and allegiances in the conflicts of the 1640s with some care. Following the death of Edmund Godfrey in 1678, some questions about the mental health of his father were to be raised. It was said that Thomas was subject to moods of depression and as a consequence even prone to violence. Indeed his church memorial noted the 'Christian courage [with which] he overcame many infirmities of his life'. There seems little to suggest any problems in his 'Domestic Chronicle', but this document ends in the 1650s and we do know that his own father's mind had deteriorated in old age. Despite Thomas Godfrey's apparently busy life and prosperity, he may well have harboured deeper problems and secrets that the family, if they knew of them, kept to themselves.[23]

THE EARLY LIFE OF EDMUND GODFREY

Among the surviving children of Thomas and Sarah Godfrey, Edmund Berry Godfrey did not stand out as unusual except in his possession of two Christian names. Edmund was born, as already noted, on 23 December 1621 and baptized in the established church on 13 January 1622.[24] The cold winter weather and the dangers of a seventeenth-century childhood not having killed him off, he grew to be, as far as we know, a healthy child. Edmund's full and uncommon name (which was to cause such problems for writers after his death) was the result of his father's combining the names of Edmund's godfathers – Captain John Berrie, a cousin and a foot soldier in a garrison at Lydd, and a former neighbour and Thomas Godfrey's 'faithful loving friend', Edmund Harrison. Two Christian names were relatively uncommon in that period. (Indeed it seems that as an adult Edmund himself always eschewed the second one, for he would commonly sign his name 'Edmund Godfrey', rarely 'Edmund Berry Godfrey', and never 'Edmundsbury Godfrey' – as some of his early biographers would have it.) Given Thomas Godfrey's interest in fostering his children's early education, young Edmund, like his brothers before him, was launched as a boarder into the world of that 'prime nursery' of Englishmen: Westminster school.[25]

As an educational establishment, Westminster school was soon to reach its pinnacle of achievement under the headmastership of Richard Busby. However, Godfrey himself was at the school under the controversial figure of Lambert Osbaldeston.[26] In many ways Osbaldeston proved a difficult man for his superiors to deal with. In 1638, the year Godfrey finally left the school to go up to Oxford, Osbaldeston had been discovered referring to William Laud (the high and mighty Archbishop of Canterbury, and King Charles I's right-hand man) as a 'little meddling Hocus-Pocus' in a letter. As a result the headmaster was brought before the Star Chamber and, perhaps to the joy of his pupils, sentenced to have his ears nailed to a pillory while standing before his own school. Fortunately for Osbaldeston, he was able to slip away before the sentence could be carried out and hid himself until the Long Parliament took its own form of revenge on Laud.[27] Nonetheless, as an educator Osbaldeston was apparently sound enough and made Westminster school a noted place for the education of young gentlemen.

Edmund's arrival at Westminster may well have been his first real view of the bustling metropolis that was to dominate his life. Although there is little doubt that the comings and goings of the Godfrey family in and out of London must have given Edmund some sight of the capital, for the next few years he concentrated on what was happening within the school walls and in the classroom. The significance of Westminster school in the seventeenth century in educating the English élite for the professions and government cannot be underestimated.[28] In between the birch, in common use at Westminster, and the book, Edmund's education would have proceeded apace. Of his schoolfellows Edmund later only spoke of the future Lord Conway, who was his 'fellow boarder' there. We do not know whether the schoolboy Edmund was either shy or boisterous in his dealings with others, but it is clear that he was a bright pupil. Education at Westminster was well suited to fit out any young gentleman for his future life. Most of the daily routine at the school was spent upon grammar and translation, some extemporary versifying, a little geography, syntax and classical history. The school also fostered a spirit of competition. Rewards and prizes were given to the best scholars, and classical and Christian ideals were inculcated at a school that on occasion also revealed its darker side. Hard knocks, bribery between the boys and their superiors, as well as moral corruption, were not uncommon.[29]

Having completed his time at Westminster, the young Edmund Godfrey was ready for the next stage of his education. In November 1638, aged sixteen, he went up to Oxford to attend Christ Church. Oxford or Cambridge and the Inns of Court were the traditional route for any young man with ambition to make something of his life. For the aristocracy, residence at a prestigious university would enable them to become more polished and refined, and for those of less wealth or a lower social standing it allowed them to place themselves among their peers with some confidence. A career in the church, at the Bar, or as an amateur gentleman administrator in local or central government beckoned for most students. By the age of seventeen Edmund Godfrey had proved himself 'diligent and industrious'.[30] He had also begun to indulge a youthful loyalism towards a monarchy that in his later life he was to view at first hand and about which he was to be less than complimentary. Like many another young man, this early loyalty took its form in poetry and it is here we catch the first real glimpse into the character of the young Edmund Godfrey. He made a contribution to a volume of verses written to congratulate Charles I on the birth of his daughter Anne in 1637.[31] It must be said that Edmund's attempts at poetry were no worse than those of many others at a time when poetry was seen as one of the accomplished arts of a gentleman. To be able to versify for friends and relatives alike was a skill, but Edmund's contribution to the collection – a doggerel verse blandly replete with clichés and catchphrases – was at least his own work, even down to the awful pun:

> No little stone, but on these happie days
> A pyramid of marble lett men rayse;
> That should you chaunce to leave us, it might be
> A faithful STEUART of your memoire[,]
> But if at last old age consume the same,
> Weele have a grater monument; your name.[32]

It is interesting that the metaphor of birth and death, two elements common to his own siblings and family life, were mixed in his verse, but one can say little more about his poetic impulse.

Of Edmund's life at university we have few clues. Had he chosen to do so, the ever-inquisitive John Aubrey might well have revealed more, for he at least knew some of Edmund's chamber fellows; but in fact he gives little away about Godfrey's university life.[33] It is not even clear whether Edmund took his degree. It was not uncommon for men of his social status not to take a degree for a number of reasons, but there is no evidence to prove that Edmund left Oxford either disappointed or in disgrace. Perhaps both he and his parents felt that the young man had acquired sufficient polish to be going on with. In the event, he was next found in Europe completing his education on a continental tour. After his death in 1678, it was alleged that while abroad at this time Edmund had kept himself free of immorality and vice, although he associated with Catholics and had Catholic friends.[34] It was also claimed that he was true to the Protestant religion. There seems no reason to doubt this claim, but given his father's liberal attitudes, Edmund's opinions on Roman Catholicism were very likely to have been formulated at this time and were certainly more liberal than most of his class. Nor in his later life, as we shall see, could he keep these opinions hidden.

Whatever the future held for Edmund, in 1640 home beckoned him once more and he returned to an England on the eve of civil war. Yet here again there is little evidence to suggest that he took any interest in the great events of the turbulent 1640s. Instead, Edmund entered Gray's Inn at the Inns of Court in 1640, where a promising career at the Bar seemed the most reasonable prospect for this younger son of the gentry. According to one source, he stayed there long enough to arrive at that 'mature proficiency as gave him a good title' to the lawyer's garb.[35] Unfortunately, at this point he was also struck down by a serious infirmity. It was later claimed that Edmund had been forced to abandon his legal studies because of ill health and increasing deafness. How serious the latter was remains open to doubt. Was this, as some have speculated, an excuse to cover up a more serious breakdown in his personal life? One early biographer claimed that his deafness 'though not very great was always natural to him'. John Aubrey, on the other hand, claimed that Godfrey had given up the Bar because he 'conceived he should gain more by turning woodmonger', but whatever the true nature of his problem Godfrey's ailment may have been sufficiently serious to prompt his association in the 1660s with the Irish healer Valentine Greatrakes.[36] In the 1640s at least, Edmund evidently thought his deafness precluded all thought of a career at the Bar, where indeed a man needed to have all of his wits about him, and he left Gray's Inn without assuming a 'graduates robe'.[37] Yet his contemporaries make little mention of his deafness in the later stages of his life. If it did remain troublesome, then Edmund's partial loss of hearing could perhaps account for some of the character traits that soon began to be observed in him. He became a rather straightlaced and melancholy young man who favoured solitariness over 'good company'. Later on, some contemporaries began to think his disposition odd if not downright peculiar, and his appearance was to be memorably described by Roger North as 'black, hard favoured, tall, stooping . . . and . . . commonly wiping his mouth and looking [up]on the ground'.[38] For whatever reason(s), Edmund in his maturity became a very grave, gloomy and somewhat querulous individual, who may have believed that he had inherited his father's tendency towards depression.

Be that as it may, Edmund's eccentricities certainly became more pronounced as he grew older and he was more set in his ways. It was alleged, for example, that he found crowds 'very irksome', as well he might if his hearing were impaired, and his association with men who were socially beneath him shocked many of his acquaintances. Godfrey, it was said, was often seen playing bowls in the company of footmen and 'ordinary' folk.[39] All of this savours of a man who became merely eccentric or simply careless of the normal social conventions of the day. There were to be few individuals around him in his personal life to curb such eccentric behaviour. According to one of the social conventions of the day he was in a minority (albeit a growing one): Edmund Godfrey remained unmarried and (as far as we can tell) never sought a wife for the remainder of his life. This was not that uncommon for the time. It may be that as a younger son he was never lucky enough to catch an heiress, and this resulted in him being among the one in six men (according to the statistics) who were still unmarried in their fifties. For whatever reason, Edmund Godfrey was never 'clogged with a wife and family'.[40] One of his early biographers, desperately attempting to give Edmund the state of martyrdom he felt he surely deserved, believed Godfrey to be completely celibate. This may or may not have been true. Naturally his sexual life remains, like many another in the period, obscure, and there were women, or for that matter men, available, especially in

London, had he wanted them. However, unlike his father and grandfather, Edmund Godfrey was to gain neither a wife nor children in whom he could confide or to whom he could turn for comfort when troubled.[41]

With the legal world closed to him, apparently for good, Edmund Godfrey retired to the countryside to rethink his future. 'Idleness being always a burthen to him', and with his busy father and brothers Michael and Benjamin as his example, he needed an occupation. The outbreak of civil war in 1642 did not seem to raise the martial spirit in the 21-year-old Edmund. Indeed the Godfreys, sensibly enough, mostly seem to have remained out of the firing line over the eight-year period of the wars. We know that Edmund for one appears to have remained away from London during the war years. According to Richard Tuke, Edmund still had some 'unhealthiness in his body' and for this reason settled in the country.[42] He was involved in a legal dispute over some land in Stevenage in 1647, but this is one of the few traces of him in the 1640s.[43] Edmund's part in the great conflicts of the era, if he ever played one, has sunk without trace. His brothers Michael and Benjamin were certainly kept out of harm's way, and perhaps Edmund followed a similar course. Benjamin remains a shadowy figure, although long-lived – he died in 1704 aged seventy-three. A businessman for much of his life, he apparently held similar political views to his brother Michael. Indeed Michael, about whom we know much more, was eventually parcelled off into an eight-year apprenticeship under Major Thomas Chamberlain of Leadenhall Street, but in August 1647 both he and his friend Thomas Papillon went abroad as a consequence of the troubles of the Civil War in England. Michael Godfrey was employed for some seven years as a factor at Morlaix and Rouen in France. His 'economy, attention, steadfastness, hopefulness and courtesy' did him no harm, and in the best tradition of such tales, he returned to London and in January 1655 married his master's daughter Anne Mary Chamberlain at St Dionis Backchurch. His apprenticeship completed in spectacular style, he was admitted to the Mercer's Company and in 1659 called to its livery. In 1681 Michael was to be labelled by his enemies as a 'stark Ph[anatic] but goes to church'[44] and we will meet him again, but it is worth noting at this point that he apparently had a shrewd eye for business. As for Edmund in the late 1640s, the prospect of being a self-made man of business in London seems also to have had its appeal, and it is to this next phase of his life that we must now turn.

CHAPTER TWO

The London Woodmonger

If [I] wo'd be throw paced [I] might be somebody among them, But
I fear [I have] a foolish & narrowe conscience, and that spoyles [me]
and all that use it.

Edmund Godfrey

A MAN OF BUSINESS

Whether by accident or design, Edmund Godfrey found a congenial
role for his talents in business. He took up the trade of woodmonger
and coal merchant in London in 1650 by entering into a partnership
with James Harrison (a relative of his father's dearest friend Edmund
Harrison). As they were armed with an estate of some £1,000 per
annum, both men were able to invest in a yard near Dowgate in the City
of London.[1] Godfrey at least proved himself a skilful businessman and
the business quickly prospered. His relations with Harrison were good
and the eventual separation of the partners was an amicable one, made
the more so by the fact that Harrison had married Jane Godfrey, one of
Edmund's sisters. It is possible that Harrison was initially the senior
partner in the business and that Edmund learned his trade from him.
When Harrison retired from the firm, however, Edmund took it over
and made it his own. His first move was an ambitious one. Evidently
seeing better opportunities in the city of Westminster (where indeed
there was less competition in his new trade) than the City of London,
he moved his livelihood into the parish of St Martin's-in-the-Fields in
1659 and restarted the business as a timber merchant and coal dealer.

On the eve of this new business venture, what sort of man was
Edmund Godfrey? His person at this time was described by Richard

Tuke, his first true biographer, as of a 'stature extenuated some what above the common size of ordinary tall men: the habit of his body spare, far from corpulencie; but well set and exactly proportioned. He was indeed (as most tall men are) somewhat inclined to stoop in his going, which might be occasioned by the thoughtfulness of his musing head.'[2] There are in fact available three reliable portraits of Godfrey from his years in London.[3] Two were painted just after his death, but one, a portrait miniature by John Hoskins of Godfrey in 1663, aged forty, and painted when he had been in business for a number of years, is possibly the most significant. This miniature shows a rather different image from the careworn figure generated by the Whig propaganda machine after Godfrey's death. It is a portrait of a rather heavy-faced man with curly brown hair worn down to the shoulders; he had yet to adopt the fashionable long wig. A small goatee beard sits upon his chin under a prominent nose and slightly pursed mouth. Heavy-lidded eyes stare off into the middle distance past the viewer and the face is a stern rather than a kindly one. Otherwise it is the portrait of a man of the City and of business who has made good in London, dressed as he is in a fine lace collar, lawn shirt and rich, black-patterned doublet. Whatever the truth of his personal life at the time, the fact is that Edmund Godfrey had soon made himself a noted figure in the bustling streets of London.

London, the home of 350,000 souls in 1659, was in fact two cities, London and Westminster; or three, if one included the growing suburb of Southwark with its stews, brothels and playhouses.[4] The metropolis was just emerging from the trauma of the Civil War in which it had played such a notable part, and in 1659 it was still the centre of Republican government. The Lord Protector, Oliver Cromwell, who had died on 3 September 1658, was succeeded by the brief, but turbulent, rule of his son Richard Cromwell. As Godfrey was setting up shop in the parish of St Martin's-in-the Fields in 1659, this rule was coming to an end. The year 1660 would see the ushering in of the Restoration under King Charles II, and in the streets of the metropolis there would be opportunities aplenty for the enterprising businessman.

London in the late 1650s and early 1660s still retained a somewhat medieval flavour, although new building and the shift of the élite population to the West End in order to surround the court based at Whitehall Palace had already begun.[5] Indeed the old city's population had already outgrown its walls and was gradually spreading west, east and north. Edmund Godfrey was to take advantage of this general movement. Earlier in the century James I and his son Charles I, fearful of any metropolitan expansion beyond their control, had singularly failed in their attempt to prevent the enterprising Londoners from expanding their residences any further.

Architecturally, however, it was a mixed metropolis that greeted the eye. London's skyline was dominated by the bulky, recently refurbished, but now sadly neglected cathedral of old St Paul's and hundreds of other obscure, and not so obscure, church spires. Below this lay densely packed houses and streets with the city clustered along the banks of the Thames from the low dens and shanty houses of the East End around the Tower to the green Moorfields stretching beyond Westminster. In the West End fine townhouses were beginning to replace the rather old-fashioned and decayed palaces once used by the aristocracy and courtiers. However, many of London's buildings, their top storeys leaning outwards and seeming to cramp the noisy streets below, were also made of wood and represented a great fire hazard. Despite this, the metropolis remained a great and noble city. However, for the more puritan members of the population, London represented a new Babylon, a den of iniquity, merely waiting for the justice of God to fall upon it, which, they noted with some perverse satisfaction, it finally did when struck by plague in 1665 and the Great Fire in 1666. For others London took on a different guise, as an 'immense crowd and hurry and bustle of business and diversion . . . the noble churches, and the superb buildings of different kinds, agitate, amuse, and elevate the mind . . . Here a young man of curiosity and observation may have a sufficient fund of present entertainment, and may lay up ideas to employ his mind in an age.'[6]

Economically, the metropolis was something of a boom town. Finance jostled alongside industry, and the smoke and fumes of the town became such that John Evelyn was later moved to write a tract against them in his *Fumifugium: or the Inconveniencie of the Aer and Smoak of London Dissipated.*[7] Parts of London were also densely overcrowded. With the end of the civil wars hordes of disbanded soldiers and their families came to the city, adding to the already high annual migration into the packed streets. Plague and other diseases periodically eliminated some of these dense pockets of humanity, but migrants still flocked to the capital seeking wealth, education, opportunity, a new life and invariably finding the streets paved with a less salubrious substance than gold. It was a city 'wither all sorts reside, noble and simple, rich and poor, young and old from all places and countries, either for pleasure . . . or for profit'.[8] In fact, the citizens of the capital were busy with both native and immigrant energy. In one of the great pictorial poems of the era, John Gay described London life in 1716 in a way that gives a flavour of what Edmund Godfrey would have found in his daily rounds of the metropolis.[9] Among the forest of houses, alleyways, streets and courts, the smells and sounds of the great crowds of city life bustled from dawn to dusk. At dawn:

> Industry wakes her busy sons
> Full charg'd with News the breathless hawker runs:
> Shops open, Coaches roll, Carts shake the Ground,
> And all the streets with passing cries resound.[10]

With the sun's rising a raucous noise began, amplified in the narrow streets by the movement of carts, coaches and sedan chairs all crowding each other over the cobbles and making life dangerous for pedestrians.[11] The different street cries also marked the seasons in the town: the 'bounteous product of the Spring! / Sweet-smelling Flow'rs . . . And when June's Thunder cools the sultry skies, /E'ven Sundays are prophan'd by Mackrell cries'.[12] As John Gay noted, one could also:

> . . . remark each Walker's diff'rent face,
> And in their look their various Bus'ness trace.
> The Broker here his spacious Beaver wears,
> Upon his Brow sit Jealousies and Cares;
> Bent on some Mortgage, to avoid Reproach,

He seeks bye Streets, and saves th'expensive coach.
Soft, at low Doors, old Letchers tap their Cane,
For fair Recluse, who travels Drury-lane.
Here roams uncomb'd, the lavish rake, to shun
His Fleet-street Draper's everlasting Dun.[13]

While the city was busy during the day, other forces roamed its streets, alleys and courts at night. Honest people went home at sundown and left the night-time to those of more curious tastes and less respectability. Gay noted that the walker at night should:

Let constant Vigilance thy Footsteps guide,
And wary Circumspection guard thy side;
Then shalt thou walk unharm'd the dang'rous Night,
Nor need th' officious Link-Boy's smoaky Light.
Thou never wilt attempt to cross the Road,
Where Alehouse Benches rest the Porter's Load . . .
Let not thy vent'rous Steps approach too nigh,
Where gaping wide, low steepy Cellars lie; . . .
Though you through cleanlier Allies wind by Day,
To shun the Hurries of the publick Way,
Yet ne'er to those dark Paths by Night retire;
Mind only Safety, and contemn the Mire.[14]

London after dark could be a dangerous place. The era remained a violent one. Civil wars and political plots were one side of life, but Londoners in particular were prone to violence. In a vigorous, bustling city, both gentleman and commoner invariably carried weapons and were occasionally forced to use them. In the crowded taverns, inns and gin shops where both men and women gathered to drink, tempers were easily lost and passions were often ungovernable.[15]

Lighting in London streets at this time was minimal. Although each householder was meant in theory to place a lantern outside their dwelling, few did so and when the sun went down shadows and darkness covered the metropolis. Thievery and violence in this darkness was commonplace. Understaffed, underequipped and untrained nightwatchmen often fought running battles with groups of drunken aristocrats. Nor were violent mobs unknown. In Drury Lane and elsewhere many of the city's prostitutes openly plied their trade with passersby. Consequently, after dark there were a number of follies the unwary traveller could fall prey to if lost in the shadows of the city's streets. In an age of uncertainty, crime and poverty stalked London alongside industry and pleasure. Amid the squalor and the misery, however, a burgeoning population, honest hard-working folk for the most part, were wary but enterprising citizens of the greatest city in Europe.

Edmund Godfrey was soon among the most enterprising. He made his first home in 1659 in Greenes Lane, part of Hartshorne Lane, in the parish of St Martin's-in-the-Fields, a relatively new area that had been developed in 1628.[16] Godfrey rented a house, yard and wharf. The lane itself was a long, low, dingy passage that ran down to the Thames and lay at the south-east corner of Charing Cross, off the main thoroughfare. It is no longer in existence, having been demolished in 1760, but it can be traced on contemporary maps. It was only one of a number of narrow streets and alleyways in the area and not that notable, although Ben Jonson had apparently lived there as a child. Hartshorne Lane was known for being 'much clogged and pestered with carts', mainly plying their trade from the wharves and sheds at its end to Charing Cross and the Strand, and back again to the wharves.[17] John Gay later described the carts:

> . . . issuing [forth] from steep Lanes, the Collier's steeds
> Drag the Black Load; another cart succeeds,
> Team follows Team, Crouds heap'd on crouds appear,
> And wait impatient, 'till the road grow clear.[18]

Hartshorne Lane, like many of Westminster's alleys and lanes off the main road, was a gloomy affair, poorly lit, airless and narrow, although still densely inhabited. It was caught between the palatial surroundings of Northumberland House, with its once fashionable architecture, courts and gardens, and the rising clamour of

Hungerford market, selling its wares of fruit and vegetables – although the latter had recently been losing business to the much more profitable Covent Garden on the other side of the Strand.[19] A number of alleys and courts led into and out of the lane, and its residents numbered the occasional professional (two doctors in 1663), small tradesmen, businessmen, carpenters, bricklayers, stone masons and cordwainers, most of whom had connections with the royal palace of Whitehall, which lay just past Charing Cross.[20] Many tenants lived in former sheds and warehouses now converted into houses, or in the more old-fashioned brick houses and numerous courts. Being enterprising souls, all of them took some care to build further additions to their property, with or without the permission of the local landlord. The landlord with overall responsibility for the area was the Hospital of the Holy and Undivided Trinity of East Greenwich, founded in 1614 by none other than Thomas Godfrey's old patron, Henry Howard, Earl of Northampton. Northampton having died in 1614, the hospital's trustees, the Worshipful Company of Mercers took over. The company numbered among its ranks Michael Godfrey and his good friend Thomas Papillon.[21] An inn called the Christopher had also once stood in the lane and this large establishment had originally been the reason for the lane's existence.

Sometime before 1660 the wharf and timberyard at the foot of the lane came under the control of Robert Scawen of Horton Place, Buckinghamshire. His twenty-one-year lease on the wharf and the adjoining tenement he promptly let out to Edmund Godfrey. Scawen died in 1669, but not before assigning the lease to his tenant. In fact, Godfrey's home was a 'very faire new brick house' in 1663, no doubt long and thin as was the fashion of its neighbours of the day. It was still standing in 1848 and had (ironically enough considering its former owner's eventual fate) been turned into a police station at some point.[22] Godfrey, by 1663 an independent, middle-aged bachelor, lived and traded there, although he was never far from his relatives. For a time James Harrison and his new wife were to live with him in the house, and his brothers Michael and Benjamin were also trading not far away in the City of London.[23] Like his neighbours, Edmund Godfrey eventually undertook some of his own building work in the area in 1664 and 1671. In 1671 the result evidently annoyed his neighbour Mrs Brocas so much that she made a complaint. She claimed that the work allowed the carriage of 'dung and [the] running of horse piss from . . . [Godfrey's] stable through a door and a passage which he hath lately made through a brick wall which was built for separation'.[24] Given Godfey's connections with the landlords, Mrs Brocas complained in vain and she lost her case. In any event she soon had other matters to think about, for her husband fell into debt and by May 1673 he was lodged in the King's Bench prison. By November 1677 their tenement was empty and in January 1678 their lease too was granted to Edmund Godfrey.[25]

As a bachelor, Godfrey only needed a small home establishment, but there were already signs of his growing prosperity. Gregory King, writing in the 1690s, claimed that the average number of servants the household of a man such as Godfrey should possess was around six.[26] Most of them would live on the premises and would consist mainly of maidservants, a cook, housekeeper with, for the very rich, perhaps a butler, coachman and a porter. Godfrey seems not to have indulged in such luxuries, or perhaps being a bachelor he thought it cheaper to live with some three servants to perform all of the necessary functions of the household. All of his later servants were to be important witnesses to their employer's last days – the aged Henry Moor, who became Godfrey's clerk in the 1670s; Elizabeth Curtis, the maidservant; and Mrs Judith Pamphlin, a somewhat nosy and gossipy widow who seems to have acted as Godfrey's housekeeper and perhaps his cook.

Edmund Godfrey's house was a business address as much as a home, and the yard attached to the property enabled him to become one of the most successful businessmen in the parish of St Martin's-in-the-Fields. Godfrey's main business was coal rather than wood, perhaps reflecting the fact that at this period the coal trade was becoming a boom market in London and Westminster.[27] Coal was taken from the fields of Durham and Northumberland, and passed through a variety of hands from pit to hearth. The London market and London hearths were part of the staple of the coal trade. Fortunes could be made from coal, as fuel and warmth were vitally important in the life of the average seventeenth-century Londoner. The wholesalers, who were woodmongers and merchants such as Edmund Godfrey, were the middlemen of the trade. They acted as brokers, buying the coal from the shippers and selling it on to smaller traders and even directly to consumers. Although London's staple fuel had originally been wood, the gradual infiltration of coal into the London market had begun in the sixteenth century and woodmongers were well placed to exploit it. By 1605 they were incorporated as the Woodmongers' Company. As it exerted a monopoly over street transport and also took great care to exploit its position as best it could, the company became a powerful voice in City affairs.

There is no doubt that the woodmongers' general reputation was poor. There were constant wrangles between the Woodmongers' Company, the Carmen, who were used to carry the fuel and the Warfingers, whose wharves they used – unless a woodmonger possessed his own. Ultimately these divisions left a bitter legacy, for although the woodmongers' strength made them important for a time their victory proved to be short-lived. In any case most woodmongers and coal merchants were thought to be naturally dishonest and were looked upon unfavourably by London citizens. They were regularly abused and accused, and in return they engaged in fixing prices and engineering shortages to make a profit. In 1673 the anonymous author of *The Grand Concern of England Explained* complained that 'I need not declare how the subjects are abused in the price of coal and how many poor have been starved for want of Fewels by reason of the horrid prices put upon them; especially in time of war, either by the merchant, or the Woodmonger, or between them both'.[28] Of course, the Woodmongers' Company denied these accusations, but its members increasing individual wealth could not be denied. London citizens, of course, naturally continued to believe the worst of them. They claimed prices were rigged and designed to bring in profit while they suffered shortages. In 1664 the court of Aldermen even set up a committee to inquire into the price of coal and the abuses of weight and measure. They found that the woodmongers had set the prices at their pleasure, bought up wharves in and about the city and leased them out under certain conditions, fixing prices and cheating in good measure into the bargain. The winter of 1666, however, caused real problems for the Woodmongers' Company. As a result of the Great Fire of September 1666 and the very harsh winter, not to mention the continuing war with the Dutch, the price of coal rocketed. Complaints rose in proportion. The House of Commons finally took a hand and established a committee to investigate abuses in the trade.[29]

Edmund Godfrey was deeply involved in this world, and he made such a name for himself that he was elected Master of the Woodmongers' Company in the 1660s.[30] He was proving to be a shrewd man of business. He was willing to put in long hours to make a handsome profit, and he had the correct proportions of gravity, shrewdness and judgment necessary for success. In 1667, however, it emerged that despite his alleged charitable nature (about which we shall shortly learn), he was not above making a profit from the poor by selling them overpriced coal. Godfrey himself was summoned before the Commons Committee touching Coals and Fuels in January 1667, and, as the Master of the Company, it was Godfrey who was found guilty (with others) of buying coal at 41s to 47s per chaldron (= 36 bushels) and selling it at 3s per bushel to the poor, making a good profit in the process. Edmund was doubly damned because most of his business lay in Westminster, and so it was thought that he had suffered little loss in the Great Fire. He was also in a doubly difficult position as Master of the Woodmongers' Company. By December 1667, after a long wrangle between the Commons and the company, the woodmongers' charter was finally withdrawn.[31] Some years of normal prices followed and the Carmen escaped from the woodmongers' control in the process, but the latter still formed a powerful company, especially as the tax on coal was being used to pay for the rebuilding of London after the Great Fire. In 1673 a further attempt was made to regulate the abuses of the trade and in response the woodmongers went to the press. They published a pamphlet in which they stated their case. In this broadside it was noted that 'The Woodmongers have most of them laid out great sums of money in building houses, stables and other buildings and the rest have taken wharves and houses at great rents, and all of them have been at great charges'. Such mouthings did them little good and problems continued until 1680 when a new act was passed to regulate the trade.[32]

But what were Edmund Godfrey's characteristics as a businessman? From the slender evidence available, it seems that, like many another in his trade, he was somewhat aggressive in his dealings with others. He certainly proved reluctant to allow bad debts to grow too high. As a result he made frequent forays into the murky legal world of the Chancery in search of debtors. Indeed his attempts to have the king's own physician Sir Alexander Fraser arrested for debt in 1669 were to backfire on him in a spectacular fashion.[33] Fraser complained to the king and as a result Godfrey ended up in custody for seven days. We catch a glimpse of Godfrey in the midst of this conflict as an obstinate, somewhat dogmatic man, who stood by the law he knew and claimed to stand for people's liberties. Godfrey's fairly immoderate statements and his refusal to admit he was in the wrong in this case did him no good at all. As a king's servant, Fraser possessed immunity from prosecution for debt, although that did not stop Godfrey's continued attempts to justify his actions even when it was obvious he would gain more by keeping quiet. This incident fuelled his reputation for arrogance. On a visit to France in 1668 such an attitude had apparently already taken him close to being whipped for his pains.[34] Chancery cases, as well as the sharp practices of hoarding and price fixing, were therefore known to Edmund Godfrey and in general seem to have been regarded by him as part of a successful business life.

During these years Godfrey endured other vexed relationships. His nephew Godfrey Harrison had been brought into the business as his assistant in 1667.[35] By the late 1660s Godfrey was spending some of his time in local politics, for he had been nominated as alderman in Farringdon Ward in 1664, but he was discharged on claiming a bodily infirmity and fined as a result.[36] In 1666 he was nominated again, but was not elected. He also staved off his election as sheriff. In the course of all of these distractions, Godfrey seems to have left his nephew to control the business. Harrison was unused to such responsibility and the business went into a severe decline. Godfrey

Harrison's part in his uncle's affairs ended with bad feelings. By January 1671 an 'unnatural kindness' existed between the pair.[37] Numerous cases were launched in Chancery by Godfrey against his nephew, but they came to naught. Edmund Godfrey struggled to regain control of his business and remained very bitter over the affair. Not only did he lose some £4,000 from his own pocket (a fortune in contemporary terms) but he felt betrayed by a member of his own family.[38]

However, other Godfrey business affairs were profitable enough. He had suffered some property losses during the course of the Great Fire, but he had engaged in a number of land deals since the 1650s to tide him over the inevitable bad patches in his trade.[39] In November 1657 he had purchased some leases, and inherited others from one of his mother's relatives' old properties in Stanwell. These included barns, stables, an orchard, as well as gardens in the manor. A house, water mill and arable lands also came into his possession. They were promptly rented out to tenants. He bought the local inn, the Swan in Fulham, as well as lands around it. Between 1674 and 1676 he also purchased the lease to some freehold houses in Blue Cross Street, and there were even some deals in property around Brewer's Yard on the eve of his death.[40] On a wider front the Godfrey business was engaged in a number of transactions with his friend, the healer Valentine Greatrakes in Ireland.[41] Land in Ireland was to be purchased from James, Duke of York (the king's brother) through the duke's servants Charles and Matthew Wren. Godfrey's connections also extended to businessmen in Bristol and Dublin, while both he and Greatrakes were to invest in a rather dubious saltworks owned by Sir William Smith on the Medway. This latter deal came unstuck in 1667 when the Dutch, during their raid on the navy base in the Medway, burned the works to the ground. All in all, however, Edmund Godfrey, like many another London businessman of his day, was hardworking, usually shrewd and occasionally just a little beyond the legal limits of good business practice. This was ironic, for at the same time as he was making a profit he was also beginning to establish a name for himself as a man of the law and as justice of the peace in his parish.

THE PARISH OF ST MARTIN'S-IN-THE-FIELDS: GODFREY, PLAGUE, CRIME AND THE VESTRY

In the later seventeenth century Godfrey's home parish of St Martin's-in-the-Fields was one of the largest and most successful in England.[42] The parish's population was on the increase, as it was in much of Westminster; the area was described in the 1690s as 'wondrous prosperous' and by that stage some 20,000 people were estimated to be crowding into its streets and its 5,000 dwellings. The growth of the population could be witnessed in the church, the focus of parish life. St Martin's Church, a spacious building constructed in the 1540s, had seating for some 400 parishioners, although John Evelyn had seen congregations of 1,000 or so cramming into its pews and aisles.[43] If the church was crowded the parish considered itself second to none, and it was certainly one of the most prestigious in the country. Located next door to Whitehall Palace and the court, it provided homes and lodgings for innumerable courtiers, ministers and civil servants. In addition to this select group of parishioners, the close proximity of St Martin's to the court also meant a profitable living for any cleric who occupied its pulpit. He alone could expect to receive £900 to £1,000 a year from his office.[44]

The traditional social composition of the parish has been seen by most historians as one of aristocracy, courtiers, gentry and their dependents, but the parish also contained large numbers of respectable tradesmen and small businessmen, as well as growing numbers of the poor and destitute.[45] St Martin's was a centre for consumer goods and services. Food, clothes and other retail goods were produced to satisfy the many wealthier individuals and their families who lived there. Many of the small tradesmen in the parish had moved out of the City of London itself because of its high rents and lack of space, only to turn up in Westminster. Other immigrants also seized the opportunities in the area. They ranged from the prospective servant to the poor labourer. Yet a darker side to the prosperity in the parish of St Martin's also existed. Overcrowded, airless and often verminous houses were packed with the poor and destitute. Such slums also brought with them the perennial problems of disease, crime and poverty. In this respect St Martin's after dark was not unlike the rest of London. As we have seen, respectable folk kept to their houses after dark, or if they did venture out at night they went in carriages, aided by link-boys carrying torches to light their way through the oncoming darkness.[46]

At the heart of parish life lay its government and in particular the place where the parish met: the vestry. During the Restoration and for some time afterwards the vestry of St Martin's was a thinly disguised oligarchy.[47] It had the reputation for strong and efficient government within its boundaries and the parish officers were also kept under tight control. The self-perpetuating and self-selected vestry of St Martin's was intent upon law-abiding order and conformity. Edmund Godfrey made his first appearance at its board in January 1660 and thereafter was regularly involved in its affairs. The select vestry (they were very careful about whom they allowed to sit at the vestry table) had been confirmed by the events of 1662 in which Godfrey also played his part.[48] In that year a new instrument had enabled the interested parties to regulate the vestry sufficiently to cut down the troubling influence of dissent and outside interference. Despite this, the parish was still noted for the presence of a small dissenting congregation.

Although he was a member of the vestry almost from the moment of his arrival in the parish, Edmund Godfrey never actually took up a parish office himself. Indeed he seems to have deliberately avoided office on a number of occasions, mainly due to the expense involved rather than any lack of a sense of duty. Although it remains surprising that given his prestigious position he was able to avoid such appointments, in other spheres he was busy enough in its dealings to become known as the 'mouth of the vestry' when it dealt with superior authorities. He was the man to whom the other members of the vestry turned whenever they had any problems with their religious and political masters.

In general, Godfrey's main interest in parish affairs turned on the problems of poverty and crime. Some parts of London and Westminster were, as the novelist Henry Fielding was to note in 1751, 'a vast wood or forest in which the thief may harbour with as great security as wild beasts do in the deserts of Arabia and Africa'.[49] Disreputable areas had always existed within the metropolis and naturally rookeries of vice and poverty were to be found in Edmund Godfrey's own parish. Indeed between St Martin's Church, Bedford Street and Chandos Street there was one such rookery known in Ben Jonson's day as the Bermudas and later as the Carribbee Islands.[50] Within such areas the problem of poverty was rife. Families were sometimes packed into old, unstable structures with little to live on and so turned to crime or the parish relief in order to survive. The local authority responsible for such problems set up systems of relief under the provisions of the act of 1601, and the dreaded workhouse was also constructed to deal with those poor who were thought worthy enough to benefit from it. The parish authorities took to punishing the incorrigible, reckless or criminal elements, or simply sending them back from whence they came. Edmund Godfrey, in his capacity as a parish benefactor, helped the needy through charity or poor relief. In September 1677, for example, he supported Thomas Beare's claim that as a poor and disabled ex-sailor he should be given a pension of 2*s* per week.[51] Yet Godfrey also had a reputation for great severity against vagabonds and criminals in general. In fact this interest in the problem of the poor had led to his support for the building of a new workhouse in the parish in 1664–5. Perhaps typically where Godfrey was concerned, after the building was finished it became the subject of a minor scandal in 1672, for the poorhouse authorities were accused of letting out the workhouse vaults, designed for interments, as a wine cellar! The Bishop of London himself was forced to intervene to ensure that the practice was stopped. This intervention appears to have been ineffective in the face of local resistance, for by 1683 the locals were letting out the whole structure for business purposes and a replacement was not to be constructed until 1724.[52]

According to Edmund Bohun, to enter upon an employment as a justice of the peace, as Edmund Godfrey did, would 'occasion [a man] much loss of time, some expense and many enemies'.[53] The hours were long and work in an urban parish could be hard with little reward. The city justice, much like his rural brethren, was a mixture of administrator, judge, arbitrator and detective. In addition, the justice of the peace in the urban environment of London had perhaps to face more squalor, violence and problems than most. To match the many difficulties he would face, Bohun noted, a good justice of the peace needed a number of attributes for success. These ranged from natural abilities, such as apprehension, judgment and memory, to civil qualities of a competent estate, good reputation and a reasonable education. The justice also had to have a religious disposition as well as the usual moral qualities of prudence, patience, sobriety, industry, courage and honesty. Few justices of the period lived up to such ideals, but Edmund Godfrey seems to have tried harder than most. In his time Godfrey gained the reputation of a useful and active justice of the peace with a strong sense of duty. Others were not so conscientious. The role of the 'trading justices' – men who abused their office and grew rich on bribes and extortion – was not unknown in London at this time.[54] Normally, however, the justice held a responsible position in society, and given his power it was important he acted fairly in his dealings.

As a keeper of the peace, the justice would be able to issue warrants against suspected persons, conduct preliminary inquires into criminal cases, deal with minor misdemeanours such as drunkenness and swearing, and take from more serious offenders recognizances or sureties for good behaviour. The justice was a local administrator: he could take certain oaths, supervise the parish officers and present them for any negligence at the next assizes. In conjunction with his fellow justices, a justice of the peace such as Edmund Godfrey could become even more powerful. Together they could grant licenses, prosecute recusants, make provision for the maintenance of illegitimate children and deal with the day-to-day life of the people in their jurisdiction. In regard to the complaints that came before him, the justice usually had three options. First, he could attempt to mediate and use his local influence, authority and standing to resolve the problem. Secondly, he could bind the defendant over until the sessions. Thirdly, for certain offences he could make a summary conviction and punish by whipping, fining or committal to an institution. More serious crimes, such as felonies, were usually dealt with more formally through the courts. Crimes that were misdemeanours allowed the justice more flexibility of response and were in fact far more common than the formal prosecutions. Thus, the justice of the peace could by his actions provide guidance to his parishioners and dispense justice when necessary.

Given his background, Godfrey's involvement with the Commission of the Peace for Westminster and Middlesex seems to have been almost inevitable. Most of his early biographers believed that his work as a magistrate was in his blood, for both his father and brothers were also justices.[55] To be included in the commission of the peace brought with it social status as well as an opportunity to associate with the great and the good, and nowhere was this more true than in the commission for Westminster. As the court was located in its precincts and the area itself was the home for many prominent figures, Westminster had its own commission of the peace. In fact, the precincts of the court were policed by being allocated to one justice in particular, the 'Court Justice', and this was the semi-official post that Edmund Godfrey soon came to occupy.[56] It was this justice who could be relied upon by the palace authorities for prompt and immediate action in an emergency, and the office needed to be occupied by an especially energetic, able and reliable man. Given that Godfrey appeared to be all of these things, he seemed a suitable choice. We can also trace some of Godfrey's work as a justice of the peace through the quarter sessions records of Middlesex. For example, in July 1673 James Mullet, a gardener, was fined for calling Godfrey a 'knave'. In May 1675 William Smith of Warwick Street was brought before the justices for 'directing a scandalous paper against Sir Edm[und] Godfrey upon punishing Hester Symonds in Westminster House [of] Correction'.[57] Some individuals were clearly rather resentful of the magistrate's high-handed manner.

Edmund Godfrey's influence in the parish and in London had been at its height during the plague year of 1665.[58] St Martin's on the eve of the plague was its usual overcrowded self, with pockets of poverty, vice and bad housing that were to prove a prime breeding ground for the disease that now emerged and multiplied. Westminster appeared healthy until around May 1665, when evidence of the disease in the squalid area of Long Ditch next to the abbey brought forth its first plague victims. The juxtaposition of palace and slum soon began to have its effect. By July deaths in the area around St Martin's Church had risen fivefold and the court of Charles II, seeing discretion as the better part of valour, moved out to Oxford. St Martin's was as hard hit as anywhere else in the metropolis, and the week of 5–12 September alone saw 214 deaths in the parish from the plague. A large pest house was established in the parish at Clay Fields in Soho Gardens, and a rudimentary cemetery was established next door for the victims of the dread disease. For a while Westminster was left to drift, cut off from higher authority with the court, monarch and many justices out of town. Eventually certain justices of the peace were chosen to 'remain and continue at their habitation in the City of Westminster . . . to the end that the people may be better govern[ed] and such orders observed in this sad season as are necessary'.[59]

One of the justices chosen for this important task was Edmund Godfrey. Alongside his colleague and fellow justice of the peace, Edmund Warcup, he ran the government of the area in the absence of most other authorities. According to him, the 'people seem[ed well] satisfied with their government'.[60] Of course he was not on his own; a few others of note stayed in the dying city during the crisis. The former Cromwellian architect of the Restoration, George Monck, Duke of Albermarle, stubbornly remained as the sole representative of the government at Whitehall. Albermarle sought to rule Westminster as he ruled the army – with a rod of iron. His lieutenant was William, Earl of Craven, while their sergeants were justices of the peace such as Edmund Godfrey. Godfrey's business as woodmonger naturally provided him with transport, and he could use wagons, carts and horses to shift the plague victims through the silent streets of the capital to their last resting place. His actions as a magistrate were often severe, but he survived the great disaster of the plague with an increased reputation. His reaction to the Great Fire of 1666 made him a notable figure at court and in Restoration London. As a result, Godfrey was well rewarded for his pains with a knighthood and £200 of silver plate. Engraved in Latin on a silver tankard that was part of his reward for his services was the inscription that he was:

A man truly born for his country; when a terrible fire devastated the City, by the providence of God, and his own merit, he was safe and illustrious in the midst of the flames. Afterwards at the

express desire of the King (but deservedly so) Edmund Berry
Godfrey was created a Knight, in September 1666. For the rest let
the public records speak.[61]

One would have thought such praise would have pleased him. Yet this
stubborn man still courted trouble by claiming that he sought no
reward and went so far as initially to refuse the honour bestowed on
him by the king.

In spite of his peculiarities, Godfrey remained careful to keep the
peace and to punish those who broke it. However, he was also known
as a very 'busy' man who seemed to have little fear of the criminal
types with whom he might come into contact. Nor does he seem to
have lacked courage when it came to exercising his office. He was first
assaulted during the 1660s: caught in an alley by an old enemy Godfrey
was threatened with a cudgel and was forced to draw his sword. The
magistrate managed to fight the man off until his cries for rescue
brought assistance.[62] His sense of duty, moderation and patience, as
well as sheer hard work, kept the area under his custodianship on a
tight leash and allowed law-abiding citizens to go about their business.
But even here the peculiarities of his character kept revealing
themselves from beneath his veneer of respectability. His sense of duty
was thought by some to be almost maniacal in its intensity; leaping into
a plague house to seize an absconding criminal was all very well, but
Edmund Godfrey proved to be someone who was often quite reluctant
to abandon the role of amateur sleuth. Indeed, he regularly took a
lead in such matters, being noted as a man who moved about at odd
hours of the night, a solitary figure who peered down alleys and lanes
in search of misconduct. He was also thought by many to be rather too
prone to taking responsibility upon himself, and at the same time
equally reluctant to give it up once he had taken it.

Even more oddly for a public official, he was seen as being soft on
dissent. It was soon known that Edmund Godfrey was very reluctant to
invoke the many penal laws against those of a tender conscience. He
had many Catholic and dissenting friends, with whom he dealt
liberally. Indeed, if we are to credit one story, he was even willing to
bend the law so as not to punish Catholics in particular. It was doubly

unfortunate therefore that on 5 September 1678 Edmund Godfrey came face to face with the odd figure of Dr Israel Tonge, who claimed knowledge of a Popish Plot, in his capacity as a herald for the even odder figure of the monstrous Titus Oates.

FRIENDS, BELIEFS AND POLITICS

As he established himself on the London scene, Edmund Godfrey naturally acquired a number of friends and acquaintances. They ranged from his dearest friends such as Sir George and Lady Margaret Pratt who lived, when in London, at Charing Cross, to the more humble friendship of the Gibbon family. Mrs Mary Gibbon, who seems to have been a cousin of the magistrate, had her home in Old Southampton Buildings where, in his later years, Godfrey took to visiting her once a week for advice, gossip and the exchange of confidences. However, there is little doubt that the most important of Edmund Godfrey's friendships of these years, and one we know a great deal about, was the relationship he formed with the Irishman Valentine Greatrakes. Their friendship began with Greatrakes's visit to London in 1666.[63]

Valentine Greatrakes was born in Affane, County Waterford, on 14 February 1628, the son of a Protestant gentry family who had settled in Waterford in the 1590s. He was well educated, but on the death of his father William Greatrakes, and the outbreak of the Irish Rebellion in 1641, Valentine was sent to live with relatives in England. He returned to Ireland in 1647 and lived a retired life upon his estates until he volunteered to serve in the Cromwellian campaign of 1649 in the regiment of the regicide Colonel Robert Phaire. During the next few years, through Phaire's influence, Greatrakes held a number of local offices in County Waterford, although with the advent of the Restoration he again retired from public life, after having first secured a pardon for his actions. He then became a respectable and wealthy member of his local community in Affane. He was described as a 'very civil, frank and well humoured man, conformable to the discipline of the church'.[64] He was also wealthy and was said to have an income of £1,000 per annum. In addition, he had made a well-connected marriage to Ruth Godolphin, daughter of Sir John Godolphin.

It was in 1662 that Greatrakes had his first premonition of the power of healing that lay within him. He soon acquired the reputation of a 'stroker' and his stroking 'cures' thereafter were often spectacular, if slightly gruesome. Indeed, Greatrakes's healing practices began to attract huge crowds at his estate who gathered to see him exercise his powers. Given his previous political background and the general fear of all dissenters at the time as possible regicides, Greatrakes was soon in trouble with the Irish clergy who naturally tried to suppress his activities. His local success at exercising his healing powers on scrofula, or the King's Evil – in itself something of a radical statement – also led to a growing national fame. This fame crossed the Irish Sea and eventually he was invited in July 1665 by Viscount Conway of Ragley to visit England in order to attempt to cure Anne, Viscountess Conway, of her severe migraines.[65] After some hesitation and persuasion (for he was apparently reluctant to come to England at the behest of any lord), Greatrakes finally left for Ragley Hall in January 1666. While his activities there did little for Viscountess Conway's migraines, the expedition did his career no harm. Viscountess Conway, herself a metaphysician and philosopher of note, had some influence among the divines, philosophers and scientists who visited Ragley Hall, and they soon gathered at the house to view the healer. Many hundreds of humbler souls also flocked there in search of Greatrakes's curative powers. In short, Valentine Greatrakes soon became a national celebrity who, in addition to his healing hands, had spittle (it was said) that could cure deafness, while his urine, which apparently smelt of violets, could cure dropsy. He began to tour the country as a healer and he generally refused payment for his services. While at Worcester in the spring of 1666, he was summoned to the court of Charles II to perform his wonders before the king, mainly it seems due to the persuasion of the king's cousin Prince Rupert and Sir Henry Bennet, Lord Arlington. Charles II, ever eager for any amusement, however esoteric, was to be disappointed in this instance. The healer failed to achieve anything in his demonstrations before the king, and instead Greatrakes became the brief subject of scientific disputation, which was of less interest to the world-weary monarch. Greatrakes's alleged powers as a healer did, however, allow him to strike up a firm friendship with Edmund Godfrey. Valentine had apparently worked his wonderful cures before the magistrate. Godfrey was so impressed that while in London, Greatrakes occasionally stayed in the magistrate's house. Indeed, upon the healer's return to Ireland in May 1666, in order to resume the life of an Irish gentleman, the two men maintained their friendship by an intimate correspondence.[66]

Edmund Godfrey wrote frequently to his friend, and this correspondence is revealing on a variety of levels. It is clear that Godfrey was not only a staunch believer in Greatrakes's powers, but may have been cured by the healer himself. It is certain that he had witnessed the activities of Greatrakes at first hand within his own family. Godfrey's letters to Greatrakes reveal boundless admiration for his friend, both as a man and as a healer. In his will Godfrey was to leave the Irishman £10 for mourning clothes, and Greatrakes had also named one of his sons after the magistrate. In part, the correspondence between the two men dealt not only with Greatrakes's healing powers, which the magistrate sought to promote at every opportunity, but also with Godfrey's views of the court, their mutual friendships, business deals, and the magistrate's own personality. Godfrey evidently saw the correspondence as a chance both to cultivate a friendship and to show off some of his learning, for he was liable to lapse into Latin tags and foreign phrases. He also gently, and sometimes not so gently, mocked Greatrakes's intimacy with his wife. Godfrey, a celibate bachelor of forty-five, appears to have been something of a misogynist at heart, believing, as he put it, that 'the Devil in Woman had prevail'd on them to Deboachery'.[67]

The two men were involved in business affairs together almost from the very beginning. In the main these interests were connected with Godfrey's livelihood as a wood and coal merchant in Westminster. Some speculative land dealing in Ireland also took place and Godfrey undertook to act as a spokesman for Greatrakes in London.[68] Greatrakes was obviously someone to whom Godfrey felt he could reveal his personal feelings. He noted at the receipt of one letter that nothing 'was more welcome unto me than ever the most kind letter from an amoroso to his Mrs. or *su e contra* from her to him,'[69] or again that he regarded Greatrakes's letters as items 'I keep carefully by me among my choicest Reserves'.[70] The correspondence reveals depths in Godfrey's character that have not previously been available to biographers. His legal struggles with his nephew, Godfrey Harrison, are revealed in the letters, recently uncovered by the author in Dublin; they drove him to despair. We also learn that Godfrey had suffered losses in property, as well as injury to his person, during the course of the Great Fire of London in September 1666. To sustain him in these bad times he called upon a deep religious belief and a remarkable faith in the powers of Greatrakes. These powers he regarded as both exceptional and God-given. The injury he sustained, due to a piece of timber striking him on his back, could, he believed, only be cured by Greatrakes's healing touch. Greatrakes had already shown his skills as a healer before the magistrate by curing Godfrey's sisters as well as other people, and Godfrey did not doubt his friend's healing gifts.

At the same time the correspondence also began to reveal Godfrey's melancholy nature, a dark side to his character that apparently could not be shaken off. This was expressed in a number of ways. It was particularly apparent when Godfrey discussed Greatrakes's wife. Although she was jestingly complimented by the magistrate, her close relationship with Greatrakes appeared to have alarmed Godfrey. His apparent dislike and mistrust of women now became more obvious and in itself was perhaps revealing of the underlying tensions that existed in his personality. It raises the speculation that Godfrey's apparent expressions of dislike of the female sex, his status as a bachelor, his deep friendship with the healer and his comments to Greatrakes may have relevance in other ways. A case could perhaps be made for suppressed homosexual leanings, although the evidence is contradictory and somewhat slight.[71] Such aspects of his personality, however, could be part and parcel of his depressive moods, which many acquaintances commented upon, as well as his failure to marry. Moreover, the known homosexuality of Titus Oates (with which we shall shortly deal), and the speculations of J.P. Kenyon about a homosexual ring in the Roman Catholic community, suggest possible reasons as to why Oates and Tonge approached an emotionally vulnerable Godfrey rather than any other justice in September 1678.[72] Certainly Godfrey's eagerness for the personal contact and companionship provided by Greatrakes is revealing of his psychological state in the 1660s and 1670s. He was a lonely man, despite his busy life. Indeed, questions about Godfrey's state of mind were also to be raised after his disappearance in October 1678. The figure that emerges from the correspondence naturally bears little or no resemblance to the Protestant martyr portrayed by Whig propaganda in the late 1670s and early 1680s. Instead Edmund Godfrey appears as a man of flesh and blood, deeply religious, somewhat misanthropic and troubled by his relatives, as much as by his odd personality. This combination of factors led him even to think of retiring to live in Ireland in the early 1670s in the company of his friend. This retirement, continually postponed for one reason or another, never happened.

The correspondence also contains much by way of political comment and for the first time reveals Edmund Godfrey's political attitudes. As a businessman with access to the Restoration political world, albeit as a minor figure on the stage, Godfrey often had close relations with courtiers and politicians at Whitehall, although in his own political life Godfrey noted prophetically that he was a man who 'If he wo[ul]d be throw paced . . . might be somebody among them [at court.] But . . . [I have] a foolish & narrow conscience . . . that spoyles . . . [me] and all that use it'.[73] Although wary of expressing his opinions too blatantly, for fear that the correspondence would be intercepted and read by eyes other than those of Greatrakes, Godfrey did comment upon the events of the day. His opinions of the court during the period of the misnamed 'Cabal' ministry in the early 1670s are generally sound. He disliked the vanity of court life, where he believed that the king's mistresses, Lady Castlemaine and Nell Gwyn, backed by the Duke of Buckingham and Lord Arlington respectively, held sway. Godfrey was equally interested in the vexed relationship between Charles and his queen, Catherine, as well as the 'pranks' at Whitehall and Newmarket. As an example of the moral poverty of the court of Charles II, Godfrey's description of the funeral of the Duke of Albermarle in 1670 was particularly damning. He described the roguery of the king and his friends at this former hero's last rites as 'a poor, pittyful sneaking show'.[74]

While discussing the court and parliament in his letters, Godfrey's political views were laid bare. As with many another magistrate, Godfrey's great fears were of division, disorder and factionalism. He feared the way in which the political wind was blowing and he was certainly aware of the manoeuvres that were taking place in the 1670s towards a French alliance and another Dutch war. He not only commented upon the visit to Dover by the court in 1670, but was also apparently in attendance himself for a while as courtiers trailed behind the king to the south-east coast of England. Godfrey believed that the purpose for the visit by Madame, Charles II's sister Henrietta Maria, was, 'besides Mistresses & pleasures . . . to try if she can prevaile with our K[ing] to relinquish the Dutch interests & adhere to the French in his designs in Flanders'.[75]

For the great fear from abroad was of the rising power of France. The ambitions of Louis XIV and his nation had been attracting critical comments in Godfrey's circle for some time. In the London business community both Michael and Benjamin Godfrey apparently shared this view. These men were part of a group who believed that the Crown's pro-French policies were damaging to both trade and religion. Indeed, Michael Godfrey took a prominent role in opposing these policies in the 1670s, expressing his dislike not only upon economic but also political grounds. Together with a number of other City merchants, on 24 November 1674 Michael signed the 'Scheme of Trade' which complained of the inequitable state of Anglo-French economic relations.[76] Michael's most notable and longstanding friendship in the City was with Thomas Papillon, with whom, as we have seen, he had travelled to France in 1647. Papillon was to have close links with Antony Ashley Cooper, the Earl of Shaftesbury, among others, but was also to be prominent among the City Whigs in the early 1680s. Indeed, as we shall see, Edmund's mysterious death may even have assisted his brother's rise among such men. The role, which Michael was eagerly to seize as kinsman to the 'protestant martyr', certainly did nothing to harm his interests, and in February 1680 he was even to give a dinner in memory of his dead brother to those arch rogues Titus Oates and William Bedloe.[77]

At home Godfrey's own fears extended to extremists in religion, whether 'fanaticks' or papists. Despite these fears, he was not in favour of persecution of either group and disliked what he saw as the purge of the Commission of the Peace in order to put the penal laws into effect. Indeed, he expressed some sympathy for the Quakers and their sufferings.[78]

The key elements that emerge from Godfrey's letters were those of discipline and good order in the home, in church, in the street (where he perceived poverty to be the gravest problem), and in politics: with discipline and good order would come freedom to worship. As the correspondence continued, he revealed that his greatest fear was that the court's policies at this time (a mixture of persecution and liberality towards dissenters and Roman Catholics) would bring disorder and dissolution into the land. At the same time, for this man of contradictory impulses, the persecution of dissenters and recusants as scapegoats for the faults of court was not the answer to public disorder and a breakdown in discipline. Politically, Edmund Godfrey remained a man of contradictions, desiring strong government but no persecution to achieve it. He also had some unusual connections in the City and among the opposition. His activities as a merchant and his political beliefs apparently led him to drift towards those hostile to the greatest power in the court at this time, namely, Sir Thomas Osborne, Earl of Danby.

In 1676–7 Godfrey's name had been seriously linked for the first time with Sir Robert Peyton and his 'gang'. The term 'gang' was in fact a misleading one. It was first used scornfully by Sir John Robinson in a letter to Sir Joseph Williamson, the Secretary of State, and has deceived some historians into thinking that it referred to a group of secret plotters. In fact, these men can be seen as part of the growing opposition to the policies of Danby and Charles II in the 1670s that cried 'up against France, against popery . . .[and the] invasion of liberty'.[79] Some members of this group were to be excluded from the Commission of the Peace as a result of their activities in 1675–7; two of them, Sir Robert Peyton and Charles Umpherville, were to be associated with the notorious Green Ribbon Club, one of a series of political clubs established during the Exclusion Crisis of 1679–83 that served as venues for meetings of the 'opposition'. Godfrey was apparently friendly towards these men and partial to some of their ideas, although he was not removed from the Commission of the Peace in 1675–7. (In fact, the only time he was out of the commission was from October 1669 to May 1671, largely because of the offence he had caused the king in trying to arrest his physician, Sir Alexander Fraser, for debt) Godfrey's links with Peyton were soon noted by the court and cannot have done him much good. Indeed, upon hearing of the magistrate's death both Charles II and his brother James, Duke of York, who had good reason to be hostile to potential Republicans at the best of times, were openly to disparage Godfrey as a 'fanatique'. This may be taken as a sure sign of their belief in his poor choice of company in the 1670s. On the other hand, Peyton himself was to switch sides in the early 1680s and become a 'fallen angel' among the Whigs in assisting Mrs Elizabeth Cellier, the Roman Catholic midwife, with her designs.[80]

Edmund Godfrey was also linked to these men by the wrangles connecting others in London in the mid-1670s. As a result of the Dutch war of 1672–4, there had been increasing disagreement both in parliament and in the Common Council of the City, where Peyton himself had been prominent, over whether parliament should be dissolved and a new election called in order to save the nation from French influence. After a rousing speech by Francis Jenks to the Common Council on 2 June 1676, Charles II and Danby had attempted to wrest the London and Middlesex Commission of the Peace, as well as the City government, back from their opponents.[81] Edmund Godfrey was almost certainly involved in these matters, even if only peripherally. He was not only a merchant but he had by now returned to the Commission of the Peace. He feared France and had openly disagreed with a court with whose dealings he had expressed some distaste both in his letters to Greatrakes and in person to the gossipy cleric Gilbert Burnet.[82] In short, Edmund Godfrey showed all the signs of increasing opposition to the court shared by his fellow merchants, and is all too likely to have been dabbling in opposition politics; not as deeply as his brother Michael perhaps, but sufficiently to have been noted by the court and for his name to have found its way on to its lists. In fact, had he not died so mysteriously in 1678, Edmund would probably in time have drifted into full opposition. Or perhaps not, for among the most notable characteristics of Godfrey were his contradictions. As we shall see, he had also retained a friendship with a number of Roman Catholic acquaintances such as John Grove, who lived in Southwark, and the notorious gossip and self-styled agent of France, Edward Coleman. This contradiction doubtless accounts for some of Godfrey's ill-fated moves in the autumn of 1678 when faced with the implications of Oates's depositions about a Popish Plot.[83] It was also apparent that Godfrey had little time for aristocratic nobility, noting 'It were a great Reformation here to see them [the nobility] affected with Civility, or Sobriety [however] nothing but an act of pure necessity will put us upon those courses'. 'To speak truth', he noted somewhat puritanically, 'nothing spoyles these Nations but ease & plenty'.[84]

As the 1670s progressed, Edmund Godfrey's status as a magistrate and a man of business gave him some authority in his community. He grew prosperous and his activities took him into many an area of government and into many walks of life; he associated with many people from the Earl of Danby (however much he disliked that overmighty first minister) to the poor of the parish. He dabbled in city politics, engaged in his justice's business, sat as foreman on a grand jury that found the riotous Earl of Pembroke guilty of murder (only to see the verdict overturned by the earl's peers) and went about his daily business selling coal and wood. Occasionally the 'black dog' of depression appears to have caught up with him, at which times he would engage in fasts and was bled to ease his cares. He was often seen wandering the streets of London, dabbing at his mouth with a handkerchief and staring at the ground as he went. Yet it seems that he led a reasonably active social life and was commonly to be found in his later years at Lady Pratt's house in Charing Cross, where she held court for her numerous guests.

One further local interest of Godfrey's should be noted. This was his presence on the Commission of Sewers for Westminster, where he took on the role of treasurer and chief accountant for the Commission. This was yet another officious city committee, whose concern was to keep up the ditches and embankments for the riverside parishes. It met regularly to listen to reports of experts, carry out surveys and assess the local inhabitants for their rates. Edmund Godfrey was not only in regular attendance at these meetings, but he threw his considerable energies into its work. So much so that the non-appearance of this energetic man at the committee's meeting on 12 October 1678 was soon noticed by the other members, and as the news spread they were not alone in wondering where the magistrate had gone.[85]

CHAPTER THREE

Titus Oates and the Popish Plot

Some truth there was, but dash'd and brew'd with lies,
To please the fools and puzzle all the wise

John Dryden, 'Absalom and Achitophel' (1681)

On the morning of 13 August 1678, Charles II, King of England, Scotland and Ireland, and 'defender of the faith', was about to take his daily exercise by walking in St James's Park. Despite the difficulties of the political situation, the king was his usual easy self. His first minister, the Earl of Danby, was still struggling in his schemes to provide His Majesty with what the king regarded as a reasonable amount of money from the increasingly difficult '500 kings' who sat in parliament. Charles II's own schemes for squeezing further cash handouts from his cousin Louis XIV, in return for remaining out of European conflicts and the sphere of French king's ambitions, had once more fallen upon deaf ears. Yet, Charles, whose mind was invariably a welter of short-term projects and designs, was no doubt looking forward to his walk with some relief. (Feeding the ducks and imagining the hordes of courtiers trying to keep up with his brisk pace through the park would amuse him.) He certainly did not wish to be bothered by supplicants such as Christopher Kirkby, whom he occasionally employed to assist him on a part-time basis with the chemical experiments in which he was prone to indulge in his laboratory at Whitehall Palace. Yet Kirkby still hovered around him, much as he had done the previous day. In the outer gallery of the palace, he even pressed a paper into the king's hand; Charles now read it as he proceeded downstairs. It talked of plots and a need to speak privately. The king, doubtless with a heavy sigh, called the man over to him. 'What plots are these Mr Kirkby?' was his question. Kirkby, an ingratiating individual in an ill-fitting wig, by all accounts hastily replied that there was a plot against His Majesty's life, and men might that very morning be lying in wait ready to shoot him. Having heard many such stories in the course of his reign, Charles said that he would talk to Kirkby on his return and then passed on his way to spend an uneventful morning feeding the ducks.[1]

Upon the king's return, Kirkby was ushered into the monarch's closet by a servant, William Chiffinch, and asked to explain himself. Kirkby laid out the bare bones of a Catholic plot. He told the king of the plan by a Benedictine lay brother, Thomas Pickering, and a Jesuit lay brother, John Grove, to shoot His Majesty. Moreover, should this fail, the queen's physician Sir George Wakeman was privy to a scheme to poison Charles. Asked for the source of his information, Kirkby offered to bring the individual himself to the king; Charles agreed to see the pair between 8 and 9 o'clock that evening. At around 8 o'clock Kirkby was once more ushered into the king's presence, this time accompanied by the somewhat wild figure of one Dr Israel Tonge who laboriously proceeded to read out forty-three articles relating to a plot. For a while the king listened with increasing impatience and then bade the doctor come to the point. The plan appeared to involve his assassination and the raising of the three kingdoms on behalf of his brother and heir-apparent James, Duke of York, but further clauses and sub-clauses were yet to be revealed. Tiring of these eccentric ramblings, but experienced enough to be unwilling to drop the information entirely just in case it could be true, the king decided to turn the two men over to his first minister to investigate. The next morning, as the king proceeded to Windsor, the 'Popish Plot' dropped into the lap of the Earl of Danby. In order to understand Danby's reaction to the 'plot' and what followed, we must begin by providing some context for the political situation in which Danby found himself, and the more general attitude toward Roman Catholicism that made the whole design more believable.[2]

A 'FLAMING METEOR, ABOVE OUR HORIZON': THE EARL OF DANBY AND THE 1670S

Sir Thomas Osborne, Earl of Danby, dominated political life in mid-1670s England.[3] With his pale face and bad stomach, the Lord

45

Treasurer had first been called to the helm of government in 1673 amidst the raging storms of a dissolving ministry and the wreck of a lost war with the Dutch. His subsequent struggles to remain in power in the 1670s were hampered by a host of troubles that mainly revolved around the ambitions of Louis XIV, a factious and uncooperative parliament, the envy and malice of his rival courtiers and the growing problem of 'popery' in high places. It must be said that in these years Danby seems to have undertaken the impossible task of reconciling the irreconcilable. His aim was to ensure that his naturally secretive monarch would journey along with a nation that had by the 1670s good reason to distrust their king. The royal court was seen as a nest of popery and French influence; previous schemes for the toleration of Catholics had unsettled the nation; and there were growing fears of what the future might bring under the king's brother James, Duke of York.

In order to achieve his own purposes, Danby attempted to project a 'Church and King' policy in which loyalty to the monarchy would be coupled with support for the established church, thereby bolstering the Cavalier interest. If he succeeded in this, Danby would be able to establish some of the basis for winning financial security for his king, while retaining his own influence within the precincts of the court. One thing the Lord Treasurer did not lack was ambition. Indeed, in order further to protect and expand his new ministry, in 1674 he sought to engage in practical management techniques with both the parliament and the court. As both bodies tended to insist vociferously upon their liberties and freedom of action, the manipulations of the Lord Treasurer were naturally much resented. Nevertheless Danby aimed to create a solid core of followers, a party of men who would do his bidding and guarantee the monarchy financial security by undertaking to manage both the House of Commons for the Crown's benefit and the court for his own. In the end, the reliability of the followers that Danby succeeded in acquiring in the mid-1670s was very dubious. And however hard he worked, Danby met with obstacles at every turn. As a result his ministry, after a first flurry of open political warfare, was soon bogged down in the trenches of the House of Commons. At court Danby had other problems: he could never bring himself to be just a 'companion in pleasure' for the King.[4] The earl was far too businesslike for the king's taste, and in the game of court politics this left him at something of a disadvantage. His attempts to compensate for his personal failing only led to further blundering associations with some of the king's mistresses, and, according to Sir John Reresby, a widespread use of a 'secret trade of taking bribes for good offices'.

Bishop Burnet noted that like many another courtier Danby was 'very plausible [as a] speaker' and he 'gave himself great liberties in discourse [but he] did not seem to have any great regard for the truth'.[5] Certainly, the Lord Treasurer's insinuating manner, by turns positive and reassuring, continued to worry away at the political life of the nation, and he retained the confidence that 'all things would go according to his mind in the next session of parliament, and after his hopes failed him, he had always some excuse ready, to put the miscarriage upon that'. At the same time, as one courtier put it, Danby was prone to 'lay about him & provide for his family'. It was suggested that ultimately this would be a double-edged sword 'for if he comes to be out with ye King his enemies will [certainly] maul him'.[6] Nevertheless, the Danby ministry was quick to emphasise its support for Cavalier doctrines, the well-being of the Church of England and hostility toward Roman Catholics, nonconformists and supporters of 'anti-prerogative' measures, and engage the nation in a genuine reconciliation of king, parliament and the church.[7]

For his part, Charles II viewed such matters with his usual jaundiced eye. He soon came round to assessing the chances of his minister's pulling off schemes to draw money from an increasingly ill-tempered and impatient parliament. Having weighed these chances up, and found them wanting, the king quietly slid back towards the French in order to finance his lifestyle, especially as Danby, faced with a possible shortage of cash, was finally forced to embark on a policy of retrenchment at court. By the mid-1670s Charles had once more settled down to the interminable secret negotiations for money with his French cousin, Louis XIV, which he much preferred. He initially did this over the head of his first minister who, once he was made aware of the situation, was only reluctantly dragged into the ever-more convoluted schemes of alliance. Danby's only counter move to such schemes was yet another attempt to ensure that the next parliamentary session was more profitable. So time and again exhaustive lists of supporters were drawn up and approaches made to various individuals in order to strengthen the ministry's hand. Yet inevitably all these schemes came unstuck in the bear-pit of the House of Commons. By 1678 the once pristine Danby ministry had virtually ground to a halt, spattered with rumours of corruption and instability. With Danby's own position still dependent on securing a benign House of Commons that would grant the financial security needed to placate the king, his only resource for so doing was to continue the anti-French and pro-church rhetoric which thus far had singularly failed to secure very much. As distrust of his methods mounted, Danby still continued to berate the King, writing: 'Till he [the King] can fall into the humour of the people he can never be great or rich, and while differences continue prerogatives must suffer, unless he can live without parliament'.[8] This, as Danby frequently pointed out, was not possible, given the condition of the Crown's revenue, and a French alliance was to him merely 'good words'. Over all of this, however, there now loomed a more sinister shadow – that of Roman Catholicism.[9]

It is difficult to convey the depth of hatred towards Roman Catholicism in seventeenth-century England. The nation's view of popery was based upon a long tradition of myth, bigotry, stupidity and, just occasionally, a little reality. The myth, founded in the sixteenth century during the age of the Reformation and religious wars, was contained in the many commemorations of victory over the popish church that were still widely celebrated in the English calendar. From Queen Elizabeth's accession (17 November 1558) to victory over the Spanish Armada (1588) to Gunpowder Plot day (5 November 1605), the English calendar was spotted with such events and they invariably kept the 'evils' of Roman Catholicism in the forefront of the English mind. As protectors of the citadel of the Protestant faith in Europe, the English should have felt secure. Yet it was commonly believed that underground sapping and mining from 'papists' still continued against both them and their religion; there were some obvious signs of this for those who would look hard enough. In Europe wars and conflicts raged and the major Catholic power of the era, the France of Louis XIV, seemed to outside observers to be bent upon a continental hegemony. There were also apparent 'traitors' in the English camp itself. They were to be found within the small but dogged Roman Catholic population who had survived all of the great traumas of the period, and in the little pocket of fashionable Catholics who clustered around the libertine court of Charles II.

Roman Catholics in general were believed by the Protestant English to be capable of any action that would bring about the triumph of their church, yet the proportion of the nation who still worshipped in the old religion was in reality quite small – about 4.7 per cent – and they did so under sporadic persecution.[10] Fines and punishment tended to fluctuate with political circumstances. Nonetheless, practical indulgence to papists was also sometimes to be found at the local level. Alongside the connivance of local officers and the mixed messages on religious policy that frequently issued from the government, the small, largely rural and gentry-based, Roman Catholic population went about their business in the remoter and more backward areas of the kingdom. If they sometimes kept out of the way, they were also part of that neighbourly feeling and county gentry community typical of English rural life. As John Miller has noted, in 'a crisis gentlemen and even priests might stress that although they were Papists, they were also gentlemen' and part of the county community.[11] So 'popery' survived in spite of the problems it faced. Yet Roman Catholics were still barred from holding office and calamities such as the plague and Great Fire of London often raised religious tensions to such heights that the Catholic community remained an easy target for persecution.

At court, on the other hand, the tolerant atmosphere engendered by Charles II proved a mixed blessing.[12] Everyone knew the court was a place of vice and luxury, and the fear that a growing clique of Catholics, as well as their converts, could control the government is visible in the periodic attempts to break up such groups through a test of official loyalty. A Test Act had in fact been passed by parliament in 1673 and it had driven many Catholics from the government, including the king's own brother James. In theory, all office-holders were to take the oaths of allegiance and supremacy, declare against transubstantiation and take the sacraments of the established church. It was intended to be a means of ensuring that Roman Catholics could not slip into office; but they soon returned. The typical court Catholic tended either to be of foreign origin – the Irish were particularly visible – or to be more cosmopolitan than their more rural brethren. Also typical was the stream of notable converts to the religion who were in close proximity to the king, including his mistresses and his brother. It was even quietly rumoured that Charles himself had also shown an interest in conversion, despite his position as head of the Church of England. Roman Catholic conversion for a while became a favourite pastime in which the rich courtier could indulge his fancies. With Catholic royal chapels based at Somerset House and St James's Palace – the residences of the queen (the Portuguese Catherine of Braganza), and the Duke and Duchess of York respectively – as well as various ambassadorial chapels available, conversion became socially acceptable. Unfortunately, serious court Catholics were prone to ideas and whispered plans for the eventual reconversion of the whole English nation. Equally significant was the presence of a high proportion of less well-known Catholics in London. Within the local population, freedom to worship in the metropolis was, if not more open, at least rather easier. Periodically, the government made attempts to prevent Londoners attending such places of worship but these were generally ineffective. One contemporary thought that there were around 10,000 Catholics in the West End alone in 1669, but as John Miller has shown in his work, in reality the numbers were much smaller. The London Catholics were also often drawn from the energetic artisan and shopkeeper class, who were an important part of the London scene, and Edmund Godfrey was not alone in coming into daily contact with them.[13]

Despite the reality of the situation, the cry of 'no popery' and the belief in a beleaguered English nation began to be ever more topical on the floor of the House of Commons and in the country at large. Andrew Marvell, the poet, Member of Parliament and propagandist, spelled out this threat most ably in plain language in the 1670s: 'There has now for divers Years, [he said,] a Design been carried on to change the Lawful Government of England into an Absolute Tyranny and to Convert the Established Protestant Religion into down-right Popery.'[14] To the true believer this mythical Popish Plot became a real one. The Pope in Rome and his secret legions, including his particular henchmen the Society of Jesus or Jesuits, were attempting to undermine English life and liberties. Secret designs were ongoing which, if they succeeded, would mean the destruction of the English Protestant establishment. In this mythological world of rant and fear, it was believed that these designs would inevitably lead to the widespread slaughter of Protestant men, women and children, the end of property ownership and of England itself as the average English Protestant knew it. Here, for example, is one author's view of what would happen to the English should the Roman Catholics succeed in their designs:

> Your wives [would be] prostituted to the lust of every savage bog-trotter, your daughters ravished by goatish monks, your small children tossed upon pikes, or torn limb from limb, while you have your own bowls ripped up . . . and holy candles made of your grease (which was done within our memory in Ireland) your dearest friends flaming in Smithfield, foreigners rending your poor babes that can escape everlasting slaves, never more to see a Bible, nor hear the joyful sounds of Liberty and Property. This, this[,] gentlemen, is Popery[!].[15]

The idea that previous attempts had been made to destroy the nation were, of course, ingrained within the English Protestant psyche, and indeed proved that these designs were both widespread and still current. The very belief itself proved the fact and logic had little to do with it. The horrors of the reign of 'Bloody Mary' (1553–8), the attempted Spanish invasion of 1588, the Gunpowder Plot of 1605, the massacres of Protestants in Ireland in 1641, the outbreak of the Civil War in 1642, even the execution of Charles I in 1649, were all considered historical proof that these designs were ever present.

English men and women avidly read gorily illustrated versions of these tales. That the plot did not exist did not make the myth any less potent and it was soon, taken in conjunction with Danby's failed attempts to govern the parliament, seen as the latest attack on Protestant English liberties and fed by growing hostility to the government's intrigues with the French. As we have seen, the latter were now being considered not just as purveyors of popery, a role once filled by Spain, but as genuine economic and international rivals.[16]

Above all of this speculation there was, however, one tangible reality: the heir to the throne. By 1678 James, Duke of York, was some forty-five years of age and possessed extensive experience as a politician, although it is doubtful whether he had really learned very much.[17] His reputation was blighted in contemporary eyes by his religion. He was a Roman Catholic convert. The man himself was certainly suspect in any case, but his openly expressed religious beliefs created enormous difficulties for the king and government. Although James was neither Lord Macaulay's melodramatic villain, twirling his moustache as he planned to force England back to Rome, nor the historian F.C. Turner's syphilitic incompetent, he did present a difficult problem both for the king, his brother, and the English nation.[18] His short-lived popularity as a soldier and sailor had not survived his open conversion to Roman Catholicism in 1673. Indeed, it was his conversion, even more than his stubborn and wilful character, that was to raise the greatest fears and become a primary justification for the crisis which was to strike the country in the late 1670s. The duke's conversion had been a long drawn-out affair, and when rumours of his inclination were finally confirmed in 1673 the fear that a future Catholic monarch would introduce tyranny and arbitrary government, and overthrow English liberties, genuinely raised the hackles of many people in government and in the country. The duke himself did not help matters, nor did he do anything to dispel a growing belief that he had violent and bloody nature. He was seen as a man who would, given the chance, take the worst of counsels in all of his affairs. He had married his second wife, an Italian Catholic princess, in 1673 in spite of parliament's protestations about the matter, and he was already beginning to be perceived as a threat to the state before the Popish Plot crisis exploded.

The Duke of York had little real understanding of the peculiarly vexed relationship between the English and popery over the years. Indeed, he held to rather simplistic views in general. Dissenters for him were merely Republicans in another guise. Church of England men were dismissed as lapsed or closet Catholics who, with a push in the right direction, could join him in rediscovering the glories of Roman Catholicism and *all* opposition was regarded as treasonous to a greater or lesser extent. The duke, much as his father Charles I had done, had swallowed the dominant ideology of European monarchy – the divine right of kings. If many saw his views as deluded, then he certainly did not. The immense personal satisfaction that the Duke of York drew from his religious beliefs has led John Miller to argue rightly that after the execution of his father, conversion was undoubtedly the most important experience of James's life. And like so many converts to a new faith, the duke naturally wanted to share his new-found religion with others. He became fervent in the promulgation of his faith, as well as hostile to those who sought to change his mind. A rather humourless man of simple beliefs, James would never become a wily pragmatist like his brother Charles. He was marked out from an early age as obstinate, narrow-minded, rigid and lacking in imagination, and all opposition appeared to him to stem from the worst of motives. Ironically the Duke of York was also one of the most English of the Stuarts and a mulish patriot of sorts. Indeed, courtiers often claimed that the country had 'a martial prince who [not only] loved glory, [but] who would bring France into [a] humble . . . dependence upon us'. But whatever his merits as a man and soldier, ultimately his devout Roman Catholicism always stood in the way of his total acceptance by the English people.[19]

The Duke of York's objectives for his fellow Catholics have been subject to continual debate since the seventeenth century.[20] The revisionist view argues that James understood, if not very well, the difficulties facing the minority religion of English Catholicism. He simply wanted equal rights for Roman Catholics, to be followed in time by secure civil rights. His apparent hastiness in religious matters has frequently been put down to his age, but it is equally likely to have been the product of years of frustration in playing second fiddle to his brother Charles. Charles's tactics often infuriated James. The king's attitude to Catholicism was an indulgent one; he seems to have found within it a satisfactory monarchical creed that was lacking in the established church. Yet Charles remained at heart a cynical pragmatist, and whatever his true attachment to the Catholicism he would never stake everything on a change of religion. Fear of a return into exile, the inordinate amount of effort required to carry out such a project and the secret treaty of Dover led the king to walk warily before bestirring the English lion of religious prejudice. In 1670 he had entered into a secret treaty with Louis XIV to launch a war against their mutual enemy, the Dutch Republic. As part of the treaty, and in return for money, Charles had agreed, at some vague time in the future, to convert to Roman Catholicism. It was not clear that the English nation itself was to follow him in this course, but Louis did agree to supply Charles with troops should the conversion go badly wrong. Had news of this secret deal leaked out, it is likely that the English would have revolted against their king's actions. Thereafter the king was more circumspect in matters relating to his Catholic subjects. In the main, he did what he could to bring toleration to bear upon suffering papists – when it suited his own needs and aims. On the other hand, James was frustrated. In January 1679 he wrote revealingly about how Charles should have followed 'bold and resolute councells, and [stuck] to them . . . measures must be taken and not departed from [and a King] should steer another course, and looke out for another passage, which no doubt may be found, to gett on's port'.[21] Above all else, a visible support for his church was in order. James had previously written, and openly expressed the view, that 'I cannot be more Catholic than I am'. His wife was also aware of how immovable his beliefs were, noting in 1674 that he was 'firm and steady in our holy religion . . . [and] he would not leave it for anything in the world'.[22] He also sought to protect his servants from persecution, and one of these servants was the cadaverous Edward Coleman.

Edward Coleman was born the son of a Suffolk parson.[23] He was a well-off Catholic convert, but he spent extravagantly in his youth and in

1671 he sought employment in the service of the Duke of York. James, of course, favoured him as a convert and Coleman, a dynamic man, was both enthusiastic and eager to convert others. When James married princess Mary of Modena, Coleman was made her secretary, but he remained very much the duke's man at heart. Coleman's vanity and meddling proved a constant theme of his career. It got him into frequent trouble and his boldness was eventually to cost him his place. He was an unprepossessing figure: lean with black eyes, a great believer in fasting, and ever eager for gossip and news. Yet Coleman must have had some charms, for his circle of friends was wide and he was a busy man in the 1670s. He maintained an open house to the important people of society. Courtiers, judges and Members of Parliament all frequented his home and provided him with the latest gossip.

Featuring in this crowd was Edmund Godfrey. It is not clear where the two men met, although Godfrey had had some business dealings with the duke's household in the past and the connection is likely to have stemmed from them. Whatever the basis for their friendship, it seems to have prospered sufficiently for Godfrey to get to know Coleman quite well. Godfrey may also have been involved in Coleman's other business venture. This was far more significant than trading in political gossip, for Coleman had initiated a correspondence, at first upon James's behalf, with a number of people at the French court and in the Vatican in order to raise funds for the monarchy. He had also forged links with the French ambassador. Most importantly, he had begun a correspondence with Louis XIV's confessor. Coleman's dealings with Father Ferrier in 1674 and then his successor Father La Chaise had been extensive. Naturally he used this correspondence to gain information about affairs in France and was quite indiscreet about affairs in England. As a believer in the conversion of the English nation to Roman Catholicism, he tended to write at length on this matter. It was: 'the mighty work . . . no less than the conversion of three kingdoms and by that perhaps the subduing of a pestilent heresy which has domineered over the great part of this northern world a long time; there was never such hopes of success since the days of Queen Mary as now in our days.'[24]

This, then, was the main business of Coleman in the 1670s, which in the end, as we shall see, was to result in his trial and execution as a prime suspect in the Popish Plot. There is little doubt that various sums of money, in addition to dangerous and indiscreet correspondence, had passed through his hands. Some of these funds stuck to his fingers, but the French ambassador had given the bulk of them to him to use as bribes. Coleman in turn bribed Members of Parliament and courtiers alike in an attempt to win their favour for what he believed were his master James's own wishes. His lavish hospitality was also used to win people over to his point of view. At his home there continued to be much political gossip and Coleman frequently exaggerated his talents of persuasion. At the same time his newsletters circulated far and wide, gathering and promulgating the views he wished others to hear. In August 1676 he fell foul of the Privy Council over his involvement in the publication of a book defending papal authority. The Bishop of London, Henry Compton, who was a Danby client and hostile to Coleman's meddling, attempted to have Coleman removed. Although James was persuaded to dismiss his servant this did not prevent him from continuing to use Coleman in an unofficial capacity. It is difficult to say to what extent James was aware of Coleman's activities throughout 1674–6.[25] The greatest period of Coleman's life occurred in 1674–6 when he was at the centre of a number of Catholic intrigues. After this his correspondence slackened as his influence waned. However, Coleman was regarded as an 'ill man' and an obvious target for informers, especially if his correspondence about the great design to reconvert the English nation was discovered.

Naturally the problem of James as the popish successor to the throne loomed ever larger over the years, especially because of the king's failure to produce a legitimate heir who could oust James from the succession. But the failure of religious toleration, fears for English liberties in the face of the monarchy's prerogative powers, the secret dealings with France in the 1670s, war in Europe, factional rivalry, and the corruption that seemed to pervade the court of Charles II, all contributed to the crisis that now developed.

The crisis of 1678–83 cannot thus be said to have had a single cause. Although James's conversion did not help, it was clear to some that the king's secret, and not so secret, deals made with Louis XIV were as much a threat to the nation as James. They were thought to be undermining the very fabric of Protestantism as well as, more mundanely, damaging English pockets. Danby's widespread abuse of the parliamentary system was also perceived as a threat to English liberties. As a result, new political patterns now began to form that eventually led to the development of political 'parties' following the dissolution of the Cavalier Parliament in 1679. Country beliefs in a staunch Protestantism, merchant-trading interests, concern with liberty, and hostility to prerogative notions and court corruption, were to emerge with the creation of a Whig 'party'. The old Anglican Royalist beliefs of 'Church, King and hereditary right', were to produce the 'Tories'. Thereafter the divided political nation was to pursue the banners of exclusion of James, limitations on his future powers as monarch, the legitimacy of James, Duke of Monmouth (the king's eldest and illegitimate son), the divorce and remarriage of Charles II himself, or simple loyalty, with equal force. Hand in hand with this went the widespread fears of court corruption and waste, of hidden court Catholics and their influence, fears of a popish successor and of the increasing power of France. The concerns of the nation were exemplified by the catchwords of the day 'popery and arbitrary government'.[26] The confirmation that something really was rotten in the state was to be found in the death of the magistrate Edmund Godfrey and the revelations of a liar with an already notorious reputation: Titus Oates.

THE SALAMANCA DOCTOR: THE EARLY HISTORY OF TITUS OATES

Titus Oates, the future 'saviour of the nation', was of Norfolk ancestry. His father Samuel Oates had been a rather down-at-heel weaver and Baptist conventicler in Coleman Street, that den of nonconformity in the seventeenth-century City of London. By 1644 Samuel had married a Hastings midwife and had also stepped from the loom to the pulpit without much difficulty. In the turbulent days of the Civil War, when religious life itself was in a state of some flux, numerous individuals were setting themselves up as preachers of the word of God, and Samuel was to the fore, preaching louder than most. Samuel Oates was thought to be a 'famous preacher' and was a popular man among his Baptist congregations, although later writers were to condemn much of his religious talk as 'sedition and nonsense'. Not that this appears to have concerned Samuel overmuch, for in the end he was not so tied to his religion that he could not change his religious colours at least once or twice in his career. In due course his ranting lifestyle naturally got him into difficulties. In 1646 Samuel was hauled up before the local magistrates in Essex, after one of his female converts died of exposure having been 'dipped' rather too vigorously in the eternal waters of life by the energetic preacher. Although he was found not guilty, Samuel was forced to leave Essex in a hurry. It was some three years before he began to prosper again. In 1649 he became a chaplain to the regiment of Colonel Pride in the New Model Army, and the same year – the year in which a Republican government was established – also saw the birth of Samuel and Lucy Oates's second son, named Titus, at Oakham in Rutland.[27]

There is no doubt that Titus Oates had a difficult childhood; his father seems to have disliked him from the first, and the preacher was hardly a model parent to his children. William Smith, who was to meet Titus's mother at the height of the informer's fame, noted that even she believed Titus odd, revealing that she thought that her son 'would have been a natural . . . and his father could not endure him'.[28] With his convulsions, runny nose and slavering at the mouth, the young Titus was singularly abused as a child. It was said that his father, coming home at night after a hard day preaching and 'doing good', used to spy the young Titus lurking in the chimney corner and 'would cry take away this snotty fool, and jumble him about'.[29] This, Lucy Oates said, 'made me often to weep because you know he was my child'.[30] In time, Titus was to prove dull or apparently just plain stupid, but then again the Oates clan as a whole was hardly much better. Titus's brother Samuel Oates junior went to sea in the 1650s and 1660s, where he served against both the Dutch and the Turks. Titus's other brother Constant Oates became a glazier in Southwark.[31] Both of his brothers were to inform against Titus in the 1680s. His two sisters, Hannah and Anne, were inoffensive enough, and his mother also seems to have been a harmless individual who, as mothers usually do with even the worst of their children, bore him some affection, which Titus was to return with abuse and harsh words.[32] As noted, his father thought little of his youngest son, but as Titus reached manhood Samuel was willing to go along with some of his early schemes and suffered as a result. Samuel senior was to end his days in 1683 in a London tavern, the Half Moon in King Street, under the 'vehement suspicion of adultery'. Yet with the Restoration of the monarchy underway in 1660, Samuel Oates desisted from belabouring his family and once more thought it politic to change his religious colours. He became a minister of the Church of England at Hastings in Sussex, and the family moved there to support him in his new ministry.[33]

In the course of the 1650s Titus had been sent up to London for his education. It is possible that for a while he attended Edmund Godfrey's old *alma mater* Westminster School, but there is little or no trace of him there. In any case, however much he tried, Titus was never a very successful pupil. Indeed, it was later claimed that he was a 'great dunce'.[34] In spite of this, by 1664 Titus had taken to attending the Merchant Taylors school as a free scholar and was under the tutelage of the master there, William Smith. In return for this tuition, Titus was alleged to have cheated Smith out of his tuition fees and was later still to accuse Smith of having a part to play in the Popish Plot. Titus proved an incorrigible pupil and he was soon expelled from the institution for his tricks. As a result, in 1665 he was sent off to school at Sedlescombe, some six miles from Hastings. As this was hardly more than a dame-school, it could not have done very much for Titus's rather peripatetic education. Perhaps his father sent him there to get him out of the way. Nevertheless, aged eighteen, in June 1667, Titus, like many another aspiring young gentleman of his day, was launched upon a university career. This proved all too brief. He went up to Caius College, Cambridge, where for some two years he continued to garner a bad reputation for his 'dullness and debauchery'.[35] He subsequently transferred to St John's College as a result but he was no more successful there, and he remained troublesome to the end as his tricks, debt, ignorance and other vices became ever more marked. He left Cambridge in disgrace in 1669 without a degree but with a capacious memory for lies, which was to serve him well in the future. However, lying and cheating were but minor crimes in contemporary eyes. His major vice, common enough at the university it seems but damned at the time, appears to have been his by now emergent homosexual leanings.

Edmund Godfrey's sexuality, as we have seen, was uncertain. However, in the case of Titus Oates there is no doubt that his sexuality holds important clues to his personality and his future career as an informer. Whether Titus Oates may genuinely be labelled 'homosexual' is a debatable point, for research into early modern sexuality has shown many men who had experience of such matters did not necessarily consider themselves homosexual or 'gay' in the modern sense.[36] There seems to be little doubt that Oates engaged in sodomy. Contemporaries mention this as a fact in the satires and pamphlets of the day. Accusations of homosexuality were often conventional in such works, but the evidence for Oates's sexuality goes beyond mere satire. A swipe at Oates upon his marriage to a follower of the religious radical Lodwick Muggleton in 1693 makes the point that Oates wed this unfortunate lady having been 'touched in [his] conscience for some juvenile gambols that shall be nameless . . . and made a vow to sow his wild Oats, and not to hide the talent which God had plentifully given him in an Italian napkin'.[37] The reference to the 'Italian napkin' was to various sodomising practices that the English, in their usual prejudiced way, naturally thought of as the activities of foreigners in general and of Italians in particular. Yet more evidence in a vulgar form, replete with *double entendres* about back entrances, makes it clear that this satirist was drawing upon an already well-known and well-founded tradition of knowledge and a story about Oates that had not died down since his first emergence into public life in 1678. Sodomy, of course, was regarded as a grave sin and certainly one against the preached norms of society.[38] It had become a criminal offence in 1562 and a distinct 'molly' culture, as it was called, had begun to emerge in London in the later sixteenth century, but only came to fruition in the latter half of the seventeenth and the first half of the eighteenth centuries.

Although accusations of sodomy often became a catch-all term for a wayward life, or any number of sins against God, in Oates's case it may have been more complicated than this. There seems little doubt that he was a paedophile. His associations with schools and schoolboys, the accusation that, as we shall see, he was to make against William Parker, and other hints suggest that he was not only an unpleasant man to be around, but positively dangerous to young boys. His physical characteristics also meant that he was hardly ever ignored. He was not a prepossessing sight, with his limp, his red face, bull neck and enormous chin, but he was certainly noticeable. His 'harsh and loud' brassy voice also began to be matched by a raucous and difficult personality. Roger North was later to note that Oates's 'common conversation was larded with lewd oaths, Blasphemy, Saucy, Atheistical, and every way offensive discourse'.[39] Yet even given this background, Oates's motivation for his career as an informer remains ultimately uncertain. What turned Oates into the man he became?

The hostility he encountered at Cambridge was but one element in a craving for respectability. He was also a man who thrived on fantasies. He saw himself becoming the saviour of the nation and making a mark in the world. Certainly his later writings were to illuminate many an imaginary invention in which he played a central role fighting against demon Popes and Jesuits. At the same time these creations reveal another craving: a craving for acceptance. It was Oates as the shrewd and secretive man of action who emerged most forcefully. In his statements and writings all the people he came across are foolishly depicted accepting him as a uniquely trustworthy individual. He portrayed himself as the arch manipulator, the hero, or superman, who despite his outward appearance managed to infiltrate their designs. He was to be England's saviour, able to convey from one important European individual to another letters concerning the great designs of the time. Of course, as these lies spun ever further out of control it must have been very difficult for Oates to distinguish between reality and fantasy. Another common theme in his life was disguise. Who he really was, what he was and where he was going remained a mystery in the increasingly unhappy and unhinged world he inhabited. So Oates's fantasy world was used to cover the sordid reality of life. In fact there were no big secrets to uncover, and even if there had been, he above all would not have been trusted with them.

Reality lay rather in back-alley meetings, stealing, begging, poverty, vice, fear, hatred and failure. Oates failed at most of the things he set out to do – except one. For a time he was genuinely honoured by some as the 'saviour of the nation', as he had always desired.

Having left Cambridge in disgrace and without a degree, Oates nevertheless contrived to slip into undeserved holy orders and he soon became a curate. By March 1673 he appeared to be prospering and was presented with a living at Bobbing in Kent by Sir George Moore, in whose possession it lay.[40] This proved another short residence as Oates's bad habits once more came to the fore. The somewhat loud-mouthed irreligious boy had by now also become a drunken thief. While drunk he tended to reveal his Baptist upbringing by proclaiming on religious matters and shocking the local worshippers. As a result Oates was soon turned out of the living, and in the manner of a bad penny immediately returned to Hastings to trouble his family once more. In Hastings Samuel Oates senior was still ensconced in his own parish church. Uncharacteristically, for a time, he showed some paternal affection towards his errant son and promptly made him a curate. The young Titus, however, had higher ambitions and he soon set his sights on the local schoolmaster's post, unfortunately occupied by William Parker, the son of a local magistrate.

Then, at Easter 1675 Titus Oates had his first known brush with the law.[41] He deposed before the mayor of Hastings allegations of Parker's sexual abuse of his charges. Naturally the schoolmaster was arrested and bound over. The fact that the charge was sexual was probably more of a reflection of Oates's desires than William Parker's, but while Parker was already safely defamed the Oates family decided to add insult to injury by further accusing the young man's father of treasonable words. This being a government matter, the mayor immediately informed Secretary of State Sir Joseph Williamson. This time the case failed and, with charges of defamation imminent, Titus Oates decided to make himself scarce by going to sea. In May–June 1675 he was appointed as a naval chaplain on the *Adventure* under her Captain Sir Richard Routh. The ship was bound for one of England's more miserable colonial possessions of the day, the city of Tangier, in order to convey the new governor Lord Inchquin to his post. On board, Oates's predilection for sodomy once more got him into trouble. He was caught, and only the fact that he was a chaplain seems to have saved him from a severe punishment. The *Adventure* reached Tangier in June. According to his own version of events, Oates had his first encounters with Roman Catholic plotters there, but the sojourn in the city was a brief one. Oates was soon back in England, and as a result of his activities he was expelled from the navy. He then lived in London for a while. With two legal actions still outstanding in Hastings – both of which might find against him – there was no point in Oates going back there, the more so since his own father was by now also lodging in London, an absentee rector as a result of the Parker affair. Moreover, Samuel had had yet another change of heart in his religious beliefs and he had returned to his old Baptist ways. Titus himself was soon picked up and arrested in September 1676 on account of the Parker affair. He was returned to Hastings and then placed in Dover Castle. By some means he contrived to escape back to London, where his life now began a cycle of poverty and misery.[42]

Around Bartholomew-tide in 1676 William Smith, once Titus's teacher, was startled to meet his former pupil in his local tavern.[43] By now dressed in the clerical garb that he almost always wore for the rest of his life, Titus was introduced to a club at the Pheasant in Fuller's Rents by the actor Matthew Medburne. Smith later claimed that Medburne had picked up Oates in the 'Earl of Suffolk's cellar at Whitehall' and proceeded to introduce him to the delights of club life; on this point there seems no reason to doubt him. Matthew Medburne was a zealous Catholic dramatist and comic actor on the London stage. Oates may seem to be odd company for such a man, but it is just possible that the association may have had sexual overtones, although this is unclear. A Mr Mekins kept the tavern in Fuller's Rents at which the club met and it consisted of several members, some of whom were Catholic and others Protestant. They included men such as William Smith himself and Edmund Everard, who may well have been a failed informer of the mid-1670s, and others, for example Jones, a priest, and one Keymash.[44] Smith was to claim that it was not a political club in any sense, and that politics in fact was banned as an item of conversation (however unlikely this seems). Paul Hammond has speculated that the club may well have been a covert place for flagellant meetings.[45] Although indeed there are some engravings that depict Oates being flogged and a number of references that refer to him flogging others, there appears to be little real evidence of this. Whatever the true nature of the club, Oates appears soon to have inveigled himself into the company of some of its members.

As a result of his membership, he was appointed Protestant chaplain to the household of the Roman Catholic Earl of Norwich at Arundel House in London. As usual, Oates was no sooner in place than he was in trouble, and after a few months he was again out of a job. Undaunted, he now decided on the Roman Catholic Church as his vocation. Having found a suitable priest, he was received into the church around 3 March 1677. In his later writings as the self-appointed scourge of Rome, Oates was to claim he was never a true Catholic in his heart but that the conversion was a cover for his first real attempt to infiltrate Catholic designs. Oates's reception into the Roman Catholic Church proved a critical point in his life and naturally enough it had more than an element of farce about it. A Father Berry, alias Hutchinson, a whirligig priest who was also somewhat mentally unbalanced, received him into the bosom of the church. A former Protestant clergyman, Berry himself had turned Jesuit, then secular priest, only to return to the established church of England and then back to Roman Catholicism once more. Given his history he proved an apt teacher for such a pupil as Titus Oates.[46] Oates was later to claim that as a result of this conversion he was shortly afterwards admitted into the secret cabals of the Jesuits, and that once admitted he was to be sent abroad as a novice to carry dispatches for the Society of Jesus. In retrospect this was highly unlikely.

Why did Oates convert to a religion that was not at all popular among his countrymen? His conversion was obviously highly insincere and it was more than likely motivated by a mixture of desperation, craving for respect, the opportunity to use his Roman Catholic 'friends' and the possible scope such dealings would eventually have for blackmail when matters went wrong. He had, however, learned of the assistance that Jesuits gave to converts, and perhaps this fact alone for a desperate, unemployed, unlovable young man, who no doubt already saw himself in the grand robes of a Catholic clergyman, may have been the real inspiration.

The second critical event in Oates's life also took place around this time. He met the slightly mad former clergyman and fervent anti-papist Dr Israel Tonge. Tonge was yet another of the mentally unbalanced clergy whom the turbulence of the Civil War had raised up and the fall of the Republic had cast upon the shores of London. A Yorkshireman in his late fifties, Tonge had been born near Doncaster and had led a peripatetic life thereafter. A former schoolmaster and clergyman, he was obsessed by the Jesuit 'menace' and after the Restoration he had ended up as rector of St Michael's Church in Wood Street. The fact that his church burnt down in the Great Fire of 1666 seems to have addled Tonge's wits still further. By 1675 his obsession with the evils of Catholicism resulted in his producing a number of virtually unreadable pamphlets on the issue. Seeking solace from those of a like persuasion, he had just moved into the house of Sir Richard Barker, a physician in the Barbican who was also a bitter anti-Catholic. Here Tonge became acquainted with Samuel Oates and through him his son Titus.[47]

Titus Oates was still unemployed and reduced to begging for a living, and an opportunity such as the one presented by Tonge did not come around everyday. While sponging off the old clergyman, Oates could also indulge in his, by now, very active fantasy life. The pair evidently saw some profit in joint authorship of anti-papist pamphlets, so they planned to 'compose . . . small treatises that would certainly be beneficial, that if possible they might subsist and live together upon the revenue of their pennies in this combat with the Romanists'.[48] With this plan in mind, Oates moved closer to Sir Richard Barker's home so he could have easy access to his new partner. At which point, with Tonge ready to scourge the Catholic hordes once more with his pen, Oates disappeared, leaving a somewhat puzzled co-author behind him.

Oates had been in the habit of going to Somerset House, the queen's residence, in the role of a converted clergyman begging for assistance. There he was certainly helped by the priests, but as usual he repaid kindness by theft; he stole some of the host, which he afterwards blasphemously used as wafers to seal his letters. Nevertheless Oates was contented enough to live upon both their charity as well as that of other Catholics. In April 1677, however, he obtained an introduction to Father Richard Strange, the Provincial of the Society of Jesus in England. Strange arranged for Oates to go to the English College at Valladolid in Spain in order that he could proceed with his education as a good son of the church. If, given Oates's previous history, this action seems a trifle silly to us, then perhaps Strange saw something in Oates that others missed. Strange's action may also have been motivated by a recommendation from Catholic friends who attended the club in Fuller's Rents, or by Medburne, or even by Oates's brief tenure in the household of the Earl of Norwich. J.P. Kenyon has speculated that a homosexual connection may have been the likeliest reason for Oates's ready acceptance by Strange and others.[49] (If so, this would not be something that the Catholics themselves would have readily admitted after Oates's fall from grace in the early 1680s.) But as it was, Oates was by now a convincing liar; he had created for his new audience the fantasy of a rich benefice, which he promptly said that he had given up so as to be admitted into the only true Church of Rome. As a willing and obviously eager convert, whatever his peculiarities, Oates appears to have imposed himself easily upon men who were in any case looking to save the soul of an ex-Church of England clergyman. Moreover, it was doubtless believed that as a former Cambridge clergyman he would have little trouble in adapting to the Roman Catholic way of life. He would need to be retrained of course, and so Oates was sent off to learn philosophy and theology at Valladolid. Satisfied with this new venture and with money in his pocket for the first time, Oates duly arrived in Bilbao in May 1677 under the alias of Titus Ambrose, or Ambrosius a poor student.[50]

Father Robert Parsons founded the college at Valladolid in 1588–9.[51] Since that time it had become a place that could provide training and education for the many priests who were to go on the English mission. Occasionally boys from the school at St Omers would also be sent there to complete their education. Oates, typically enough, arrived after the academic year had ended and he was forced to wait around until the new term began. He soon proved troublesome. The rector of the college, Father Manuel de Calatayud, later noted: 'I admitted him, very much against the grain though it was . . . Little more than a month went by, and he was in such a hurry to begin his mischief that I was obliged to expel him from the College. He was a curse. What I went through and suffered from that man, God alone knows.'[52] In fact, the college itself was somewhat in the doldrums at the time of Oates's residence. In a number of ways, he was rather more typical of some of the new recruits to the Catholic church than many would later admit. With declining Catholic numbers in England and attached, as they usually were, to a dwindling number of Catholic gentry, some of the most recent converted priests were prone to drunkenness, lechery or simple ignorance. Control over the church's English affairs had become sporadic, and boredom and laziness proved a great attraction to many of the mavericks of the day.[53] The priest who received Oates into the church was a case in point. At least Oates did not remain long within the college walls. By October 1677 he was again on his travels, having been asked to leave. Lacking even the basic skills for survival in Spain, he soon returned to England.

Two incidents of note had occurred while he was in residence in Valladolid. Oates had awarded himself a degree from the University of Salamanca and back in England was to proclaim himself as 'Dr Oates' at every opportunity. He had also met William and James Bedloe.[54] The Bedloes were a likely pair of rogues who, when Titus was at Valladolid, were on a European sojourn during which they benefited not only from the scenery but also from fraud and other crimes along the way. William Bedloe was born in Chepstow, Wales, in May 1650 and spent much of his childhood both there and in Bristol.[55] In fact much of Bedloe's early life was clouded in obscurity and he himself intended it should remain that way. What is clear is that Bedloe had skirted close to Roman Catholicism. It was said that he had been thought a promising enough young man for Father David Lewis to attempt his conversion. As a reward, Lewis was later to be executed at Monmouth during the time of the Popish Plot crisis. In reality Bedloe, like Oates, seems to have seen the Catholic church as a milch-cow to use as and when he saw fit. In any event, at twenty years of age Bedloe evidently fell out with his stepfather and made his way to London. Here, in the wild alleys and lanes of the metropolis, William Bedloe found his real talent as a gamester, sharp and footpad. Although Bedloe's early biographers related many of his subsequent adventures in the city in detail, most of these tales were fictions, adapted from the readily available rogue literature of the time.[56] There is little doubt that Bedloe had been on the wrong side of the law, and he had spent at least part of the 1670s in jail. His usual crime was fraud, in which he passed himself off as a person of quality and indulged his victim's vanity as he liberated their goods. This doubtless called for some acting ability, as well as a suit of fine clothes to carry it all off. That he was successful shows something of his imposing personality. The handsome, bold and bad William Bedloe thus passed his days as a Restoration rogue. With his imposing airs, many a trick and scheme was hatched and Bedloe worked his way through the fringes of London life. One of these schemes was undoubtedly brief employment as a message carrier for the Catholic community in London. While most of the tales about Bedloe are somewhat implausible, it is clear that he did serve for some time in a Catholic household, possibly that of Lord Bellasis, the soldierly Catholic noble who was to be imprisoned in the Tower in the course of the Popish Plot crisis.[57]

It is also clear that Bedloe had come across Titus Oates before their meeting in Spain. He may well have met Oates when the latter was a member of the household of the Earl of Norwich. Whatever the truth of the matter, England soon became too hot for Bedloe and so he decamped to Europe with his brother James. They reinvented themselves as one Lord Cornwallis and his servant. The bold Bedloe boys, heavily disguised in the best Restoration comedy tradition, turned up in various places as master and man and doubtless had many adventures as they worked their way though Europe. William, dressed in a number of aristocratic disguises, proceeded to defraud his victims to meet his own and his brother's living expenses. He awarded himself a captaincy and the pair stole a number of horses here and there. They were not prone to using violence in their schemes, as far as we know, but their fraudulent behaviour enabled them to work their way gradually through France and into Spain.

But at Salamanca their bogus lifestyle finally caught up with them. Having engineered one fraud too many, the brothers were conveyed under arrest to Valladolid, still disguised as an English milord and his servant. Once William had disentangled himself from this little local difficulty, both he and his brother were destitute and in need of assistance. Help was at hand, however, as they soon heard that an English scholar of their acquaintance was idling away his time at the local college. It was thus that Oates found himself with two unwanted guests. The dauntless 'scholar' Oates and the criminal Bedloe were later alleged to have concocted a scheme at this time in which William and his brother would play witnesses to Oates's information, but in fact the Bedloes and Oates parted with some bad feeling. William and James robbed Titus of some money and promptly disappeared while Titus was generously obtaining them some dinner. Little else was to be gained from their meeting this time.[58]

Oates soon found himself back on the streets of London and resumed his begging from various Catholics to sustain himself. Once more Richard Strange indulged this odd 'scholar' and sent Oates to St Omers in December 1677 to study among the rhetoricians there.[59] St Omers was a boys' school designed for the teaching of young well-to-do English Roman Catholic boys, some of whom might go on to the priesthood. Oates arrived as the tobacco-chewing 28-year-old Samson Lucy – it was advisable to travel under an alias – and naturally presented the authorities at the school with a problem: what could a boys' school make of this by now foul-mouthed and bull-necked monster? Oates swiftly revealed his ignorance, as well as his unsuitability for attending the school; the school authorities soon curbed his tobacco habit, and Titus treated everyone with bad grace. The boys seem at first to have regarded Oates as a figure of fun; one of them later bragged of smashing a pot over his head. Later Oates became more dangerous as he indulged himself at their expense. He was given a 'distinct table alone' at dinner, but within a fortnight he was found to be 'of a bad & hypocondriacal humour, rash, indiscreet, turbulent and vindictive, a grand flatterer, boaster & lyer'.[60] The new English Jesuit Provincial, Father Thomas Whitebread, who had replaced Strange, visited the school in June 1678 and finding Oates in residence had him expelled.[61] Nevertheless, from this experience Titus had learnt a number of things about Jesuit life, for he had whined that he wanted to be admitted to the order, and to keep him quiet he had been briefly sent to the Jesuit seminary at Watten. As with everything else, he had disliked it and was unable to understand the teaching there. However, by now his investigations had enabled him to learn much about the society and its frequent councils in England. Although he was never involved in any Jesuit schemes, such information provided him with a number of useful names.[62]

July 1678 was a hot month in London. Edmund Godfrey, just back in the city after a French holiday, went about his daily business. Around the same time a dejected Titus Oates once more arrived back in London. Again, on the fringes of the great hubbub of city life, there was now only the crazed Israel Tonge to indulge and sustain the fantasies of glory and attention that Oates still harboured. Although ideas of being the saviour of the nation had mostly evaporated in the face of his failures at Valladolid and St Omers, startling revelations now proceeded from the mouth of the younger man. To the dazzled and credulous Tonge they seemed to confirm all of his worst fears. Yes, there had been a plot and this dated from at least 1639. Had not he, Titus Oates, heard and seen things that would make the old man's blood turn cold? Had not he, Titus Oates, risked life, limb, and his immortal soul, to uncover the devious plotting of these wicked men? Was not Tonge himself a major target for the plotters who resented his books, the same works that had also revealed their wickedness? Eagerly, Tonge asked Oates to write it all down. Oates, just as eager to have an audience who listened for a change, did so. He soon visited Tonge in his new abode, the house of Christopher Kirkby (the king's chemist) in Vauxhall. There he read a long and no doubt laboured tale to the increasingly panic-stricken Tonge. This plot went beyond anything Tonge had believed possible: names, dates and events, all flooded out, all confirming his view of the evils of popery. Tonge asked Oates for a copy. It had to be made in secret, as Oates claimed that even now the Jesuits were hunting him and would murder him if they found out he had revealed their plot. [63]

By 11 August Oates had left a copy of the forty-three articles relating to the plot under the wainscot near Tonge's lodgings in Sir Richard Barker's house. This convoluted postal method had been chosen to protect Oates, but also doubtless to give both parties an added air of excitement over the affair. Oates may also have attempted to sell his creation to the Jesuits at this point, but if so he was quickly rebuffed. All would soon be revealed, however, for this information, according to Tonge, must be taken to the king directly – and who better to take it to Charles than Tonge's good friend, Christopher Kirkby. The latter shared Tonge's views on Catholics and, moreover, he had bragged of having access to His Majesty. Kirkby agreed to try to get an audience with the king. He approached Charles, as we have seen, on the morning of 13 August and after dinner that day, at about 8 o'clock, Tonge and Kirkby were ushered into the king's presence. Having been fobbed off on to Lord Treasurer Danby, Tonge and Kirkby's next move was to attend him. At first Danby was too busy to see them. Then at last at about 4 o'clock on 14 August they were finally ushered into the presence of the Lord Treasurer, who had the incriminating papers before him. It was soon clear to Danby that neither Tonge nor Kirkby was the real informer in the case. Tonge related how the papers had come to him. Danby encouraged him to explain further and Tonge stated that the method by which the informant worked required secrecy as he was deep in Catholic councils. Danby then asked his servant Mr Lloyd to attend the doctor and observe how the Roman Catholics went about their work.

With his ministry only stumbling along, it may well have occurred to Danby that a new opportunity had just presented itself. His biographer Andrew Browning has noted how just a few months prior to Tonge's arrival the earl had wished for a 'some small insurrection' to present itself in order to unite the monarchy and the nation.[64] In Danby's eyes this was now a possibility. Danby was a shrewd politician and he was to use similar tactics later in his career.[65] He soon engaged himself in trying to uncover the plot's authors. The original informant remained teasingly obscure and Tonge rather evasive. Indeed, the minister's attempts to arrest Pickering and Grove, the two men named as the actual assassins intending to kill the king, proved equally fruitless. As Tonge, Kirkby and Lloyd scurried about the streets of London in their search for apparently non-existent assassins, both the king, who had been kept fully informed, and his minister began to lose interest. Danby had kept the plot close to his chest rather than passing the information to the secretaries of state for investigation, and it was proving unprofitable.

Both Tonge and Oates now seem to have realised that their policy of secrecy was beginning to rebound. A further attempt to set a decent trail was now in order. On 30 August Tonge sent information to Danby that a number of revealing letters from Fathers Whitebread, Ireland, Fenwick and Blundell had been sent by the conspirators to the Duke of York's confessor, Father Bedingfield, at Windsor. In fact, as Danby hurried off to Windsor, Bedingfield was already examining the mysterious coded communications that had turned up in the post and, not knowing what to make of them, but suspecting they boded no good for himself, he hastened to lay them before James, Duke of York. James was, as usual, outraged by the attempt to implicate one of his servants in a plot and took the letters to his brother the king. As these imprudent forgeries were circulated, the king grew still more disgusted and even Danby began to back out of any plans he may have had to exploit the plot. Rather than leave well alone at this point, James insisted that the matter be brought out into the open before the Privy Council. Either he, or his advisers, may well have seen this as an opportunity to stifle the fraudulent plot at birth. Charles reluctantly agreed.[66] Unaware of these events and believing that their evidence was now in danger of being ignored completely, Tonge and Oates sought to find some other way to bring it to public notice. With Oates fancifully claiming that he was now betrayed to the Jesuit provincial and indeed that he had been flogged as a result, Tonge was concerned. Fearing retribution, they fell upon the easiest way of bringing the plot out into the open: namely, by having their depositions sworn before a legal authority. At first they tried to bring their evidence to the notice of Secretary of State Sir Joseph

Williamson on the 5 September 1678.[67] Williamson, who had previous dealings with Tonge, was well aware of his crazy reputation, even if he did not recall Oates's name from the Hastings affair of 1675. He flatly refused to see either man. Tonge was now at a loss and so he took advice from some of his 'honourable friends about such a Justice as they might trust with so weighty a business. They, after some consideration, commended Sir Edmund Bury Godfrey' to him. And so Edmund Godfrey finally entered the plot that in one way or another was to cost him his life.[68]

CHAPTER FOUR

The Last Days of Edmund Godfrey

Nothing is more common, than to have two men tell the same story
quite differently one from another, yet both of them Eye-Witnesses to
the fact related.

Daniel Defoe, Serious Reflections during the life and surprising adventures
of Robinson Crusoe: with his vision of the angelick world *(1720)*

I am tied to the stake, and I must stand the course

William Shakespeare, King Lear

SEPTEMBER 1678: THE PLOT IN THE BALANCE

After Sir Joseph Williamson's refusal on 5 September Israel Tonge
went alone to Edmund Godfrey's house on the same day and told
Godfrey that he wished to have some information sworn, but at this
point he was reluctant to say what it concerned.[1] Naturally the
magistrate was equally reluctant to take such an obscure matter any
further; being ever sensitive to the legal nature of such transactions,
he expressed his caution before committing himself. A desperate
Tonge then persuaded Godfrey at least to visit the 'honourable
friends' and confer with them. This meeting then took place,
although we do not know where, nor who these 'honourable friends'
actually were. In the event Edmund Godfrey was sufficiently
persuaded to agree to meet with the informants the next day. On 6
September, Tonge returned to Godfrey's home in the company of
Oates and Kirkby; Oates and Godfrey met for the first time. It is not
clear what the magistrate thought of Oates, but the interview itself did

not go well. Godfrey again expressed his reluctance to take any depositions without knowing their contents, and, according to Tonge's version, he also asked the men to go elsewhere. Given Godfrey's officiousness in similar dealings this seems unlikely, although it is possible that having now seen the trio in person his disquiet with the affair had grown. Tonge claimed that he knew no one else to whom he could turn and the matter was a weighty one. He also said that Godfrey had come highly recommended. More significantly, Tonge now admitted that the matter at hand was one of high treason and that the king himself already had a copy of the depositions. Indeed, so serious was the matter that His Majesty had thought fit thus far to entrust it to only one member of his Privy Council. He mentioned no names but it must have been obvious that he meant Danby. Godfrey persisted in his inquiries as to the nature of the information, this being his right as a magistrate. It was 'fireing houses & towns' said Tonge. Godfrey then knew that the matter could be a serious one and as an experienced magistrate it may also have crossed his mind that even such outlandish folk might have some genuine information.

He therefore now began to question Oates about the matter. Oates told Godfrey that it concerned a fire in Southwark, which, he said, had been started by the Catholic priest John Grove. Godfrey may well have frowned a little at this for he not only knew John Grove personally but was also aware that he had been very active in stopping the fire even to the extent of losing his own property.[2] Nevertheless he still allowed Oates to swear to the papers and he even underwrote them. Tonge also swore on oath that the matter was known to the king. In spite of this the men would not leave any of the documents with the magistrate. It is very unlikely, however, that Godfrey would not have insisted on reading at least some of the documents. Thus far he had kept to his duty and he was well aware of the law on misprision of treason. Any failure to inform the proper authorities of treasonable matters could land not only Oates and Tonge, but also himself, in grave trouble. Indeed one source claimed that not only did Godfrey read the papers but he also made notes from them.[3] If he did, it was likely that Godfrey merely considered the documents wild and

exaggerated nonsense. Oates had already been caught out about
Grove, and Godfrey may well have decided to drop a hint to some of
his Catholic acquaintances about these eccentric individuals and their
claims. Oates's version of this interview was a typically crude one. In a
later idle bar-room moment he claimed that Godfrey was such 'a
Cowardly rascal, for when I went with my depositions to him, he was
so frighted that I believe he beshit himself, for there was such a stink I
could hardly stay in the room'.[4]

In fact, the very next day after seeing Godfrey Oates was to show his
own particular form of bravery by hurriedly leaving his lodgings in
Cockpit Alley, claiming that the Jesuits were after him and that one of
them, a man named Stratford, had beaten him. In reality Stratford, a
drunken neighbour, had been beating his wife and Oates had
intervened, complaining about the noise rather than the action itself,
so the man had fallen on Oates instead. The 'saviour of the nation'
swiftly retreated to lodge with Tonge at the Flying Horse tavern, where
he gave his credulous partner a more suitably heroic version of the
affair. Next Oates claimed that the Flying Horse itself was being
watched, so the pair agreed to repair to Kirkby's home in Vauxhall for
greater security.[5] Over the next week or so, as Kirkby and Tonge
attempted to kick start their plot by loitering around Danby's home in
the hope of a conversation with him, Oates, to while away the time,
began to put his depositions in order. He later claimed that he felt
more fearful than ever, now that his name would be well known to
Catholics as Godfrey must have told them of the plot.

In fact, sometime between taking the depositions and the next time
he was to meet Oates and Tonge, Edmund Godfrey had acquainted
his Catholic friend Edward Coleman with the details of what had been
revealed to him. One commentator noted that this was his usual
'custome, keeping faire with both sides'.[6] Indeed he had apparently
'wished him [Coleman] to wait upon the Duke of York' and to know
whether the duke had heard anything of the affair.[7] It is entirely
possible that Godfrey had also warned his other Catholic friends
about the plot. In any event at this meeting, which seems to have
taken place at Colonel George Weldon's tavern in York Buildings,
Godfrey apparently advised Coleman if he knew anything to

'impeach, which it is sayd hee did, and swore something before Godfrey which hee entered into a pocket booke'.[8] Whatever the truth of this, Coleman certainly informed James, Duke of York, of the design. The duke was soon insisting that the whole plot should go before the Privy Council together with the fraudulent letters sent to his confessor, Bedingfield. So, thanks to Godfrey's meddling, Danby's plan to keep the whole plot a close secret until it could be revealed in such a way that would benefit him had been spoiled. Worse still, Godfrey had influenced the constant rivalry in court affairs between the Duke of York and Danby by giving the former this advantage, damaging Danby's own credibility at court in the process.

Danby knew Godfrey well, of course, although, according to Gilbert Burnet, the two disliked one another. It is entirely possible that one of Danby's own servants had been one of the 'honourable friends' who had recommended Godfrey to Tonge. Indeed, Danby's servant, the ubiquitous Lloyd, seems a likely candidate in this respect, for the latter had been dealing with Tonge on an almost daily basis, mostly by blocking Tonge's access to his master. Equally there seems little doubt that at some stage either Danby summoned Godfrey or the magistrate paid him a visit of his own volition. At that meeting Danby appears to have railed against the hapless Godfrey for his part in the affair. The magistrate, given what we know of his previous reactions to authority and his staunch belief in the rule of law, is unlikely to have taken these complaints calmly. There may well have been an argument, with Godfrey defending his rights and Danby furious at being thwarted. Only afterwards would the magistrate have realised that the Lord Treasurer was not someone to be taken lightly. It was undoubtedly Danby to whom Godfrey referred when he met one acquaintance, Mr Mulys, in St James's Park, and was asked by him about the plot, rumours of which were by now in general circulation. Godfrey replied 'what was common Discourse of the Town – But I must not talk too much . . . for I lye under ill circumstances: Some Great Men blame me for not having done my Duty, and I am threatened by others, and very great Ones too, for having done too much.'[9] He was also alleged to have said to another acquaintance 'I shall have little thanks for my pains . . . I did it very unwillingly and would have fain have [had] it done by others.'[10] It appears that Godfrey believed that his action or inaction had already stirred up trouble. We must consider that Godfrey had met a trio of men by this time who had told him of a popish plot and he had begun to obscure the evidence, or had at least decided not to pursue the matter as vigorously and publicly as he should have done. Godfrey was thus beginning to flirt with the crime of misprision of treason, and over the next few weeks his dealings with Oates and most of all with Edward Coleman were to lead him on to still more dangerous ground.[11]

Over the next week or so Tonge and Kirkby made a number of further excursions to see either Danby or his crony the Bishop of London. On 19 September Tonge managed to see Danby, who asked him about Oates, whose name the Lord Treasurer now knew. He wanted to know whether he was a Yorkshire man and in any way related to the Oates who had been involved in the Yorkshire plot of 1663.[12] Otherwise he had little to say. Tonge then approached the Bishop of London to act on his behalf, but this appeal also fell on stony ground; the bishop mouthed platitudes and little else. An approach by Tonge to the ever-busy cleric Gilbert Burnet was also made around this time.[13] Burnet had previously known Tonge as a man who was ever 'full of projects and notions' and he at least was amazed by what he heard. Indeed, Burnet decided to make his own inquiries through the secretary of state's office, which claimed it knew of Tonge's discoveries. The officials there also thought that Tonge was merely inventing stories in order 'to get himself . . . made a dean'.[14] After this Burnet was to claim that he saw no reason not to discuss the business with others and did so. His cynical acquaintances saw it as 'design of Danby's to be laid before the next session [of parliament to] . . . put an end to all jealousies of the King, now the papists were conspiring against his life'.[15] George Savile, Marquis of Halifax, even told Burnet that he thought the discovery, whether true or false, would soon get out of the court's control and it was dangerous for that reason.

On 27 September, however, a summons finally came from the Privy Council.[16] Tonge and Kirkby rushed to attend but arrived too late. They were now ordered to attend the next day. One would have thought that this might have satisfied the informers, because this meant they were due to appear before the highest in the land. Yet a combination of factors once more led them to the door of Edmund Godfrey. Tonge appears to have been fearful that Oates might slip away again, or worse still that the dangerous Jesuits would remove him from the scene. Indeed, he seems to have thought that with the 'Jesuit assassins' lurking in every doorway, according to Oates at least, this might well be a distinct possibility. Something must be done to make the plot more public, lest the Privy Council stifle the information, as the Lord Treasurer had apparently done. Faced with this possibility, Tonge decided that they must revisit the magistrate whom they had previously visited on 6 September.[17] So on 27 September they returned to Edmund Godfrey's house, and there Oates swore before the magistrate two copies of his information. Faced with something in the region of eighty-one articles of fact, Godfrey signed both copies and the whole was witnessed by Tonge and Kirkby. This time Edmund Godfrey also insisted on retaining one copy for himself. Tonge reluctantly agreed and after this he and Kirkby left to go to the Privy Council meeting.

What was in these depositions? In their various forms the documents detailed clause by clause a number of attempts to murder King Charles II and the comings and goings by Oates and his Catholic acquaintances associated with the plot.[18] In a laborious fashion the depositions related tales of Scottish, English and Irish rebellions and a Europe-wide conspiracy that were guaranteed to warm the hearts of any rabid anti-Catholic. In his version of events Oates said he had seen numerous letters detailing the plot and had been informed at various times of most of its crucial details by rather loquacious, or plainly stupid, Roman Catholics: Charles II and perhaps his brother James, Duke of York, (unless as a Catholic he agreed to the plot) were targeted for assassination by bullet or poison. Oates also claimed to have seen other letters detailing the actions of the bungling Honest or Trusty William, an alias of John Grove, and Thomas Pickering, the would-be assassins. The pair were supposed to have made several farcical attempts to shoot the king, only to be foiled by poor guns and failing flints. There were hints of large sums of money to finance and sustain the plot, ranging from £10,000 to £15,000. A number of letters to Father La Chaise, conveyed by Oates to France, which detailed the extirpation of Protestantism in England and the stirring up of the Presbyterians to rebellion in Scotland, were also noted alongside derogatory references to Charles II and his father Charles I – these references implied that one or the other had been illegitimate. (In fact, this was an old canard common enough among the defeated Republicans of the early 1660s.)

Most of Oates's claims could easily have been taken from the published accounts of the real or imagined Republican plots of the 1660s.[19] Hints of the gathering of armies, secret commissions, rumours of bribes and the encouragement of rebellion among English Catholics were all familiar fare to anyone well versed in this earlier plot mania. By far the most significant aspect of the depositions lay in the tale of a general and secret meeting of the Jesuits held at the White Horse tavern in London in April 1678; Oates claimed that matters of treason were discussed and that he was an actual observer of these dealings. Oates went on to spice his tale with his supposed knowledge of the botched firing of London in 1666 and Southwark in 1676. He also added more material about Edward Coleman giving away state secrets, further attempts to kill Charles II and information against some of his old acquaintances from the club in Fuller's Rents and elsewhere.[20]

Why had the informers once more returned to Godfrey, the man whom they already knew was reluctant to have anything to do with them and whom they believed had told the authorities Oates's name? In retrospect (because we know that Godfrey was shortly to die) their action could be seen in a sinister light, but their motivation is unlikely to have been anything more than the fact that they still lacked any real contacts who could have been more helpful to them at this stage. They had been rebuffed by the most obvious contact in such matters – the secretary of state's office – and Godfrey was perhaps their last chance. The magistrate, however, must have greeted them with some dismay. Although he still strove to commit himself no further than any justice should have done, he was obviously left vulnerable and troubled. He was now in possession of what he believed was a grave, secret design against the monarchy. What was he to do with it? One would have thought that the obvious answer would have been for him to pass his information on to a higher authority, but Godfrey appears to have made a series of major misjudgments at this point that are redolent of his troubled personality. Instead of following Tonge and Kirkby straight to the meeting of the Privy Council, he seems to have turned once more to Edward Coleman for advice. The two men discussed the problem of the informers and Godfrey seems to have shown Coleman the papers he had acquired. At some point these papers were handed over to Lord Chief Justice Scroggs and he eventually sent them to the Privy Council, but the magistrate still remained troubled by the whole business.[21]

THE PRIVY COUNCIL: 28–29 SEPTEMBER 1678

The meeting of the committee of the Privy Council 28–29 September at which Tonge and Oates were to be interrogated was to be of vital importance in forwarding the plot.[22] The king himself introduced the affair in the first morning session, where he related how Kirkby and Tonge had approached him and that he had passed the affair on to Danby. The Bedingfield letters were then produced and examined by the wary ministers, who 'by the ill spellings of names; and other suspicious marks, thought [them] to be counterfeit matter'.[23] At which point Tonge was called in and proved to be singularly unhelpful. Charles asked him who Oates was and Tonge revealed that he and Oates had been before Edmund Godfrey to have the deposition sworn. It seems that Sir Joseph Williamson at this point made the logical suggestion that Godfrey himself should be summoned; however, nothing was done on that score. It may be that a still annoyed Danby blocked the suggestion, or perhaps the ministers thought the affair so unconvincing as not to be worthy of such serious consideration. Instead they adjourned for the morning. In the afternoon the Duke of York came before the committee to explain his part in the affair and the 'ill contrivences' of the letters. He then left. The committee finally called in Titus Oates and asked him to justify this strange affair. Now for the first time the main informer had an audience of the great and good to impress. He was not to waste his chance.

Where the committee members had smiled a little at the eccentric Tonge, they sat up and took notice of the booming voice of Oates.[24] Without the king or the Duke of York in their midst to control proceedings, they proceeded to listen to Oates as he effortlessly related his tale without any reference to the papers before them. Oates introduced himself as a clergyman who had once possessed a small parsonage near Sittingbourne, and who had subsequently been a chaplain at sea and in the 'Dutch fights', latterly on a voyage with Sir Richard Routh. After hearing of the many schemes of the Catholics, he had decided to penetrate their meetings. Once more Oates portrayed himself as the shrewd man of action who had determined, at some personal risk, to infiltrate Catholic designs, whatever the cost. He claimed he had decided to pretend to convert, and eventually he became trusted enough to be employed as a message carrier. He had been paid to take a packet of letters from Richard Strange and others to Madrid on behalf of the Jesuits. On reaching Burgos, however, he claimed that he had unsealed the letters and read the contents. At that point he related much of what had now been entered into the deposition that Godfrey had seen: trouble in Scotland and in Ireland, money and men supplied to provide for the attack, the planning for the death of the king. He also revealed that a number of meetings had been held about these matters in London itself. Oates was able to supply places and dates for these, as well as the names of those in attendance. He claimed that in Spain he had been swiftly taken into the confidence of the Jesuits and that on his return to London he had been sent to St Omers where he learned still more of the plot. Seizing the chance to return to London when it was revealed that the Jesuits had planned to kill off old Dr Tonge because of his writings, Oates had offered to poison Tonge for £50 (though he had in fact revealed the scheme to Tonge, he said).

Oates also told the council that he had continued to be employed to carry a number of papers between the conspirators. Assassination was their real game. The killers were to be Trusty William, Pickering and Coniers. The latter had dogged the king in St James's Park in

A previously unpublished John Hoskins portrait miniature of Godfrey the businessman of St Martin's-in-the-Fields, c. 1663, shows him in a different and less sympathetic light than later portraits.

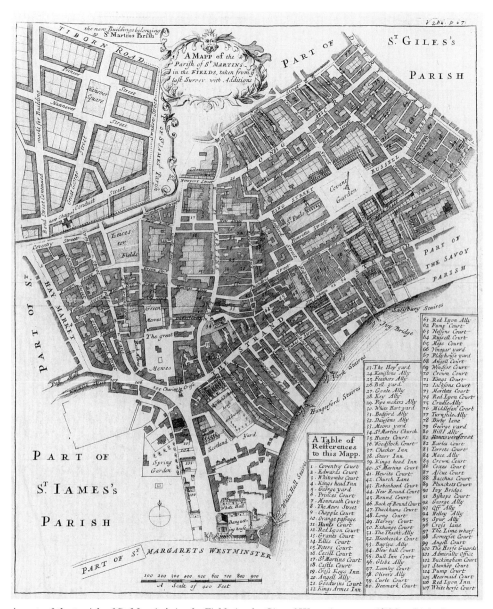

See detailed table of references below the map.

A map of the parish of St Martin's-in-the-Fields in the City of Westminster, c. 1720, which gives a good idea of the crowded nature of the area in which Edmund Godfrey spent much of his life.

King Charles II in a portrait by an unknown artist, 1675. The king always doubted the genuineness of the Popish Plot, but was ineffectual in preventing its exploitation by politicians opposed to the Earl of Danby's government.

A panoramic view of the city of Westminster showing the area between the palace of Westminster and Somerset House by William Morgan, 1682. The Palace of Whitehall is located to the centre left of the

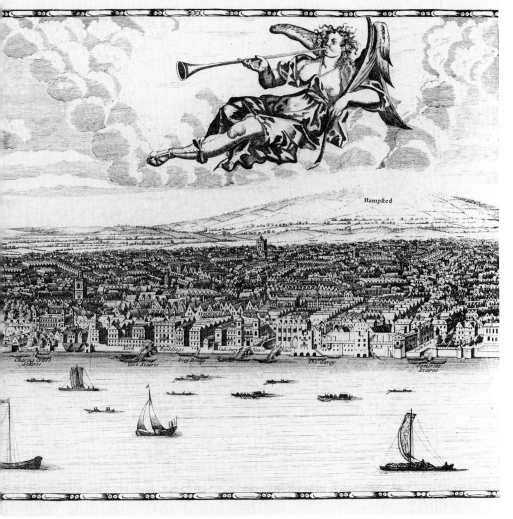

picture, while Somerset House, the reputed scene of Godfrey's murder, is on the far right. In the centre, marked by Charing Cross Stairs, lies Edmund Godfrey's home and woodyard.

This portrait of Titus Oates by Robert White, 1679, shows the main informer of the Popish Plot in all his borrowed glory as a clergyman.

Dogmatic, obstinate and a fervent convert to the Roman Catholic cause, in many respects James, Duke of York, was a primary source of the crisis which struck the country in 1678. This portrait is by Sir Peter Lely, c. 1670.

A shrewd and often forthright politician the Earl of Danby's mishandling of the Popish Plot was ultimately to end in his dismissal and imprisonment in the Tower of London. Many contemporaries also suspected him of involvement in the 'murder' of Edmund Godfrey. This portrait is by Sir Peter Lely, c. 1680.

June and July 1678, and when Charles went to Windsor Coniers had undertaken to attempt to murder him with a dagger, aided by four Irish ruffian priests. He had even purchased a set of daggers from Wood, an old Roman Catholic maker of cutlery in Russell Street. Pickering, on the other hand, was used to more conventional means of murder. He was hired to assassinate the king, but various technical problems had prevented it. John Grove and Coniers had both confessed to Oates himself that they had been hired to kill the king. Pickering and Grove even had a pistol with silver bullets to do the deed and had been promised £10,000 for their services from Father La Chaise, Louis XIV's confessor. They had greedily asked for £15,000 and this also had been promised. Failing the bullet and the knife, the king was to be poisoned by Sir George Wakeman. Oates claimed that Fathers Ireland and Fenwick had personally told him of these plans at a Catholic meeting.

The most significant part of the interrogation then followed. Oates took a hint in the questioning and claimed that the money for these schemes was to pass through the hands of none other than Edward Coleman. It seems this hint may well have come from Danby, anxious to get something at least out of this plot that he could use as a lever in his war at court with the Duke of York. Oates also claimed that emissaries had been sent throughout the country to spread the word that the king intended to sell his nation to a foreign state. Other methods were also to be used to incense the people and divide the nation from its rulers, whether king or parliament. Oates knew some of these emissaries through the club in Fuller's Rents and they were, he said, the devil's representatives. With this matter in hand, further differences were to be engineered between king and parliament, thus creating chaos in the land. Oates's informants also mocked the king personally and claimed that Charles was so negligent that he minded nothing but whores.

Oates was also shown the forged and mysterious letters and, naturally enough as Tonge had written them, he claimed to recognise the disguised hands of Fenwick, Blundell and other Jesuits. The Jesuits had even attempted to suborn London conventicles, but the Londoners were too clever to be taken in by their schemes. On 19

August there had been another meeting in Fenwick's chamber at which Coniers and one Anderson were chosen to go to Windsor to further the plot. Indeed, Oates claimed that he would have had six or seven more packets of secret papers to show had not the plot been discovered. But the story had got out and the secret letters intercepted at Windsor had alarmed the conspirators.

Oates had by now left his Privy Council audience spellbound and more than a little perplexed. There is little doubt that he had appeared convincing, especially as he had all the answers, dates, times, places and names of those involved. The ministers came to believe, or were at least half convinced, that there might well have been something in his tale.[25]

The next day, 29 September, a further meeting of the Privy Council was called and this time King Charles himself decided to attend.[26] As he sat down he must have viewed the whole affair with his usual cynicism, but he *was* willing to listen. Opinions differed as to his reaction. There is little doubt that he caught Oates out on a number of points, yet he did not press him. For example, Oates mentioned Don John of Austria, but Charles caught him out on a description of the man, whereupon Oates feebly responded that he had been told it was Don John 'and he could say no more than he was tould'.[27] The king pressed Oates as to where he had met Father La Chaise and Oates grew confused. He also pressed him as to where the Jesuit Provincial consult had met in London, and Oates boldly claimed at the White Horse in the Strand. But the king knew very well that the Jesuists had actually met in St James's Palace, the residence of his brother James.

The cutler Wood was also called in but he, of course, denied everything. Oates rather feebly claimed that as Wood was not in his work clothes he could not recognise him. Some in the room thought the king was showing his courage in making light of the affair, while others thought he had been half persuaded that the Jesuits were guilty of something. The king is reported to have said openly that Oates was a 'lying knave', but he did little more than this to ruin Oates's chances of success and indeed seems to have been criminally irresponsible in now deciding to play no further part in investigating the affair. Coleman's name had been mentioned, however: 'Mr. Oats testifyed touching the . . . concern of Mr. Coleman in these matters' and particularly of his correspondence with La Chaise, Louis XIV's confessor.[28] Perhaps the king, who had personally disliked Coleman's meddling, thought it worthwhile to expose the man and finally remove him altogether. Whatever the reason, he lazily allowed the Privy Council to issue a number of warrants to seize some of the persons Oates had mentioned. As this was announced, Danby chipped in that Coleman's papers ought to be seized as well as his person. It was to be a fateful remark, but was possibly based upon the information that Godfrey had given him.

The warrants were issued but many of the birds had already flown. However, Oates and a guard of soldiers were entrusted to search the buildings and streets of the metropolis for Jesuits and others who had offended. Fathers Whitebread, Fenwick and Ireland were soon arrested. Thomas Pickering, John Grove, and a number of others were also caught up in the net. The most notable catch proved to be Edward Coleman and his interesting papers.[29] At further meetings of the Privy Council the arrested men were interrogated. They naturally denied the affair, but not their knowledge of Oates. They were incarcerated in any case. Oates stumbled his way through ever more elaborate accusations and could not even recognise Coleman when he was summoned, but Coleman's fateful papers did appear to confirm some of the plot. In fact, King Charles was disgusted at what they contained and now once and for all washed his hands of the affair. Even the Duke of York, proved reluctant to assist Coleman.

The papers themselves were examined by a small private committee of the Privy Council: Prince Rupert, the Earl of Nottingham (who was Lord Chancellor), Danby, the Bishop of London, Secretary Coventry and the Chancellor of the Exchequer. They too were dismayed by what they read. Indeed, Sir Robert Southwell noted that the plot was getting out of hand, just as Halifax had predicted, and that it: 'will unavoidably devolve into the cognizance of the parliament, and then God almighty knows where the matter will stop. For this imprudent man [Coleman] has by his natural madness taken upon him to involve a person of high consideration as a party in his chimeras and the dangerous correspondence maintained between him and the confessor of the French King.'[30]

Still the plot was not really proved as yet. Oates was so far the only witness to these schemes and he was proving a feebler instrument in such matters than he might have hoped. Other than Coleman's correspondence little evidence had been found by interrogating the prisoners or by searching their papers. Once more it seems that the plot and its informers, now safely lodged in Whitehall Palace, were at a standstill. But the ripples of unrest began to spread. The guards at Whitehall were doubled; the Privy Council sat and interrogated many prisoners. There was little doubt that for his folly Coleman was certainly doomed, for the king was incensed at both his actions and the descriptions in the documents. With parliament now due to meet on 21 October, however, the Privy Council began to slacken off in its pursuit of the plot. With less zeal than before, the judges had been asked to rule on whether the evidence of one man made a sufficient case for treason. Unfortunately, on Saturday 12 October the whole situation altered. For on that day Sir Edmund Godfrey disappeared and as the news spread the nation was to be thrown into the greatest crisis of Charles II's reign.

EDMUND GODFREY: THE LAST WEEK

With the plot in the balance, rumours began to circulate in London and further afield. It was not easy to keep the investigations quiet, especially as Oates and his guards were rampaging around the city picking up victims for interrogation. Edmund Godfrey, however, had not been called before the Privy Council. Surprisingly, the magistrate to whom Oates had first delivered his depositions had not been invited to play a further part in this affair. In fact, Sir Joseph Williamson's suggestion on 28 September that Godfrey be called into the Privy Council to be questioned over what he knew about the design had not been followed up. Neither does the magistrate appear to have volunteered for interrogation. On the contrary, he seems to have become ever more depressed by the situation in which he now found himself.

Fortunately, there is sufficient evidence, although it is sometimes contradictory, to track Edmund Godfrey's movement over his last days.[31] While Oates was before the Privy Council, Godfrey went about his normal business. By Monday 7 October, however, his friend Edward Coleman had been arrested together with a number of other Catholics. In fact, despite Godfrey's warning Coleman's vanity had placed him in deep trouble. When he had talked to the Duke of York on 29 September, he had been reassured that if there was nothing incriminating in his papers he should hand himself over for interrogation. Coleman had also talked to others before his arrest, including Lord Chief Justice Scroggs. In due course Coleman had surrendered to Sir Joseph Williamson. The members of the Privy Council who began, as we have seen, by examining his papers had come to some swift conclusions. Yet still no one had approached Edmund Godfrey about the matter.

Mrs Mary Gibbon was a family friend of Godfrey.[32] She was also, arguably, an important witness to his state of mind just before his disappearance. Her evidence, however, has been somewhat neglected. Yet on at least four separate occasions she related her tale which, the more one reads it, the more it strikes one as a genuine view of Godfrey in his last days. Although she occasionally elaborated on her evidence, taken all in all, it still retains a ring of truth.[33] Mary was the wife of Captain Thomas Gibbon and was also 'somewhat related' to Godfrey. He appears to have looked upon her as something of a confidante. In fact, their parents had been friends and he frequently went to visit her at her home in Old Southampton Buildings. Interestingly, she was a Catholic and her daughter, also called Mary, appears at one time to have been in the employ of Edward Coleman.[34] In any event, she later claimed that a much-troubled magistrate had visited her on the Tuesday prior to his disappearance. As he closed the door of her chamber, he, in a disordered state, asked her 'If she did not know the news which was all over ye Towne that he was to be hang'd?' For, he added 'the entire Town is in an uproar about me'. She asked him what the plot was, to which he replied 'Oates had outswore himself and so it would come to nothing', but he had 'tooke Oates, & Tongs Examinations yesterday . . . moneth, and had never spoken of it to any man, although he had dined at my L[or]d Chancellors and Sir Wil[lia]m Joneses, the Attouney Generalls'.[35] At that point, they were interrupted and a confused Godfrey said he would come the next day to let her know more. He did, but as she was not yet dressed, he left without further discussion. She later told Sir Joseph Williamson, however, that Godfrey 'believed that surely there was a plott. That Oates had sworne largely, so as to confirme ye truth of what he said.'[36]

MONDAY 7 OCTOBER

Monday was the quarter sessions day for Westminster at which Sir Edmund Godfrey attended as a justice of the peace.[37] After court was recessed, Godfrey went out with his old friend Thomas Robinson, a fellow justice of the peace, to follow their usual custom after the sessions of dining with the head bailiff. In the course of the dinner, or just after it, Godfrey and Robinson openly discussed the latest news of the plot and the character of Oates. Robinson asked him if it was true that he had taken several statements and Godfrey confirmed his reluctant part in the affair. He also claimed that he no longer had the papers but had already delivered them to 'a person of quality'.[38] It was also during this conversation that Godfrey expressed the view that he was to be the first martyr in the case. Robinson indicated his surprise and Godfrey claimed he would not part with his life tamely, nor would he go about with any servant to protect him. In another version the words appear to imply that Godfrey was rather more concerned about the way in which parliament, which was shortly to meet, would see his part in the affair than about any threat of personal violence. He was right to be fearful, for Godfrey already had a reputation as someone tolerant of papists and his failure to reveal the full details of the plot to higher authorities could well have landed him in a case of misprision of treason. At the least, a subsequent trial may well have led to his incarceration and the loss of his property; at the most his own life might have been in danger.

TUESDAY 8–WEDNESDAY 9 OCTOBER

Godfrey's friend and business acquaintance Thomas Wynnel was later to claim that he met Godfrey in the days that followed and that the magistrate was both disordered and very unhappy. Later still, Wynnel was also to claim that he had repeatedly reasoned with Godfrey about his general unhappiness and that the magistrate had said that he had not long to live.[39] Despite his personal problems, however, Godfrey was coherent enough to engage in business and promised to dine with Wynnel on the coming Saturday to discuss some houses that Godfrey was going to buy. Wynnel also claimed that he talked to Godfrey at around the time when the Roman Catholic lords accused by Oates were committed to the Tower. He said that Godfrey told him that the lords were innocent but that Coleman would die; that Oates was foresworn and perjured, and the design was against the Duke of York. He was melancholy, he said, because he was 'master of a dangerous secret, that would be fatal to him; that his security was Oates's deposition; that the said Oates had first declared it to a publique minister: and [secondly] that he came to Sir Edmund by his direction'.[40] However, the Roman Catholic lords were not arrested until 21 October, so Wynnel's story falls rather flat at this point and like many another's evidence it may well have been exaggerated or tampered with.

THURSDAY 10 OCTOBER

Captain Thomas Gibbon later claimed that around 10 o'clock that Thursday morning, Godfrey had sent once more for Mary Gibbon. As she was attending her sick mother, the captain went to the magistrate by himself and later claimed to have found Godfrey in some disorder. Gibbon subsequently told this to both his daughter and wife on his return to the house. As we know, it had been to Mrs Gibbon that Godfrey confessed his melancholy about the affair in which he was involved. Later she claimed that some time before, when he was unwell, he had sent to her to make him some jelly, and on visiting the magistrate she found him very upset and intent on eating only whey instead. When she fussily asked him why he asked her to make the jelly and then resorted to whey, he spoke of fears for his sanity: 'Oh! Cousin, my father's sharpe melancholy I cannot shake it offe, it is hereditary; I am the only child of my father that takes after him: I was . . . [let] blood severall ounces yesterday, and some ounces before.'[41] He was also alleged to have said: 'I am best alone; I cannot get off this Melancholy'. Her daughter supported this tale and claimed that Godfrey said he had been bled. Captain Gibbon and his wife were naturally concerned about their friend, the more so since Mrs Gibbon was later to claim that it was well known in Kent that the Godfreys had been notorious for such distempers. Indeed, she was later to say that Thomas Godfrey himself had been subject to fits, and that at times she had seen him forcibly tied to his bed. She also said that Thomas had at one stage attacked three of his children and the surgeons had been called in to save their lives.[42]

FRIDAY 11 OCTOBER

On Friday 11 October a meeting of the parish vestry took place and Edmund Godfrey was, as usual, in attendance. The vestry business was full of mundane but, to the men themselves, important matters. The vestrymen made a number of decisions.[43] Richard Wheeler was at this meeting and he was to state that the magistrate had looked quite miserable and had even tried to pay off his debts. However, George Weldon saw Godfrey that night, when the magistrate was dining at his public house with others.[44] He later said before the Lords Committee that Godfrey was in good humour when last he saw him. The magistrate also showed him his pocket book (presumably the one in which he made notes of depositions and which was later missing from his dead body) but gloomily said he would not see him so often at Weldon's house from now on. Weldon went on to say he was a good friend of Godfrey and that the magistrate had previously said that he would be a sacrifice at one time or another. As Godfrey left on the Friday, however, Weldon asked him whether he would dine with him next day and Godfrey replied that he did not know whether he should. However, Weldon later seemed to change his story about

Godfrey's mood several times. Or perhaps the magistrate's mood really was fluctuating between despair, hysteria and sanguineness, for some at the vestry said he was in a pleasant enough mood there. Whatever the truth of the matter, in the late afternoon (4 or 5 o'clock) Edward Birthy and his wife claimed that they saw Godfrey walking down Drury Lane looking down at the ground and seemingly pensive, melancholic and even distraught enough not to know them.

There is little doubt that Godfrey did return home for some time that day. His servant Judith Pamphlin was later to relate what happened there. She claimed that on the Thursday Godfrey had been so distraught he had torn his band from his throat and flung it into the middle of the room. Nor was the Friday evening much better, as Pamphlin claimed that Godfrey had 'tumbled over all of his writings, and burnt as many papers, as her apron would hold'. She was very concerned about this, as she thought that in his distraction he might also have burnt the deeds for a cottage that she had mortgaged to him. The maidservant Elizabeth Curtis was to claim that a man also brought a note to Godfrey that same evening, but the magistrate 'didn't know what to make of it'.[45] Whatever the truth of the matter, it is certain that Henry Thynn was later to tell Sir Robert Southwell that he had seen Godfrey looking very glum indeed that evening at the house of the magistrate's great friend Lady Margaret Pratt.[46] The Pratts were old friends of the magistrate. Sir George Pratt of Coleshill in Berkshire had died a few years previously, but his wife Lady Margaret still held court in her house in Charing Cross and Godfrey frequently visited her there. Significantly, despite being a vital witness she appears never to have been interviewed by the authorities as to Godfrey's mood that evening.[47]

SATURDAY 12 OCTOBER: THE DAY OF DISAPPEARANCE

About this, the day of Godfrey's disappearance, there are a variety of eyewitness accounts. Some of them are plainly contradictory, while others seem to hold elements of the truth. At 6 or 7 o'clock that morning Richard Adams was to claim that he went to Godfrey's house and was told the magistrate had already gone out. However, the maid

Elizabeth Curtis was to claim that before Godfrey went out a man named Lawrence Hill had called and talked to Godfrey in both English and French. As we shall shortly see, this was to prove another nail in Hill's coffin at his trial. Curtis claimed that she had seen Hill in the parlour that morning when she brought in Godfrey's breakfast. Nevertheless, Curtis had not recognised Hill when she was taken to Newgate to identify him before the trial. Godfrey's clerk Henry Moor said that his master had some judicial business prior to 9 o'clock, then the 'company' left. This was as far as he would venture. It is clear that whatever the order of the earlier events, at around 9 or 10 o'clock that morning Henry Moor was with Godfrey in the parlour of his house. It was there that Moor helped his master on with his new coat. Then Godfrey changed his mind and replaced it with his old one and his sword. Godfrey left the house, crossed the yard and briefly paused at the gate, before leaving and turning out of Moor's sight.[48]

Richard Adams was to claim that he had returned to Godfrey's house at around 11 o'clock and found the servants there in great consternation: they appeared to fear for their master's life. Yet this is very unlikely. Although we know that Godfrey's manner had struck them sufficiently over the last month to worry them, he had only left the house an hour before and why he should cause such worry so soon is unknown.[49] It may well be that Adams actually got his days mixed up, for at around 9 o'clock that morning in St Martin's Lane, Mr Parsons, a coachmaker and churchwarden, claimed that Godfrey had stopped to ask for directions to Primrose Hill. Parsons, eager to pass the time of day, had cheekily asked the magistrate whether he was going to buy the place and Godfrey had sharply replied, 'What is that to you? I have business there or else I should not ask'd you or to [that] effect.'[50] But in another version of the meeting with Parsons, Judith Pamphlin claimed that what Parsons had really said was that Godfrey was looking for the 'woods'.[51] His business being that of a woodmonger, this does not seem so unnatural. Importantly, however, Sir Joseph Williamson, a trustworthy witness, confirmed in his notes upon the case that this meeting did actually take place.[52]

By 10 o'clock, Thomas Mason of Marylebone, who claimed he knew Godfrey by sight, saw the magistrate going towards the fields between

Marylebone Pound and Marylebone Street. He also said that he passed the time of day with Godfrey. It was also alleged that Godfrey was seen again at around 10 o'clock in the fields walking towards Marylebone, and that he was met there by a brewer of St Giles who talked with him. One witness claimed that at around 11 o'clock Godfrey was seen passing by the Lady Cook's lodgings near the Cock-Pit, after which he was seen in St Martin's Lane once more. He went by the church and down by Church Lane into the Strand. Richard Cooper, Mrs Leeson (his sister) and James Lowen all later alleged that they met Godfrey at this time in St Martin's Lane and said good morning to him. They also claimed that he looked melancholy. But Cooper was to admit that he could not remember the day this happened and that it might not have been the Saturday at all. For what it was worth, Henry Moor confirmed something of this tale. Yet another witness, a Mr Collins, claimed to have seen Godfrey at around 10 o'clock near his barn, hard by Marylebone Church.[53]

Thomas Snell, who lived in Holborn Turnstile, said he saw Godfrey pass by on his way to Red Lyon Fields at around noon that day, although he admitted that it was someone who actually knew the magistrate who told him it must have been Godfrey. In his pamphlet on the affair Nathaniel Thompson noted that his informant told him that Godfrey was undertaking some business at a churchwarden's place around midday. In the meanwhile, Thomas Wynnel, who was due to meet Godfrey at noon for his business meeting concerning some houses owned by himself in Brewer's Yard, was making his way to George Weldon's public house in York Buildings. As we have seen, Weldon's public house appears to have been a regular haunt of Godfrey, and other members of the vestry usually retired there after their meetings. Wynnel turned up early, but there was no sign of Edmund Godfrey. By noon he had sent Colonel Weldon's servant to Godfrey's house to seek his luncheon guest. This man soon returned and said the magistrate was not at home. Wynnel stayed on a while, then he himself wandered down to Hartshorne Lane. At Godfrey's house he saw Judith Pamphlin (or Curtis the maid) and Henry Moor looking both sad and surprised. They said Godfrey had gone out two hours before, which would place his departure between 10 or 11 o'clock. Wynnel naturally asked whether Godfrey would be dining with him that day, but Moor could not say. Wynnel then told Moor to tell his master that he was returning to Weldon's establishment. Wynnel later claimed the two servants appeared to be in great disorder. He, in the meantime, returned to Weldon's public house. Moor remembered the visit, but little else.[54]

Wynnel talked to Weldon that afternoon and he later claimed that Weldon believed he would see Edmund Godfrey no more. A puzzled Wynnel asked why, knowing it was common enough for Godfrey to go out early after he had finished his judicial business and not to return until quite late. To which Weldon replied that the magistrate's brothers, Michael and Benjamin Godfrey, had just been with him and said the papists had been watching their brother and were confident they had got him. This seems unlikely and it may be that Wynnel, whose statements are rather dubious at times, but who clearly was an important witness, confused Saturday with Sunday.[55] Whatever the case, Joseph Radcliffe, a vestryman and seller of oil in the Strand, alleged that he had met Edmund Godfrey near his door at 1 o'clock that afternoon. He also claimed the magistrate had looked melancholic. Radcliffe was to give his evidence at the inquest into Edmund's death so he may be taken as a rather more reliable witness than most, although he was also to complain that his evidence there had not only been interrupted but tampered with at a later date. It was also alleged that Moor had attempted to silence Radcliffe later that week for unexplained reasons of his own. Whatever the truth of this, Sir Joseph Williamson was to note that Godfrey had allegedly been seen around 'Arron Cookes [and the] L[ord] Tr[easurer's] daughter after one about near two'.[56] It was also alleged that two gentlemen had seen Godfrey in the back court of Lincoln's Inn. They had observed him making a sudden turn there and going out by the back door, by which they also left, and they had then seen him turn the corner wall between there and the Turnstile. A barrister at law met him there. Although Williamson noted that Godfrey was 'said to be near Turnstile near 3, but on inquiring of his brother there was nothing found in it', in fact Michael Godfrey was to state that the last real trace of his brother Edmund came at around this time, 2 to 3 o'clock.[57]

Thomas Grundy and James Huysman claimed that between 2 and 3 o'clock they had seen a person much like Godfrey close to the White House near Primrose Hill and that they had followed the man for about twenty yards. He looked very melancholic but they were only to connect him with Godfrey later on. A person living near Primrose Hill, on the other hand, was said to have declared before many people that he had seen Godfrey at about 3 o'clock that day and that the magistrate was walking in the fields there; indeed, he claimed Godfrey often walked there. Thomas Burdet later claimed to have met with a flustered Mr Wynnel not far from Green Lane between 2 and 3 o'clock. Burdet was startled when Wynnel said 'what have your people [the Roman Catholics] done with Sir Edmund Bury Godfrey, the town says you have murdered him.' Wynnel then told him the reports of the magistrate's disappearance, but once again this witness was not sure that it was on the Saturday that the meeting actually took place. Even so, rumours of the magistrate being missing seem to have begun very early. Judith Pamphlin later said she heard Moor's wife claim Godfrey had killed himself some days before the dead body was even found. Captain Thomas Paulden, a regular at the Duke's Coffee House, later stated that rumour had reached the establishment at around 3 or 4 o'clock on the Saturday that Godfrey had been killed by thieves or by his own hand. Whatever the rumours, it is clear that by 3 o'clock Edmund Godfrey had disappeared.[58]

SUNDAY 13 OCTOBER

Early on Sunday morning a worried Henry Moor set off from Hartshorne Lane for the house of Michael Godfrey. Once there he told Michael that Edmund had been out all night. Michael Godfrey told Moor to keep quiet about the matter at least until the afternoon when they would talk again. Moor was back at Godfrey's house by 9 o'clock in the morning. The nosy Judith Pamphlin, who disliked Moor and was still worried about her mortgage deed, which she believed Godfrey had burnt in haste on the Friday, saw him come in. Naturally she asked him where Godfrey was. Moor replied 'you silly foole he hath bin gon[e] out these two houres'. Later that same day both Michael and Benjamin Godfrey turned up at the house in Hartshorne Lane. They agreed with Moor that inquiries about Edmund should be made and they sent Judith to the Gibbon's home. Moor went with the Godfrey brothers to see Edmund's friend Lady Pratt at Charing Cross and to several other houses. As they did not find Edmund anywhere, they once more asked Moor to stay quiet about the matter at least until Monday. This seems dubious now and at the time it also struck some as suspicious. In fact, the whole affair was beginning to look odd, as Roger North was later to note: 'What a matter was it, that a justice of the peace did not dine at home, to raise such a Hubbub as this? A thing that must, sometimes, happen to everyone, as Business or Friendship may engage them abroad.'[59]

In the meantime, Judith Pamphlin had turned up at the Gibbons' home and asked whether they knew where Godfrey was. Mary Gibbon senior said she had not seen him and Judith replied that he must have been with her as she had heard him say that he needed to see Mrs Gibbon. Gibbon senior was later to claim that she herself had gone to Godfrey's house on the following Tuesday and questioned Moor. He claimed that Edmund was 'upon his fayth . . . as well as she'. When later challenged on this obvious lie, Moor said that Michael and Benjamin had told him to lie to save the estate. But Michael and Benjamin themselves came to the Gibbon's home on the Monday to ask whether Edmund was there. Gibbon said she had not seen him. They asked what sort of humour he had been in; she told them about Godfrey's actions and that he was much disordered. At this Michael Godfrey, she said, had 'lifted up his eyes and hands and s[ai]d L[or]d we are undone, what shall we doe'. But they refused to say why, only that they believed their brother to be at church on the Sunday and so they thought he would have come on afterwards to Mrs Gibbon's house. They left saying that she should hear more soon.[60]

MONDAY 14 OCTOBER

On the Monday morning the two Godfrey brothers went several times to see the Lord Chancellor, the Earl of Nottingham. Sir Robert Southwell was later to state that it was on this Monday morning that

Nottingham came into a Privy Council committee and told the members that the Godfrey brothers had consulted him about Edmund's absence. He joked that the pair 'would needs believe that their brother was murthered by Papists; but his L[o]rd[shi]p told it in such a sort (seeing the man had been not missing by 2 nights) that little notice was taken of it and noe order' was made on the matter.[61] Rumours of the magistrate's absence had, however, leaked out. North was to claim that rumours 'always used to run as wildfire in a train, and spread all over the Town . . . And so went the report that Godfrey was missing. It was in everyone's Mouth, Where is Godfrey? . . . they say he is murdered by the Papists.'[62] Robert Whitehall, sitting in George's Coffee House in Freeman's Yard, had heard the rumours that the magistrate had been murdered on Sunday or Monday. Around Primrose Hill, however, all was quiet. A servant of the owner of the fields near the hill turned up in the meadows alongside a butcher and two boys and proceeded to search for a missing calf there. They had little luck and saw nothing at that time. They searched for the calf again the next day (Tuesday) but again found nothing.[63]

TUESDAY 15 OCTOBER

On Tuesday Henry Moor attended a funeral.[64] He had heard on Sunday evening that the event was to take place, and with the Godfrey brothers' permission he now sought to divulge to the crowd there that Edmund Godfrey was missing. It was at the funeral that Parsons, the churchwarden, told him that he had seen Godfrey on the Saturday morning about 9 o'clock or so in St Martin's Lane and that the magistrate had inquired the way to Primrose Hill. Armed with this knowledge Moor went up to look at Primrose Hill, and Mary Gibbon was to claim that Moor had told Judith Pamphlin that he must have been within a few yards of the body, if it had been there. Yet despite this, Moor was later that same day denying to Mrs Gibbon that anything was wrong; the clerk's actions appear very suspicious. About 10 o'clock, however, Thomas Mason saw a man who must have been Moor walking under a hedge near his house. Moor inquired of Mason whether he had seen his master Godfrey in the fields since Saturday.[65] Mason told him that he had indeed seen Godfrey at around 10 o'clock on the Saturday morning. It is unclear, but obviously important, whether this meeting took place on Tuesday or Sunday. But what is clear is that Moor *was* lurking about Primrose Hill at some point after the Saturday. Now, however, the 'alarm took, and all people ran about, strangely busy, enquiring what was become of Godfrey'. Some of the rumours flying about were that Godfrey had been married to a widow of a lawyer, who may have been Lady Pratt, that he had been discovered in bed with a whore, that he had retired into the countryside or simply that he had been murdered.

Robert Southwell later confirmed that Nottingham came to the Privy Council again on the Tuesday morning. This time he was less jovial and said the two Godfrey brothers were still following him about and that he could give them no other answer than to attend the committee. Michael and Benjamin were thus called in and, according to Southwell, they made such a commotion that he now had an order to draw up a proclamation concerning Godfrey's disappearance. Southwell held off printing it, however, for that afternoon Henry Thynn came in with the story of how melancholy Godfrey had looked at Lady Pratt's on the Friday evening. The Godfrey brothers complained to him about the delay. Nevertheless, Southwell said, he had now heard of how melancholy Edmund had been and perhaps the miserable man had just stepped into the country for a few days. Even a concerned Southwell would not damage the honour of the Privy Council by issuing a false proclamation until the situation was far clearer.[66]

Chaos still reigned in the house at Hartshorne Lane, however. That same Tuesday Mrs Gibbon went to Godfrey's house again and had a talk with Judith Pamphlin, who, no doubt with a wink and a nod, hinted that they would not see Edmund Godfrey again; a worried Mrs Gibbon asked why and Judith replied that she could not tell her. It was after this that Moor had still maintained everything was all right. A few weeks later Judith did finally come to Mrs Gibbon to ask why she (Judith) had not been examined. At the same time she hinted of things she could tell: 'I and ye clerke can say a great deale, if we were examined upon oath, [for] the clerke knows more than you can imagine'.[67] Mrs Gibbon later gave some notes about this and other matters to the Lords Committee that examined Godfrey's death, and when she was called in to explain, the Earl of Shaftesbury roundly belaboured her for her pains. However, Captain Gibbon talked to George Weldon and learned from him that Godfrey had been very out of sorts ever since Oates's examination. Mary Gibbon junior confirmed Judith Pamphlin's complaint that she thought it strange she had not been examined. Judith's explanation of the situation was that Michael and Benjamin Godfrey were not happy for her to appear. Indeed, they wanted to keep her quiet and told her that if she had to say anything then she should say that the papists had killed Godfrey, or she would lose her position.[68]

Another witness, Richard Wheeler, went to Godfrey's house on the Tuesday to ask whether he had turned up, he found the mace-bearer of the mayor there talking to Henry Moor. Moor confirmed that nothing had been heard of the magistrate but what the churchwarden Parsons had told him and what a new witness, a man sawing wood in Soho fields, had said. This individual, called Sawyer, claimed to have seen Godfrey in Soho. Furthermore, Sir Joseph Williamson was later to note that: 'On Tuesday evening [a man who from other sources we learn was named Thomas Morgan] went round by that place [Primrose Hill] to dresse a horse & washed his hands in a pond, &, saw nothing.'[69] Robert Forest later claimed to have been hunting with his pack of hounds earlier on Tuesday at the place where the body was to be found, and there was no body there at that point. With his friend Henry Harwood he also hunted there on Wednesday, and he claimed that they had both beaten the area and the ditch in search of quarry. The pair may well have been the 'soldiers' whom the landlord of the White House near to Primrose Hill saw there looking for hedgehogs. Either way, such a lonely spot seems to have been quite crowded during those few days.[70]

WEDNESDAY 16 OCTOBER

Robert Southwell was at the Privy Council early on Wednesday and once again he noted that the Godfrey brothers were in attendance. But the Duke of Norfolk had that day come in with another tale that

Edmund Godfrey had gone off in secret to marry a lawyer's widow, one Mrs Offley. This once more 'putt the matter into laughter for that day'.[71] Some time during the week Richard Adams was also talking to the Earl of Powis at the end of Lombard Street, when he saw Mr Harrison, the estranged nephew of Godfrey, and crossed the street to talk to him. Adams asked Harrison for the truth about his uncle and the latter replied that the report was that papists had murdered him. Also at some point in the week Elizabeth Dekin, a servant to Mr Breedon of Hartshorne Lane, was told by her fellow servant John Oakley that he had seen Edmund Godfrey on the Saturday evening walking near the Water-gate at Somerset House in the Strand. He also said that there was a man or two near Godfrey at that point. Oakley was positive that it was the magistrate as he doffed his hat to him and Godfrey did likewise. Although this witness came forward long after the event, we will return to the placing of Godfrey near Somerset House when Miles Prance enters the tale.[72]

THURSDAY 17 OCTOBER: THE DISCOVERY OF THE BODY

Around midday on Thursday 17 October Adam Angus, the curate of St Dunstan's-in-the-West was browsing at a bookshop in St Paul's churchyard.[73] A young man in a grey-coloured suit who was passing by stopped, touched Angus on the shoulder and said that the missing Edmund Godfrey had been found in Leicester Fields, by the dead wall with his own sword run through him. He then walked off. A worried Angus went off to the vicar of St Martin's-in-the-Fields, Dr Lloyd, who earlier in the week had been making inquires of his own among the vestrymen. Angus told Lloyd of the mysterious incident. At around the same time, about 1 o'clock, William Bromwell, a baker, and John Waters, a farrier, both from the parish of St Giles-in-the-Fields, were dodging the raindrops as they trudged over the fields towards the White House tavern near Primrose Hill. While crossing one of the fields on the south side of the hill, the pair saw a sword scabbard, belt, a stick and a pair of gloves, lying together hard by the hedge. Presuming they belonged to a man who had gone into the ditch to relieve himself, they left well alone. They soon reached the White

House and over their drinks mentioned their find to the landlord John Rawson. Rawson, a man with an eye for an opportunity, asked them why they had not picked the goods up and brought them into the alehouse. He mentioned that there had been several soldiers earlier in the week hedgehog-hunting out there and that it might have been one of them who had left the goods behind. Having heard the men out, Rawson evidently thought it worth his while to get hold of the goods, so he offered both of them a shilling for a drink if they would go back with him to look for them. But it was now raining hard and as a result the men sat back, supped their ale and waited for the skies to clear.[74]

In a newsletter of the time, William Griffiths was to give a slightly different version of these events in that he added an extra two characters to the tale.[75] He was to claim that Edward Linnet, a butcher from St Giles, and his dog were also in the company of Bromwell and Waters and that it was the butcher's dog that uncovered the body. Yet Linnet makes little appearance in other evidence thereafter. He was not called to the inquest and made only a brief appearance in the Shaftesbury papers. Was he the butcher who was in the fields on the Monday and Tuesday? The mysterious butcher and his dog, however, were to reappear as an important factor in some historians' views of the affair, as we shall see below.[76]

Whatever the truth of who was there, what do we know for certain of the tavern called the White House? Summoned before the Lords Committee that investigated Godfrey's death, the landlord, John Rawson, said that he was a Protestant. Although he had few visitors during the winter, his tavern was much busier in the summer when many Londoners came to take the air on Primrose Hill. The coroner John Cooper was to claim that the building itself was a poor place with little to commend it, having no hangings or accommodation and scarcely a glass window to keep out the draughts. While its regular patrons were a mixed lot, some of the most interesting regulars were a group of tradesmen who kept a club there. Mr Horny, a tailor of St Giles, thought he heard Rawson call these men 'papist dogs', and he thought the clubmen were all papists, except one Greenway.

It is clear that some of these men were in the tavern at the time of the inquest, for the club was to meet on the Sunday after this event.

As a club the men were later noted for having discoursed freely about any number of things. They included one Swannet or Stanwick, a waterman who kept a victualling house in St Giles by the pump near by Noah's Ark. Another member was none other than Mr Moyle or Mulys, a gentleman's stewart who lived with his son Blundell, a milliner, also a member of the club, in St Giles. Mulys was an acquaintance of Edmund Godfrey and indeed was to claim that he had had a conversation about Oates with the magistrate some five or six days before the 12 October. The other members of the club included: Edward Grove, a strongwaterman who lived over against the Horse Shoe tavern in Drury Lane; Cawthorne, a joiner whose business was hard by New Market; William Brand, a silversmith; Greenway, a Protestant oilman in Russell Street; Currey, a silversmith; and Cosey, a Protestant pewterer over by Drury Lane. By far the most important member of the White House club, however, was 'Mr. Prince a silversmith in Holborn'. This was none other than the Miles Prance, who was to be an important figure in the trials that followed Godfrey's death. Prance later confirmed his attendance at the club before the Lords Committee, mainly by denying that he had been to the White House in the previous twelve months, although he may well have been closer to events on Friday 18 October than he later revealed. Rawson claimed the men themselves did not game but did spend a groat apiece on entertainment. Greenway said that they were not a club as such, but they met sometimes and discoursed about various things – but not, he hastened to add, about state matters.[77]

In any event after further talk both Bromwell and Waters finally agreed, in return for a shilling, to go back with Rawson to try to locate the spot where they had seen the discarded goods. It was now about 5 o'clock. They succeeded in locating the place and there found the goods, but as Rawson stooped to pick up the scabbard, he thought he saw a body in the ditch on its belly with a sword through it sticking seven or eight inches out of its back. At this the men seem to have panicked; they went immediately to the churchwarden of the parish house to tell him of their discovery. But he was ill and they soon found themselves before the door of Constable John Brown, who lived in a house near St Giles Pound.[78]

As soon as word was brought to Brown he immediately called upon his neighbours. So it was that William Lock and thirteen or fourteen men went with Brown to view the scene. The body was located in a drainage ditch on the south side of Primrose Hill. The hill was surrounded by various fields fenced in by high mounds and ditches, and the drainage ditch lay some two fields away from the White House, 'so cover'd with the Bushes and Brambles, that it was a hard matter to see the Body, till one were come just upon it'.[79] There were some deep, dirty lanes to be crossed to approach the ditch, and the gates between the fields were generally left unlocked. That week's weather had been rather stormy, and it was later alleged that area around the place was so dirty that the constable and his men, who carried the body, got filthy up to their saddle skirts. With an English propensity for noting the weather, however, others claimed that much of the week had been fair with only a few showers of hail or rain. Griffith's newsletter noted that the gates through to the grounds where the body lay were found to be 'forced, and . . . tracks, it was first thought of a coach . . . upon better examination [were] found by Serjeant Ramsey [Serjeant at Arms to the Lord Treasurer Danby] to be only those of a cart'.[80] These marks, it was claimed, were fresh and there was also much hay strewn about the fields either to feed the animal that had pulled the cart there or, in a more sinister interpretation, abandoned after being used to cover the body of Edmund Godfrey.

With John Rawson and the others in attendance, however, Brown and Lock got into the ditch. Brown's own words describe the scene. There was, he said, 'A dead body lying in the ditch of the field, called Primrose Hill, with the face downwards, and sword run through it, coming out at the back; but this deponent not knowing who the same was, lying on the face, turned the said body, and found it to be Sir Edmund Bury Godfrey and this deponent, well observed the place where the said body lay in the ditch.'[81]

In the gathering gloom, for by now it was nearing 8 o'clock and coming on blustery, Brown made his decision. Having noted the posture of the body, he drew the sword out of it and, together with his men, heaved it out of the ditch. They confirmed that it was indeed

Godfrey. The sword was noted as having a point covered in blood, but the part embedded within the body was black without any blood on it. They then carried the body back over the fields to the White House.[82]

It is worth noting at this point the original posture of the corpse. Godfrey was lying in the ditch with a sword run through him just under his left breast; it came about seven or eight inches out of the right side of his back. The hilt of the sword was three inches from the ground. One of Godfrey's hands was doubled under and he seemed to lean on it, while the other hand was lying upon the bank of the ditch. His 'hair chamlet' coat was thrown back over his head. His hat and periwig were lying among the bushes over his head. No band or cravat was found on him. It was later claimed that Godfrey had had a large laced band on when he left home; this was now missing. However, Judith Pamphlin later told Mrs Gibbon that Godfrey had himself torn off his band on the previous Thursday.[83]

Once at the White House, Constable Brown had the body placed on a table and searched. By the light of candles they found in one pocket six guineas wrapped in paper, four broad pieces of gold and half a crown also wrapped in paper. In the other pocket were two rings (one with a diamond), one guinea, £4 in silver and two small pieces of gold. On one of the magistrate's fingers was another ring. But the pocket book, which Godfrey used to make notes of his examinations and interrogations, was missing. The other goods, the sword, scabbard, belt, gloves and stick were all later confirmed to have belonged to the magistrate. Some said that they were quite weather beaten.[84]

Thomas Paulden was once more indulging himself in the good company of the Duke's Coffee House that evening when two men came up on horseback and shouted for help. The company all rushed out and they were told the missing Edmund Godfrey had finally been found. In the meanwhile Brown and the others went to Godfrey's home to break the bad news to Henry Moor that his master had been found at last. It was nearing 10 o'clock by the time they arrived at Hartshorne Lane. There they found not only Moor but Michael and Benjamin Godfrey, as well as their relative Mr Pluncknett and Danby's man Serjeant Ramsey. At first Moor and Godfrey's brothers queried whether the body really was that of Edmund, but Pluncknett said he would go with the constable and his men to examine it while Ramsey excused himself to go off to break the news at court. Brown was told to meet him for further orders at the Chequer Inn in Charing Cross by 1 o'clock that morning at the latest.

Pluncknett, Brown and his neighbours rode through relatively quiet city streets and out into the dark countryside. Once at the White House Pluncknett was shown Godfrey's corpse and, recognising it, cried out 'This is my Brother Godfrey[!]'. He then insisted on arming the company with lights in order to visit the ditch. Only then did Pluncknett, Brown and their followers make their way back down to Charing Cross where Ramsey by now awaited them. Ramsey now dismissed the weary Brown, who was no doubt reassured by his statement that the Coroner of Middlesex, Mr Cooper, had already been informed and the matter was now in his hands. Brown was to be available, nevertheless, for the inquest that would surely follow.[85]

THE CORONER'S INQUEST: 18–19 OCTOBER

Friday 18 October now dawned. As required by the law in such cases, a coroner's jury, assembled by Mr John Cooper, Coroner of Middlesex, met to consider this most mysterious death. Established in 1194, the Coroner's Office was an important institution in matters of sudden or suspicious death. While not generally a medical man in the seventeenth century, it was usual for a coroner to be of some social standing.[86] The attitude of the coroner and his jury was to prove of some significance in the assessment of the case that now lay before them. The inquest was, of course, a public drama, and as such it was subject to the usual pressures brought by family and friends of the deceased. In addition, it would soon have been realised that the case had unique political overtones. In itself the inquest had to rely upon lay interpretations of the way in which Godfrey had met his end. Although in this instance expert medical men were also to be called in to assess the nature of the magistrate's death, in fact, their medical evidence has been subject to examination and criticism ever since. It was also later claimed of this particular jury that much art and ingenuity was used against it to get it to deliver the right verdict. It was said that the jury was first of the opinion that the verdict was *felo de se*, or suicide, and that it had to be persuaded otherwise.[87] In addition, it was claimed that the jurymen were refused an autopsy on the body, which appears to have been untrue, and that John Cooper turned the body over to Godfrey's family as soon as he could. The reality was somewhat different.

In general, the inquest followed the rules of others of the era, but it began badly. Cooper had not even begun his difficult task when the Coroner of Westminster, Mr White, turned up. He claimed that he was there at the request of some in St Martin's parish who evidently mistrusted Cooper's abilities. White offered either to assist in or wholly take over the case. Naturally offended, Cooper rejected both moves outright and stood his ground, alleging, quite legitimately, that the case belonged to his jurisdiction. There followed a 'warm contest' between the two men over their jurisdiction and Cooper refused to allow his rival any part in the affair. After the two coroners had argued and made fools of themselves, someone finally made the peace and the two eventually came to an agreement that satisfied Cooper. Mr White withdrew and was given a guinea for his troubles by Michael Godfrey who, together with Dr Lloyd, had apparently been behind this move.[88]

It is said the jury, John Cooper (the coroner) and Constable Brown then went at around 10 o'clock to view the place where the body had been found. There was also a 'great concourse of people' either already there or trailing along behind them and messing up the ground. Indeed, the crowd seems to have included the two Godfrey brothers, a surgeon, Zachary Skillarne, whom Michael had invited along, Godfrey's clerk Henry Moor and, on Danby's behalf, his Serjeant-at-Arms Ramsey.[89] In fact, quite a lot of people came to view the place and then the body. They saw the ditch where it had lain and then they went to see Godfrey himself, still lying on a table where he had been placed the previous evening. Brown claimed the body's neck was broken: 'It was very weak and one might turn his head from one shoulder to another.'[90] One Hobbs later claimed he had told a Dr Goodall that it would be very well if Michael Godfrey would send for a surgeon and a physician from the court to satisfy all persons. He also claimed that he thought Godfrey's face was not only 'blotted', but the violence done to him could be seen in his bloody eyes; he did not observe any fly-blows. This, it was claimed, was an important point, as it proved that putrefaction and insect infestation had not yet set into the corpse.[91]

At some point the body was stripped. This seems to have been done after the Chases and Mr Lazinby saw it for the first time. Mr Chase, the king's apothecary, and his son came to view the body and noted the two wounds and a great contusion on the left ear, and that the magistrate's whole face was very much bruised. Chase later claimed that he was asked by the interfering Dr Lloyd to go once again to see the body on the Saturday, and on that second viewing he found a swelling on the left ear, as if a knot had been tied there. He thought Godfrey had been beaten from the neck to the stomach. Four years later, in 1682, Mr Lazinby, from the king's court, was called to testify and he said that on seeing the body he thought that Edmund Godfrey appeared to have been strangled. Indeed, the cloth that strangled him had been kept about his neck until he was cold. He went on to say that in cases where people are hanged and let down while still warm, the blood would drain away and their faces would become very pale. In Godfrey's case, however, the blood could not drain away and it had made his face look bloody. He also saw some blood near the ditch. From the neck to the stomach and breast, Lazinby noted, the body was very discoloured and black. After he and Chase senior had seen the body, Lazinby went off for a glass of beer while Chase junior remained behind. It was he who unbuttoned Godfrey's collar and found there two great creases both above and below it; Lazinby was once more sent for to have yet another look. He put the collar together and observed it made a mark, like a straightening upon a finger, the neck being swelled above and below the collar by strangling with a cord or cloth. The body's eyes were also bloodshot, as if Godfrey had had a great cold or had sustained a blow on the forehead or temple. Lazinby noted that Godfrey's clothes were not wet, which surprised him, as there had been a 'storm' the previous afternoon. Apparently there was a great fire blazing in the ale house, which may have accounted for this drying out.[92]

We know that the body was not re-dressed and that at least four medical men saw it on that Friday. One Fisher, a carpenter to Lord Wooton, who had come to see things for himself, assisted in removing the dead man's clothes. He noted that Godfrey's shoes were clean. Much was made of this fact, it being thought that it was a clear sign that Godfrey had been carried to the ditch before being dumped there. In undressing the body, however, they removed three pairs of stockings, a pair of socks, his breeches, which were black and his drawers. They then propped the dead man up, unbuttoned his coat and pulled it off; there was blood on the back of his flannel shirt. About his throat were marks of something that had 'girt' him and his neck was so weak that it might be turned in any direction. Fisher noted that they could not bend Godfrey's arms to take off his shirt because of rigor mortis, so they were forced to split open the shirt in order to remove it.[93]

Doctors Zachary Skillarne (or Skillard) and Nicholas Cambridge must have then turned up, and they viewed the body in the presence of the coroner John Cooper and his jury at around noon in the White House. If there were some argument about a post mortem, it would have been at this point; some claimed that the Godfrey brothers would not allow the body to be opened. However, that there was a post mortem of sorts is clear, for there are hints about the matter in Sir Joseph Williamson's notes. It was not likely to have been comprehensive if the family was resistant. Probing the body with medical lances, Skillarne noted that the breast appeared to have been beaten with some obtuse weapon or with the 'feet or hands or something'. The neck was distorted: 'you might have taken the chin and set it upon either shoulder'. Two wounds were also noted; one of the surgeons probed these. One wound was an inch deep, then came up against the ribs; the other wound went through the body. There was also a claim that neither the flannel shirt nor waistcoat were penetrated, but in retrospect this does not seem to make much sense. Skillarne said that no more had been done to Godfrey's neck than in ordinary suffocations, but that the second wound went through his heart. This wound had not killed the magistrate; it had been inflicted after death.

The next point of debate was whether Godfrey had been strangled or hanged. Skillarne was to note that in his experience a lean man's muscles, if he had died of wounds, would have been turgid, but that strangled people never swell as such an act hindered the circulation of the blood. The dead man's face was somewhat swelled and of a fresh colour; he was noted for being pale in his life. As to the time of death, the doctor stated that it occurred some four or five days previously. This would place the death on Sunday or Saturday. He also said that the body might have been kept a week and not swelled, for Godfrey was a lean man. Putrefaction, he later noted, had only set in after the post-mortem examination.[94]

Nicholas Cambridge also saw the body on that Friday and he found the neck dislocated, the breast greatly beaten and two puncture wounds under the left breast, one against a rib, another right through the body. These wounds, he said, were made after death. Other notes available claim that there was also a green circle about the dead man's neck as if he had been strangled, and that the blood had settled about his neck, throat and upper part of the breast. Both surgeons agreed the wounds were not the cause of his death, but could not agree on the means of his demise, settling for a general notion of strangulation. Coroner Cooper was later to state before the Lords that he did not know who had killed Edmund Godfrey, but that he believed it was murder and that the man had been strangled. He also noted a bruise near the dead man's throat, on his breast, and that the body had been in a posture where Godfrey could not have fallen or put himself. Moreover, the fields over which he would have had to pass would have been dirty and there was no dirt on his shoes. Additionally, it was Cooper who observed the tracks of a coach in the ground where, he said, no coach used to come. But Serjeant Ramsey, who examined these marks, declared them to be merely cart tracks, as one might expect in a field. Cooper also claimed that the dead man's joints were limber and pliable, and that his clothes were weather beaten. However, his idea that the body was fly-blown was refuted at a later date.

Cooper also made a more important report to Sir Joseph Williamson on 20 October 1678. In these notes we find mention of the fact that the hilt of the sword, which had passed through the body, had been three inches from the ground on the corpse's discovery. There was no blood near the place, nor where the body had been placed, nor any under the hilt of the sword. Mention was made of a bruise located on the top of the breast, just under the collar, and a circle round Godfrey's neck indicating he had been strangled. This report to Williamson also noted that the dead man's shoes, or at least the soles, were extremely clean. Contrary to the surgeons, Cooper claimed that the body showed signs of putrefaction. The dead man's face was not only redder than ordinary, Cooper said, he had not died from the wounds in his breast. Godfrey's neck turned all one way to the left and his eyes and mouth were closed. His stomach was 'extreme empty, therefore had not eaten in two days or more'.[95]

Elizabeth Curtis had been set to washing the body at the magistrate's house when it was finally brought home. When asked at a later date for her opinion, she said that she had not noticed any spots of blood on it. As for the clothes of the dead man, she was ordered to look at them by Henry Moor to search for some note that was said to be about Godfrey. We are not told what this note was supposed to be, and whatever it was it was not found. Was it the note Godfrey was alleged to have received on the Friday at his home and did not know what to make of? Gobbets of blood and some dry spots of a greenish colour were found upon his waistcoat, linen and drawers, as well spots of white wax. This was seen as the sinister signs of papists who used wax candles. More logically, of course, it could merely have been the result of the blunderings by Brown and company in the dark or of the subsequent post mortem, which was carried out in the poor conditions of the White House. When Elizabeth washed the body, it did not smell, nor were the clothes ragged or tattered, but sound and whole. They were those he had on when he left the house.

The body had already been stripped at the White House, and, wrapped up in a blanket, it was now returned to the relatives. Indeed Moor, Michael and Benjamin and the sisters had gone to the White House to see the body on the Friday, and the coroner issued a warrant for its release to them on the 18 October, but it seems to have remained in the White House until at least noon on the Saturday.[96]

The inquest itself was proving difficult to resolve. If we are to believe the tales of some of the jurors involved, who were later interrogated by Sir Roger L'Estrange, some were unconvinced by the medical evidence, or just plain confused by the surgeons' reports. Surrounded by a great crowd of people and the dead magistrate's relatives, they were unable to come to any verdict. As one of them later said 'the Jury could not tell what to think on't, it was so ticklish a Bus'ness'. As the debate swayed between a verdict of suicide and murder, Cooper called a halt to the proceedings for the day. The jurymen complained about this, for it meant they would lose another day's business by having to reconvene the next morning. Also, apparently flustered by the crowd, Cooper decided to change the venue to the Rose and Crown in St Giles.[97]

SATURDAY 19 OCTOBER

Saturday found the jury now sitting at the Rose and Crown, where it was to remain until midnight. Why did a verdict take so long? It is unlikely that the number of witnesses called necessitated such a long debate. So it seems that there was some genuine disagreement over the verdict. Only four verdicts were possible: accidental death, homicide, suicide or an act of God. The coroner and the jury would have sought the most likely verdict by examining the victim's words and deeds, and the witnesses would have been called merely to bolster their already formulated views. We have noted that the inquest was not carried out in the quiet contemplation of the fact as in a present-day coroner's court. On the contrary, the rooms at the White House had been packed with people, some of whom had vested interest in the 'correct' verdict, and those at the Rose and Crown were unlikely to have been a less impartial venue. In the end, the interested parties and the family appear to have got their own way. The verdict was that Godfrey had been murdered by persons unknown and that he had been strangled. Skillarne and Cambridge, in between arguing with one another, had apparently been the most important witnesses, and it was their testimony that had persuaded the jury that Godfrey had been murdered.

Some of the other witnesses called were a poor lot. They included John Wilson, a saddler in St Martin's-in-the-Fields, who said that he had seen Godfrey some two weeks previously and that the magistrate had told some people that he was in danger for his part in discovering the Popish Plot. Thomas Morgan also testified that he had been around the spot where the body was to be discovered earlier in the week and had seen nothing then. Bromwell, Waters and Rawson told their tale. Caleb Wynnel and Richard Duke said that they had seen Godfrey talking to Joseph Radcliffe after 1 o'clock on the Saturday afternoon. Constable Brown was recalled to tell how he had been sent for and what actions he had taken. Significantly, Godfrey's clerk Henry Moor was called but poorly questioned. He was only asked at what time Godfrey had left the house on the Saturday and whether he had been wearing a lace band or not! Radcliffe, however, told his story of meeting Godfrey at the vestry on the Friday and of his temper there, although he was later to claim that his evidence had been tampered with and his impressions there of a miserable and melancholy Godfrey had been altered by the coroner. He also told of a second meeting with Godfrey at 1 o'clock on the Saturday and his wife backed up his story. Finally, there was Mrs Gibbon, ever anxious to tell her tale, but she also later claimed that her evidence had been altered. Nonetheless, as the crowd broke up the jury still appeared to be confused. In fact, one of them later confessed that he had not understood any of the evidence and did not understand even now how Edmund Godfrey had met his end.[98]

Nor were some other individuals apparently happy with this verdict. Cooper's actions had not only been called into question, but complaints were made that the body had been released too early. It was said Cooper had performed badly, having been pressed by Dr Lloyd and the Godfreys to come up with a verdict; the witnesses had been of little help, aside from the two surgeons, and his jury was still confused.

Some days later the Godfrey brothers were said to have visited the Gibbon's home. While there, Michael and Benjamin talked to Captain and Mrs Gibbon about Godfrey's behaviour ten days before his disappearance. It soon became apparent that they were there more to persuade the Gibbons that their brother had been murdered than to hear their opinions. Indeed, three or four days after the body's discovery another visit had been paid to Mrs Gibbon's home by two of Godfrey's sisters, Jane Harrison and Sarah Pluncknett. They told Mary Gibbon that Godfrey had been clearly murdered at the Duke of Norfolk's home (Oates's old employer when the former had been Earl of Norwich), for that household was all in mourning. Putting on mourning seems like a serious mistake for a murderer to make, and Mrs Gibbon was unconvinced. Mrs Harrison desired Mrs Gibbon to speak 'sparingly of what she knew of S[i]r Edmund; saying to her, that she knew more of his minde than anybody'. Mrs Gibbon went to see the body next day with Mrs Harrison, who now asked her if she believed the papists had killed her brother, but Mrs Gibbon only replied that Edmund had done many kindnesses for the papists. Despite this she was invited to the funeral, and while there she quizzed Henry Moor about why he had told her his master was not dead; 'he then saide his Master[']s two brothers ordered him so to do'. With Godfrey safely dead, however, the moves to uncover his murderers now began.[99]

CHAPTER FIVE

Reaction

The king is safe, but Godfrey's slain, now traytors look about yee; You
are afraid of every Bush, the truth of God will rout yee.

New Verses Concerning the Plot (1679)

'Do you think he [Prance] would swear three men out of their lives
for nothing?'

Sir William Scoggs at the Trial of Green, Berry and Hill (1679)

THE FUNERAL: 31 OCTOBER 1678

Given Titus Oates's revelations to the Privy Council in late September,
the death of Edmund Godfrey confirmed the reality of the Popish
Plot to many Londoners and there were soon moves afoot to discover
his killers. The verdict of the coroner in the case, as we have seen, was
one of wilful murder and almost inevitably the blame was soon laid on
the Catholic community. Few paused to ask why Catholics should
murder such a liberal magistrate and apparent friend to themselves as
Edmund Godfrey.

Given the nature of his death in the midst of a growing political
crisis, the magistrate's lying-in-state proved significant. Initially the
family moved the body from the White House to Godfrey's home in
Hartshorne Lane. A large crowd, who went to pay their respects,
converged on the body as it was laid in the street 'exposed to the view
of all comers'.[1] The curious and sightseers who saw the corpse
apparently went away distressed and 'inflamed'. Gilbert Burnet noted
that this unofficial lying-in-state had the effect of sharpening men's
spirits, leading to fears that an enraged London mob would soon rise
and precipitate a massacre of all the Catholics in the city.[2]

Nonetheless, although a number of arrests were made of Catholic suspects, the presumed killers of Godfrey still remained at large.

However, Edmund Godfrey's recreation as a Protestant icon – a martyr who had died so that others might live – was a more rapid affair. A thick layer of propaganda soon submerged the person he had been. A number of iconographic images were manufactured through a series of set pieces, pamphlets and drawings largely engineered by the growing opposition factions who, because of the crisis, were now coalescing into a political party that many were soon to label as 'Whig'. Godfrey's image went through a variety of transformations, from the actual use of his corpse in public display and in a mass funeral, to the use of his image in tableaux and parades, to the illustrative and poetic material of pamphlet literature and popular culture. These set pieces, almost public dramas, that appeared over the next few years were designed to push home the Catholic threat to the nation and the fact that Godfrey had been a martyr for the Protestant cause.[3]

Naturally the constraints of Godfrey's own will, which he had written in the previous year and which was meant to dictate the nature of his funeral, were studiously ignored. In that interesting document Edmund Godfrey had willed, as an ever-practical man of business, that on his death as little fuss should be made as was possible. Indeed he had desired a pauper's grave and no 'pompe or pagentry [or] attendants'. He was also eager that his burial should take place early in the morning or late at night, so as to 'avoid being troublesome to the world . . . especially to the streets'.[4] As he saw it, death was not a mere commonplace, but neither should it be the subject of wasteful extravagances or damage to business. By this stage, however, the body had fallen into the hands of those who wished to press home political and religious points; a massive, semi-official funeral was the result. The growing influence of the leaders of the opposition must be suspected here. Michael Godfrey had already stepped in to take command of Edmund's affairs by seizing his brother's papers. Michael also possessed indisputable links with the opponents of Danby's regime that went back at least to the early 1670s. With parliament now in session – it had begun to sit on 21 October – the moves to exploit the crisis began to grow apace.[5]

It was at this point that the small figure of Anthony Ashley Cooper, Earl of Shaftesbury, John Dryden's 'daring pilot in extremity', entered the scene.[6] By 1678 Shaftesbury was a disaffected politician of some note, although his efforts to undermine Danby and the king's designs in the 1670s had by 1678 reached something of an impasse. Indeed, a recent spell in the Tower because of his activities had done little to assist either his cause or the ailing health of the 57-year-old former Cromwellian and Restoration minister. He was perhaps beginning to doubt that any success would ever come his way again, for as an inveterate enemy of the court there seemed to be no way back into Charles II's graces for him. So in the summer of 1678 Shaftesbury journeyed south to his estates at Wimborne St Giles, hoping that the autumn session of parliament might just present fresh opportunities for his shrew, tactical skills.[7]

The 1670s had seen Shaftesbury move from government service to outright hostility to the regime of Charles II and Danby. His distrust of the king's plans and religion had only grown gradually, but like many another politician of his generation he would naturally seize upon the opportunity to re-emerge as a more appropriate adviser to the wily Charles Stuart. Although he was occasionally accused of actually inventing the Popish Plot scare for his own ends, in retrospect this seems highly unlikely. Oates, as we have seen, was an opportunist with his own agenda, but this did not prevent the cunning Shaftesbury from adopting him and his famous plot. Indeed, the frustrations of the previous three years doubtless dropped away as Shaftesbury learned more details of the plot: the opportunity to exploit the fears of popery and arbitrary government, which to some extent he shared, and to lock horns with Danby were too great to resist. 'Let the Treasurer,' he is alleged to have said, 'cry as loud as he pleases against popery, and think to put himself at the head of the Plot, I will cry a note louder and soon take his place'.[8]

Upon his arrival in Westminster, therefore, Shaftesbury soon made up for lost time. Already there were many disaffected former courtiers such as George Villiers, 2nd Duke of Buckingham, seeking to exploit the crisis now brewing in the nation. And as the plot began to suck in both great and small, it was to be used to gain many a courtier some advantage at the court of Charles II. While Shaftesbury may personally have doubted Oates's claims, the informer and his brethren, who were soon to come forward, could be encouraged to target their accusations against those in the government who mattered most in Shaftesbury's mind: Danby, the Duke of York and even the king himself if necessary. Danby he wanted removed and as for the Duke of York, as a Catholic he was to be subject to a policy of limiting his powers as a future monarch, or even exclusion from the succession should that policy fail. In the great political contest that was to follow the death of Edmund Godfrey, the victim himself became merely a pawn to be moved across the board, as both Shaftesbury and the king sought to resolve the crisis of the succession.[9]

At the opening of parliament in October, Charles II had only briefly mentioned the plot, much to everyone's frustration. This was partly deliberate. Behind the scenes his first minister, Danby, and his brother, the Duke of York, were engaged in continual squabbles over what to do about the affair. Danby still hoped to exploit it for his own purposes, while Charles appears to have hoped that the whole affair, which he regarded as a pack of lies in any case, would soon blow over. This, however, only gave the initiative to the opposition: for if the king and his government were unwilling and unable to exploit the plot, then the opposition was. Dominated by men such as Shaftesbury, the Commons and Lords now began rather aimlessly to interrogate everyone in sight, to nobody's particular satisfaction. In the meanwhile, Titus Oates was brought before the Commons and for three days running he kept the shocked Members of Parliament enthralled with his tales of the devilish designs of the Catholics against the Protestant nation.[10] With his credit rising once more, mainly due to Edward Coleman's papers and Godfrey's death, Titus was now in his element. Well paid, well fed and in his own apartments at Whitehall, he made frequent forays as 'saviour of the nation' to visit the House of Commons and reveal yet more long-forgotten details of the plot, or to try to discredit many an old enemy among the Catholic community.

As a result, the arrests of various prominent, and not so prominent, Roman Catholics continued. On 24 October warrants were issued for the arrest of five Roman Catholic peers, Lords Arundel, Bellasis, Petre, Powis and Stafford, all of whom had been accused by Oates of possessing commissions from the Pope. As yet Oates had refrained from any accusations that would bring him closer to the king, but York and Danby were becoming all too obvious targets and his backers were not about to let them off the hook on which all now found themselves. Indeed, under Shaftesbury's patronage, the hunt for papists and closet plotters began to widen. Shaftesbury's aim in this affair appears to have been to keep the agitation over the plot simmering as a useful political tool, but he was also concerned, as every 'true' Englishman was, with a defence of parliament and English liberties against Stuart schemes of popery and arbitrary government. With this in mind a series of attacks on Danby and the Duke of York began to form, but Shaftesbury also had time to inquire into the death of Edmund Godfrey.

Within parliament the opportunity was taken to form a committee on 23 October in order to investigate the Popish Plot.[11] By 28 October the House of Lords had also suggested that a subcommittee on Godfrey's murder should be created. It was soon packed with 'opposition' or opportunistic peers: George Villiers, Duke of Buckingham was the first to be appointed to the committee, alongside the Marquis of Winchester, Viscount Halifax, the Earl of Essex and, bringing up the rear, Danby's own man, the Bishop of London.[12] Initially their task was to secure witnesses as well as to gather and examine evidence; however, Shaftesbury, who soon joined the committee, governed its actions. The committee's methods left much to be desired. Indeed, far from conducting a sober dissection of the Godfrey case, it was politically biased from the very beginning. The committee members had little time for those with tales of Edmund Godfrey that did not fit into its already preconceived notions that the papists had murdered him.[13] That plain fact was what they intended to prove to themselves if to no one else. So witnesses were treated to a mixture of threat and financial inducement in a series of robust interrogations. For example, both of the men who had discovered the body, William Bromwell and John Waters, were thrown into prison for their pains as their stories did not match, while John Rawson, the landlord of the White House, was forced to admit that a Catholic club often met on his premises. Francis Corrall, a hackney coachman, was hauled before the committee for foolishly claiming while in his cups that four men had forced him to convey Godfrey's body in his coach.[14] He was treated with bluff threats and thrown into Newgate prison to rot for his intemperance. Little else emerged from the hearings and interrogations, and given this fact, the gift of Godfrey's funeral, soon to take place in the streets of the city, was not to be lightly passed up.

A state funeral for Godfrey was naturally out of the question. Despite Burnet's claim that he had persuaded the king otherwise, Charles II and the Duke of York, according to the French ambassador at least, still believed Godfrey had been a troublesome 'fanatique' who had committed suicide.[15] Both men were also well aware that the magistrate's death could be used to stir up even more political agitation against the government, given that the regime was generally seen by the public as reluctant to investigate the plot at all. Undaunted by this royal obstacle the 'opposition' were willing to give their martyr, as they now saw him, a suitable farewell by organising a hero's funeral themselves.[16]

For some time the body had been lying in-state at Bridewell. On 31 October 1678 Godfrey's coffin, draped in a black cloth with armorial bearings and carried by six men, left Bridewell and proceeded in a massive funeral procession along Fleet Street and the Strand to Godfrey's old church of St Martin's-in-the-Fields. Seventy-two divines and over 1,000 mourners of 'quality' attended the cortège, and considerable numbers of citizens from London also joined the procession. This prodigious crowd packed the church to hear a bombastic pulpit performance by Dr William Lloyd. As if to emphasise the danger to the entire congregation, and to give an added frisson to the occasion, Lloyd was also protected by two burly clergymen deliberately chosen for their size. As they squeezed into the pulpit with him, in case the papists, ever more daring it seemed, should make an attempt upon the life of the pastor, the congregation settled down to hear a vivid explanation of the troubled times in which they all lived.[17]

Lloyd's sermon, which was to run to several editions when printed, was upon the text 'Died Abner as a fool dieth'. In a number of ways, or so Lloyd thought, the comparison with the biblical Abner was appropriate. Abner had also 'spent [his] life serving [his King, doing] justice and shew[ing] mercy', only to be murdered for his pains. Abner was an eminent and dignified man, useful among his people 'and not forgetful of the church', and therefore to Lloyd the biblical figure was Edmund Godfrey written into scripture. So to contemporaries even the Bible itself had foretold the terrible events of Godfrey's sad demise in 1678. Unfortunately, Lloyd's parallels between the two men soon began to be somewhat laboured, so he returned to the subject at hand, which was Godfrey the man. Edmund was, claimed Lloyd, a 'Just and Charitable man, a Devout, a zealous and contentious Christian'. Lloyd's personal recollections of Godfrey's character were in fact to set the pattern for the magistrate's future iconography. The official image of Godfrey was to emphasise the magistrate's kindness among the dissenters and recusants, as well as his fitness for office through his 'Nature and education . . . study and practice'.[18] To Lloyd, Godfrey was a man who had given his life for his country; his parish and its affairs were his wife and children. The image, in short, was of a devoted, caring individual who had put aside worldly pleasures in favour of duty. Godfrey's dubious business dealings, his complex politics and odd behaviour were firmly suppressed. However, in dealing with the current rumours of depression and suicide, Lloyd proved remarkably circumspect. He dismissed the rumours as either a ploy of Godfrey's killers, a slander on the family, or, more dubiously, something that proceeded from Godfrey's own 'thoughtfulness'. Even so, Lloyd openly admitted that he had not at first entirely dismissed the possibility of suicide, 'till I saw the contrary with my eyes' on viewing the body.[19] Having dealt kindly with Godfrey's memory, Lloyd then moved on to the reason for his death. Here, he firmly laid the crime at the door of the Jesuits as part of a wider popish plot. In his sermon Lloyd was able to lay the foundations for the recreation of the confused and troubled Edmund Godfrey as a Protestant martyr.[20]

WILLIAM BEDLOE, MILES PRANCE AND THE SOMERSET HOUSE TALE

Titus Oates was naturally of little help in finding the murderers of the dead magistrate. He now proclaimed himself an intimate friend of the safely dead Godfrey, to whose demise, as even he himself admitted, he owed much of his success. But Oates had been under guard in Whitehall Palace at the time of the death and in any case he had bigger fish to fry. What were needed, therefore, were other witnesses to come forward who could throw some light upon the mystery. As an inducement, a proclamation offering a reward of £500 was issued in the hope that someone would turn up with some information.[21]

As it happened, the first of the informers to crawl out into the light and claim knowledge of the strange death of Edmund Godfrey was none other than Oates's old Spanish acquaintance William Bedloe.[22] On 2 November 1678, the Secretary of State, Henry Coventry, received an intriguing letter from William Bedloe who was in Bristol. In this letter Bedloe claimed that not only did he know something of the murder of the magistrate, but he was now prepared to make revelations about the affair. The small-time thief had in fact only just been released from gaol, where, ironically, he had been supported by some Jesuits and as far as we know he had never even met Godfrey. Not that this mattered to William Bedloe, of course, for if he could fool many in Europe with his frauds, why not seize this opportunity at home when it presented itself? Bedloe, like Oates before him, sensed that his hour had come. He was swiftly brought up to London and on 7 November he was taken before the Privy Council. There he was to prove to be a rather more cautious witness than Oates, but only after he had gradually dropped his improbable stories of vast hordes of men disguised as pilgrims waiting to cross over from France.[23]

Bedloe's story was that he had been four years among the Jesuits, and he had also been in Spain and other parts of the Continent acting as a messenger for them. The most important new evidence that he presented was that he knew the papists had murdered Godfrey, because he himself had been asked to help shift the body from Somerset House, the residence of the queen, by the killers. Sometime in October 1678, he said, two Jesuits of his acquaintance by the names of Le Fèvre (or Phaire) and Walsh, who were attached to the queen's entourage in Somerset House, had met him and sought to secure his help in a deed of great note. Le Fèvre, a mysterious Englishman who passed himself off as a Frenchman, had promised William a sum of money if he would join their design. A great obstacle to their business, Le Fèvre claimed, had to be dispatched. Although Bedloe was intrigued by the affair, his associates were unwilling at first to say who was to be murdered. Bedloe, reluctantly, refused to participate and he did not attend a second pre-arranged meeting. He then claimed to have met Le Fèvre once again, this time by accident in Fleet Street on 13 October. The latter had rebuked him for his lack of courage, but despite this he was still willing to offer Bedloe a second chance. A further meeting between the two was arranged at Somerset House the next day. Here, in the middle of a courtyard after dark Bedloe was told that the business had already been done and he could now see the body. Bedloe was taken to a small room and there was shown the dead body of the murdered Godfrey. Also at this meeting, it later transpired, were Walsh, a person who attended the queen's chapel, and Samuel Atkins, a clerk to Samuel Pepys. As the body clearly could not remain there, Bedloe had promised to return to assist the gang to remove it elsewhere. Once more he had thought better of it and did not turn up the next evening.

Walking in Lincoln's Inn Fields the next day, he had again chanced upon Le Fèvre and yet again the patient Romanist had rebuked Bedloe about his lack of zeal. Nevertheless, Le Fèvre had then rather absurdly proceeded to tell Bedloe the circumstances of the murder. He, Walsh and one of Lord Bellasis's gentlemen had succeeded in luring Godfrey into Somerset House at about five o'clock on the Saturday afternoon on the pretence of making further disclosures about the plot. Once there, the magistrate had been forced into a small room in the palace and a pistol had been placed at his head. The plotters had then demanded the return of the depositions sworn by Oates. Godfrey refused and so they stifled him between two pillows and, sensing he was still alive, had finished him off by strangling him. On the Monday night, having first shown the body to the unreliable Bedloe, they carried Godfrey in a chair and then a coach into the fields near Primrose Hill and there placed his body in a ditch with the magistrate's own sword run clean through him, so as to make it appear that he had killed himself. On learning of all this, Bedloe had fled London on 23 October and then returned to Bristol.

Bedloe also took the opportunity to relate an edited version of his origins and European activities to the Privy Council. He had been born in Chepstow, he said, and bred a Protestant. He had also briefly served in the Prince of Orange's army, but had been seduced by the religious houses on the Continent.[24]

What is one to make of Bedloe's tale? It was, given his previous history, deliberately vague, for as yet he had not been coached by anyone in any other version. However, we may note some details from it for now and pass on. It seems to have been Bedloe, or his sponsors, who first established Somerset House as the scene of the crime. The murderers had also been given a purpose in killing Godfrey: they wanted to prevent some secret he held from going any further. Additionally, the killers had been a mixed bunch of Catholic priests and laymen. Godfrey had been stifled, strangled and then run through with his own sword to make it appear that he had committed suicide. Conversely, Bedloe's timing for those events was very dubious and difficult to reconcile with the discovery of the body on the Thursday.

The next day, a rather more confident William Bedloe went before parliament and there he began to describe a more elaborate story to his new audience. Indeed, so confident in his tale did Bedloe now appear that the king was certain someone had further instructed him overnight. Nevertheless, William's rise was now rapid, in spite of the fact that when faced with the unfortunate and innocent young Samuel Atkins, who had recently been accused of being a conspirator to murder, he had not been able to recognise him.

Samuel Atkins was a servant of the former diarist and civil servant Samuel Pepys, who was himself a client of the Duke of York. The arrival before the Lords Committee of one Captain Charles Atkins (no relation of Samuel's), who claimed knowledge of the murder, had led to Samuel Atkins's arrest. It was hoped that the young man would soon collapse under pressure from the committee, inform upon his master and thus become the key witness for the opposition in the murder of Edmund Godfrey. Unfortunately, Samuel proved a stubborn suspect and moreover he had a reliable alibi in that he had actually been lying dead drunk on board a ship at the time Godfrey was supposed to have been murdered. Bedloe was pushed forward to confirm Atkins's presence at the scene of the crime. The plot to frame Samuel Atkins fell through but despite this, William Bedloe became, alongside a rather jealous Titus Oates, the darling of the nation. Further revelations flowed from his mouth and pen as he grew ever more confident in his accusations. Now he revealed that he had also been an agent of the Jesuits on other business and was well aware of their dealings. As the poor unfortunates whom he had caused to be arrested began to have their time in court, Bedloe also joined Oates as a witness for the prosecution. Although he was to perform poorly in court, of far more importance was the fact that Bedloe, after some prompting, had now managed to implicate Miles Prance, a Roman Catholic silversmith, in the strange death of Edmund Godfrey.[25]

Miles Prance was born in Eastwood in the parish of Marsh in the Isle of Ely.[26] His father was Simon Prance, a gentleman of some note in the parish and in the Cambridge area until his Royalist sympathies caused him to lose both his estate and his liberty. Thereafter Simon Prance spent some time in prison, where he converted to Roman Catholicism and became something of a zealot in its cause. He even had his children educated as Roman Catholics. Indeed, it was said that two of his sons became secular priests in France and the Indies, and two of his daughters became nuns, one in Lisbon and the other in Rouen, Normandy. Miles was sent into an apprenticeship as a gold- or silversmith. He became quite accomplished in his profession and his Catholic contacts enabled him to have 'a beneficial employment among men of the Roman profession . . . in regards of the many . . . trinkets of silver-work, which are used by the professors of that outside religion'.[27] Prance, based in St Giles-in-the-Fields, also took work in the household of Queen Catherine at Somerset House in the Strand and became a familiar figure there, although he later lost his employment. At the time of the plot's discovery, Prance was living with his wife on Princes Street in Covent Garden, alongside a number of fellow Catholics. He had also joined the club that regularly met at the White House tavern and he drank at the Plough Inn, another regular haunt of the Catholic community. Up until that point there appears to have been little sinister in Prance's life and nothing much to mark him out from any number of other Catholics who lived and worked in London.

None the less news of the death of Edmund Godfrey had meant that suspicion had fallen on many innocent Catholics. Prance was soon picked up because his neighbours had grown suspicious of his ill-considered remarks in favour of the Jesuits, and in subsequent inquiries at his home the lodger, who owed Prance money and could not pay, had maliciously revealed that his landlord had been away from home at the time of the murder.[28] Prance never could explain his absences over that week. Together with the fact that he had been employed by the queen's chapel and did most of his business with Roman Catholics, this was sufficient ammunition for the authorities to proceed with his arrest. As the Lords Committee dragged Prance off for his interrogation, he was unfortunate enough to be spotted by the opportunistic patrons of William Bedloe. Bedloe conveniently claimed that Prance had been one of the very men he had seen near the body of Godfrey as it lay in Somerset House. After a short examination by the Lords, in which he denied being a party to any murder, Prance was conveyed to Newgate, loaded with irons and placed in a cell. The combination of freezing cold and lack of care over forty-eight hours led him to confess that he did in fact have things to reveal.

Brought before the Privy Council, Prance made many circumstantial revelations about Godfrey's murder and incriminated three acquaintances. Once placed in better quarters, however, Prance soon changed his tune. Five days after his first confession he was brought before the king and recanted his previous tale. The king sent Prance before the Privy Council again and they, suspecting that the plotters had got to him, soon returned him to the cold cells of Newgate with the threat of the rack for company until he was able to see the error of his ways. There seems to be little doubt that while in Newgate Prance was pressured to stick to his original version of the 'truth'. He later claimed that he had been visited there by a number of 'advisers', who attempted to persuade him that not only a pardon and the truth were at stake but also his life. These advisers included William Boyce, a friend, as well as Gilbert Burnet and Dr Lloyd, whom we last saw giving the sermon at Godfrey's funeral and prior to that interfering at the inquest. Under the circumstances, Prance once more gave way. He now claimed that his first confession had in fact been true, but fearing a loss of trade with the Catholic community he had recanted. Now, he said, he saw the truth of the matter and henceforward he was even willing to add to his confession.[29]

Prance's tale began in a quiet way in Michaelmas 1678.[30] He alleged that one Mr Townley and his two sons came to London on their way to Douai. While in the city they lodged at the house in Drury Lane of a man called Aires, where John Fenwick, the Jesuit, also lived. After Townley and his sons went off to Douai, one of his brothers revealed to Mrs Prance and Adamson, a watchmaker, that there were designs to raise men for the Catholic cause; he boasted that they also had commissions from Lord Bellasis and other Roman Catholic lords. This information was related to Prance at a house in Vere Street where yet another Catholic club met. Other evidence also emerged of Catholic stirrings and gradually Prance had developed a clear idea of the plot and forces being raised. He also had enough evidence to be able to implicate some of his Catholic friends. However, as a good Roman Catholic, at this point he saw no need to reveal the plans.

The plot against Godfrey came to Prance's notice on the Sunday before the actual killing through Fathers Girald (or Fitz-gerald) and Kelly, both of whom were Irish priests. At the Plough alehouse by the Water-gate off the Strand, Girald asked Prance whether he knew Edmund Godfrey the magistrate. Although Prance, like many Londoners, had both seen and heard of Godfrey, he knew little of him. Girald then told Prance that the magistrate was in fact a bitter persecutor of the Catholics and 'particular enemy of the Queen's servants', as well as a fixed enemy of the schemes of the Catholics in general. Indeed, so desperate an enemy of Catholics had the magistrate become that he needed to be stopped and, Girald hinted, whoever did this good deed would get a reward from Lord Bellasis and his backers. Prance was invited to join in their plans. At first he reacted in horror to the suggestion that anyone could commit a cold-blooded murder, to which Girald replied that it was really no sin but actually a work of charity to kill such a man. Kelly agreed. Despite this assurance, Prance still needed persuading. Again he was told that 'Godfrey was a busy man, and was going about to ruine all the Catholicks in England, and that it was necessary to destroy him, else they should all be undone'.[31] Others soon came into the business: the elderly Henry Berry, porter to the queen on the upper Court Gate at Somerset House was one; Lewson, another priest and Philip Vernatti, a former paymaster at Tangier and now a servant of Lord Bellasis, were two others; there was also Robert Green, an old Irishman whose task it was to lay out the cushions in the queen's chapel at Somerset House; and finally there was Lawrence Hill, the son of a shoemaker and now a servant to Dr Goddin, who was the doctor of the treasurer of the Royal Chapel at Somerset House. In the week following, Prance claimed that he met with these men several times to plan how to do the deed, and in the meantime they had decided to follow the magistrate's movements.

Throughout the week as they dogged Edmund Godfrey, he went about his business. They were even daring enough to go to Godfrey's home on the pretext of having some business with him. By Saturday 12 October they were ready. That morning Girald, Green and Hill were observing Godfrey's movements as usual. Kelly in the meantime came to Prance's house to get him ready. Hill actually went in to see the magistrate and engaged him in some business, while the others hung about outside. Between 10 and 11 o'clock Godfrey finally left his home. Prance noted that he came out 'all alone[,] as his manner was, for, being a Plain stout gentleman [*sic*], he never or very seldom went abroad attended with any servant, which they very well knew'.[32] They then followed the magistrate in his wanderings, until at about 6 or 7 o'clock in the evening he came to a great house in St Clement's, where he dined. Green went off to Prance's house, but actually found him in the pub nearby. They then hurried off to Somerset House to alert Kelly and Berry. While they waited in the yard there, at about 9 o'clock Edmund Godfrey came out of the house. Seeing this, Hill rushed before him to warn the others he was coming. Their plan, it seems, was to wheedle the magistrate into the yard on the pretext of a quarrel occurring there. Godfrey was to be called in as a magistrate to put a stop to the quarrel and thus fall into their hands. Hill stood by the Water-gate, while Kelly and Berry began their pretended quarrel. Godfrey was walking along the Strand when Hill finally accosted him. Hill knew him well – Prance claimed that they had done some business together over coal: he hastily asked Godfrey to step in and stop the fight. 'Pough, pough, said Sir Edmundbury, refusing at first to trouble himself'.[33] Eventually Godfrey was persuaded by Hill to go to assess the situation. Hill entered the yard first with Godfrey behind him. Girald and Green pushed in behind. Prance was up against the wall in the shadows and when they had passed he went up to the gate to keep watch. Green then threw a twisted handkerchief around the magistrate's neck and calling upon God, he secured the magistrate's sword. He then throttled Godfrey. Not content with this, he proceeded to beat the magistrate's breast angrily. Seeing Godfrey was not quite dead, Girald was intent on running his own sword through him, but the others held him back. Green then punched the prostrate magistrate once more and broke his neck. The bloody-minded Girald, seeing Godfrey lying dead, said 'Well, if we could not have inticed him in here, I resolved I would have followed him down Hartshorne lane that leads to his own house, and there would have run him through with my own hand.'[34] Now that they had killed Godfrey, what were the murderers to do with the body?

Prance soon joined them and Berry, who had stood at the other gate, also appeared. Together they carried the corpse up a flight of stairs into a long entry that led to the upper court by the coach house, then into Dr Goddin's lodgings where Hill lived. There they put the body into an empty room. And there, according to Prance, it lay for all of Saturday night, Sunday and most of Monday. It was only after dark on Monday at about 10 o'clock that Prance returned to the place. Hill told him that the body had been shifted once more, this time across the upper court of Somerset House to another room. He then retired to the Plough alehouse where Green, Girald and Kelly were drinking. Hill came in later and together they went to move the body again. They shifted it back into the original room. Clearly they could not go on lugging a dead magistrate about a crowded royal palace forever without someone eventually noticing, and so a solution to their troubles had to be found. Girald and Kelly, perhaps under the orders of their masters, or so Prance thought, came up with a new plan. This was to dump the corpse in the fields in an obscure place 'in such a manner as that whenever he should be found it might be supposed that he had murthered himself, which would much serve the interest of the church, when it should be publickly known, that he was so busy in charging Catholicks with a Plot . . . that he made away with himself'.[35] To lend some credence to this design, none of Godfrey's property nor his money was to be removed. Prance did not see any pocketbook taken from the corpse in his presence nor did he see what happened to Godfrey's band. This latter, he presumed, was lost with the continual moving of the body. In the event they agreed to carry the body away after midnight, and Hill undertook to get a sedan chair to carry the corpse. They all agreed to meet Hill by 11 o'clock on the Wednesday night.

By the time they finally got the corpse into the sedan it was nearly midnight, and when Girald and Prance came to take up the chair they found that it lacked leather carrying straps. The enterprising Hill, however, was able to provide them with some cord to carry it. The soldiers on guard at the gate were now a problem, but Berry was able to inveigle them into a drink and a smoke elsewhere. Thus, grunting and gasping with the dead weight in the sedan chair, the men moved the body out of Somerset House. Hill ran on ahead to get a horse. Girald and Prance carried the sedan to Covent Garden at the end of James Street, and then Kelly and Green took it up. They wandered through King Street, New Street and so up and along Rose Street and at that point, somewhat exhausted, they stopped once more. After a brief rest they again took up the sedan chair and now they proceeded past the Greyhound Tavern and the Grecian Church. Here Hill finally turned up with a horse. The sedan chair was then pushed into a building and the body was bundled up on to the horse. Hill, Girald and Kelly then went off with the horse and its burden, while the tired Miles Prance went home. He finally got home shortly before 1 or 2 o'clock that morning after an exhausting night's work.

The next day Girald told Prance that they had laid Godfrey's corpse in a ditch near Primrose Hill and transfixed him with his own sword. On the Thursday the body was found. That night Prance was in the Horse-Shoe tavern drinking with Philip Vernatti, who pumped him for details of the killing. Vernatti later met Girald, who gave him a blow-by-blow account to tell to Lord Bellasis. It was only after much pressure that Prance began to reveal the names of those involved. A formidable liar, Miles Prance was now to be responsible for the arrest, trial and deaths of three of the men named by him – Robert Green, Henry Berry and Lawrence Hill, all of whom were acquaintances of his. Of the missing Girald, Dominick Kelly and Philip Vernatti there was no trace: they had fled.

THE TRIAL BY JURY: 5–10 FEBRUARY 1679

Robert Green was an elderly Irish Catholic and generally a reliable sort of man, although he, like his monarch Charles II, was subject to some occasional lapses in his faith. Indeed both Robert and his wife were frequent visitors to their neighbours Mr and Mrs Warrier and, with a fancy for a little sinful meat, occasionally put their dinner in a Protestant pot, so as not to offend the Catholic fathers whom Robert served in the chapel by eating meat on a Friday.[36] The pair were happy and contented, although Mrs Green was insistent that in such troubled times Robert should come straight home after his visits to the Plough Inn and not wander the streets of London. Green spent at least some of his time drinking there with his fellow workers, one of whom was Miles Prance. This habit was to cost him dearly for on 24 December 1678 Green, alongside his fellow Catholic Lawrence Hill and the Protestant Henry Berry, was arrested by the king's messengers and placed in the cold damp cells of Newgate charged with the murder of the magistrate Edmund Godfrey.

The series of trials that followed the death of Godfrey and the revelations of the Popish Plot were mostly overseen by the Lord Chief Justice with whom Godfrey had been acquainted: Sir William Scroggs.[37] A corpulent, red-faced, intemperate man, who had seen many a prisoner to his fate since being called to the Bar in 1653,

Scroggs had risen to his eminence only four months prior to the outbreak of the Popish Plot affair. Having worked his way through the lower courts, he was now at the height of his powers. At the best of times Scroggs would perhaps have sympathised with Robert Green's ambles to the local public house, for he himself was a formidable drinker and prone to scandal in his private life. His talent in court, noted Roger North, was 'wit' and he was also a 'master of Sagacity and Boldness . . . and many good turns of thought and language.'[38] He was, however, fearful of 'noe man where his kinge and countrie were concerned' and no doubt looked askance at the Romanist prisoners now before him in the dock of the Court of the King's Bench on the morning of Wednesday 5 February 1679. Here in the coming days Green, Berry and Hill, the prisoners at the bar, found themselves on trial for their lives over the death of Edmund Godfrey.

The trial began soon after the three men were brought up from Newgate prison to the King's Bench. In this case, as with any other murder trials of the day, the accused appeared to have little chance of a successful defence. They were allowed no defence lawyers to advise them, that position, on the technical points of the law, being taken, if he was so inclined, by the presiding judge. After spending some considerable time in a dank gaol that was usually injurious to health, the accused would of necessity have to think on their feet in court. They were generally allowed pen and paper to make notes and were entitled to cross-examine witnesses, but the trials of the day were designed more to convict an accused person than to engage in any search for the truth. Indeed, to most people the fact that the accused were in court in the first place was in itself sufficient evidence that they must be guilty of something; the trial was conducted merely to discover what crime(s) they were actually guilty of.[39]

In this case Mr Justice Wild, the clerk of the court, read the arraignment to the prisoners. In this it was claimed that on 12 October 1678 they 'having the fear of God before your eyes, but being moved and seduced by the instigation of the devil' had murdered Sir Edmund Berry Godfrey with a 'certain linen handkerchief of the value of six-pence' about his neck. All three men were then asked how they pleaded and all three pleaded not guilty.

They were then taken down and the trial was ordered to be suspended until Thursday 6 February, and then after a brief discussion it was put off until Monday 10 February in order that 'the king's evidence might be the more ready'.[40]

Monday 10 February saw the three men once more before the bar of the court. A suitable jury was swiftly sworn in, and the first of the opening statements was made, outlining to the crowds who packed the court the heinous nature of the three men's crimes. Mr Serjeant Stringer once more related the crime and the Attorney General, Sir William Jones, another former acquaintance of Edmund Godfrey's, opened the case against them. In their absence Girald, Kelly and Vernatti were also arraigned. Jones's opening statement was clear enough. He began with a peroration on the crime of murder, a crime of so deep a stain, he noted, that nothing could wash it away. Jones also presumed that everyone knew of Godfrey as a useful and active justice of the peace. This was not unlikely, as some of the jury had known Edmund personally. Jones then related how Godfrey had taken some depositions concerning the plot. His next theme was how the magistrate's industry had found out some of the principal actors in that design. Discovering this the Jesuits, foreseeing the danger they were in, had decided to prevent any further revelations and had trailed the magistrate, dogged his every step and met frequently at the Plough to plan Godfrey's elimination. Jones noted that of the six offenders in the case, the priests had fled for they are 'always the first to contrive the mischief, so are they always the first that fly the punishment'. He then related Prance's version of the events that led to Godfrey's murder and the dumping of the body on Primrose Hill in such a manner as to 'murder his reputation . . . that the world should conclude he had killed himself'. The Recorder of London, the formidable Sir George Jeffreys, then called on the first of the Crown witnesses, Titus Oates, to give his evidence in the case.[41]

Oates, by now a practised hand in court, pretended intimacy with Godfrey and related his part in the affair, which, for him, was quite limited. He spoke of the depositions and of how Godfrey had visited him on Monday 30 September and had expressed his concern that some great persons were unhappy with the magistrate's part in the affair. Godfrey had said that he was damned on both sides and threatened with an appearance before parliament. Oates then went on to say that the week before his disappearance Godfrey had again visited him and claimed that he had been threatened by the popish lords in the Tower and had been 'dogged' by suspicious people. Yet, he went on, Godfrey did not want to take his man along with him when he went out to do his business, because he was a 'poor weak fellow'. Oates had encouraged the magistrate to stand firm.

The next witness was Thomas Robinson, who related his meetings with Godfrey after the quarter sessions on 7 October and their discourse about the plot. Robinson noted how Godfrey had believed that he would receive little thanks for his work in the affair and for the fact that his involvement was an unwilling one. Although he did not have the examinations about him at the time, Godfrey had agreed to let Robinson see them when he had them back from 'a person of quality'. It was to Robinson that Godfrey had claimed he would be the 'first martyr' but he did not fear open enemies and would not go about with his clerk to protect him.[42]

The next, and most important, witness was Miles Prance. He related his version of the murder and the roles played by the accused in a sober fashion much as we have already seen above. He was then cross-examined and in the main stuck to his story, even adding the occasional incidental detail to give it a genuine air. Such as in this exchange:

Att. Gen:	What had you for dinner [at the Queen's Head]?
Prance:	We had a barrel of oysters, and a dish of fish. I bought the fish myself.
L.C.J.:	What day was it?
Prance:	The Friday after the proclamation.[43]

Prance's story appeared to hold together as by now, of course, he had rehearsed it several times for a number of audiences. Despite Lawrence Hill's protests that Prance's evidence was perjured and that it had been extracted under torture, only to be retracted and then emerge afresh once more, Prance was a generally convincing witness.

Not that he was ever deeply pressed by either Jones or Scroggs. Indeed, at one point the Lord Chief Justice went out of his way to defend the witness against Lawrence Hill's wife by flatly stating 'Do you think he would swear three men out of their lives for nothing?'[44] During the questioning which followed, the three accused men made a valiant attempt to trap Prance but only came to grief by admitting that they knew him and that they had in fact been drinking partners.

William Bedloe was the next Crown witness. His version of events was now cautiously told. Borrowing the rhetoric of Oates, William now proclaimed himself as the man of action who had tried to infiltrate Jesuit designs. He had been recruited as a potential killer but, of course, he had refrained from the deed. He had, however, seen Godfrey's body in the dark by a light with five or six others around it in Somerset House. The bad light had hindered his views of the others and he was careful not to swear against Hill or old man Green. Berry he had seen a number of times as the porter at Somerset House. He then related how he had spotted Prance in the lobby before the committee room and had spoken out against him as one of the men around the body that night. Hill in fact claimed he had never seen Bedloe in his life, but Bedloe did state that he knew both Green and Berry well, nor did they deny it.[45]

The next three witnesses were also very important: Constable John Brown, together with Zachary Skillarne and Nicholas Cambridge, the surgeons who had examined the body. Their evidence will be re-examined in the next chapter. Another witness was Elizabeth Curtis, Godfrey's maid, who spoke up against Hill, claiming that he had visited the magistrate on the Saturday morning and that Green had been there a fortnight before the murder on some other business. Both men denied this. She also mentioned the note delivered to Godfrey on the Friday that the magistrate did not know what to make of. The note had since disappeared. Various witness were then called to prove that the accused men had been seen in the company of Prance and the priests at the Plough Inn and the Queen's Head. Of more importance was Sir Robert Southwell, who related how Prance had come before the Privy Council and had then been sent in company to Somerset House and there had found the rooms and places in which the killing had taken place. Cross-examined as to whether Hill had admitted before the Privy Council to knowing both Girald and Kelly, Southwell confirmed he had, but Hill protested that he knew *a* Girald but not *the* priest. Lord Chief Justice Scroggs mocked this equivocation mercilessly and the trial moved on to Berry's part in keeping people out of Somerset House on the nights of the 12–14 October. In vain Berry protested that he had orders to do so. The prosecution wound down with a neighbour of Berry's, who claimed that Mrs Berry had been with him the previous week in an attempt to get him to remember that he was with Berry on the Wednesday night when the body was allegedly moved. Unfortunately, he could not remember this at all.[46]

It was now up to the accused men to prove their innocence. Hill tried hard to prove he had not moved out of doors on the Saturday after 8 o'clock, but once more Scroggs mercilessly took his testimony apart – all the defence witnesses were Catholics and as such in his eyes they were willing to swear anything to support each other. Hill's attempt to prove that the body could not have been hidden in Dr Goddin's chambers was also roundly dismissed. For his part Green called his landlord Mr James Warrier and his wife in an attempt to prove his whereabouts on the 12 October. They also suffered from the merciless questioning of Scroggs. One witness, Mr Ravenscroft, summed up the men's plight by commenting that they were 'all simple people, without defence for themselves'.[47] The three soldiers who had actually been guarding the gate of Somerset House on the night of the 12 October, and who swore that they had been at their duties, were also dismissed by Scroggs as liars and drunks, although they stuck to their story with dogged determination and refused to be budged or intimidated: the sentinels were in place, said the corporal. Nor had they left to go for a drink or smoke at any time, nor was there a sedan came out, but there was one that came in and as they had no orders to stop anyone going in or out they allowed it to do so.[48] Lastly, attempts to prove that Prance had been tortured into changing his evidence were cut short by Scroggs and the defence floundered.

The Attorney General then began to sum up the case. There was a weak defence, he claimed, and the proof against the prisoners was very strong because Bedloe agreed with Prance on some minor but telling details. Moreover, he went on, the staff at the Plough Inn concurred about the meetings that the accused held there, just as the maid agreed about the men visiting Godfrey on the Saturday. The evidence of the constable and two surgeons proved that Prance's version was the correct one 'so that', he went on, 'I think, there was never an evidence that was better fortified than this'.[49] As a final flourish he then attacked Roman Catholicism.

The Solicitor General took a different tack by dismissing talk of Prance changing his mind, and he explained it away easily. He concluded by saying it was 'impossible that Mr. Prance, a man of that mean capacity, should invent a story with so many circumstances, all so consistent, if there were not truth at the bottom of it'.[50] It was left to the Lord Chief Justice to conclude. Scroggs began by assessing the evidence of Oates, Prance and Bedloe once more. He praised Godfrey as a willing and able justice of the peace. He dismissed talk of Prance's change of mind, as he was not on oath at the time. Bedloe, whom allegedly Prance had never met, he claimed confirmed Prance's story in particulars. Scroggs was quite certain that it was not possible for a man like Prance to invent such a story and yet have it confirmed by people he did not even know. On the other hand, it was very possible for the priests, who were capable of anything, to contrive such a deed. On the matter of the soldiers, Scroggs was less dismissive, but he still sowed doubt in the minds of the jury as to how much weight could be placed upon their testimony. He then went on to attack priests in general as 'the preachers of the murder'. There was, he said, monstrous evidence for the whole plot and the delusions of popery. Naturally enough the jury was brief in its deliberations and quickly returned with a verdict of guilty. The accused were then sent down and brought back on 11 February to hear sentence. Green claimed he was as innocent as a child, Berry that he was not guilty of anything in the world such as this crime and Hill that God Almighty knew of his innocence. The trio were doomed and were sentenced to be executed by hanging.

At the first two executions on 21 February 1679 both Hill and Green died still protesting their innocence to the last. Berry, being a Protestant, had been held over in the hope that he would make further discoveries. But on 28 February he also was executed while denying all knowledge of the crime. While on the scaffold 'he lifted up his hands towards heaven, and said, As I am innocent, so receive my soul, O Lord Jesus', and many there wondered at his words.[51]

EDMUND GODFREY AND THE HISTORIANS

To contemporaries the killing of Godfrey was thus quite quickly settled. The papists had murdered him as part of a wider Popish Plot, and, three of the men accused – Green, Berry and Hill – died upon the scaffold for their crime. Attempts to alter this verdict only came in the 1680s when the heat of the plot had begun to die. The first real attempt to give a different version of Godfrey's death took place in 1682 and resulted in Nathaniel Thompson, William Pain and John Farwell being placed on trial for libel. These men had produced a pamphlet called *A letter from Miles Prance in relation to the murder of Sir Edmondbury Godfrey*, in which it was implied that Godfrey had killed himself and that the coroner's jury had been persuaded to bring in a verdict of murder rather than suicide. The pamphlet also criticised the forensic evidence and the witnesses of the day to prove its point. Thompson and Farwell were swiftly tried, found guilty and placed in the pillory, while Pain was fined £100 and imprisoned until he had paid his debt.[52]

After these punishments, few people were willing to enter the lists against the accepted version of Godfrey's death. It took a sea change in English politics in the mid-1680s to allow Sir Roger L'Estrange to finally take up the challenge of the investigation.[53] By February 1685 the Duke of York had finally succeeded to the throne as James II, and as a Catholic he was naturally rather unhappy with the blame for the plot and the murder still being laid on his co-religionists. So the new king took his revenge. Titus Oates was tried and punished, Miles Prance felt the weight of the law as a perjurer and L'Estrange was given a warrant to begin a new 'strict and diligent Enquiry into such matters'. L'Estrange, it must be noted, was neither an unbiased historian nor a disinterested party. Indeed, as a fervent Royalist and 'Tory' he had been at the centre of the publication war during the crisis of 1679–83, nor had he held back from attacking the great informers of the day from Titus Oates to Edward Fitzharris. In his work he plainly spoke of his 'horror for this villainous deceit [the plot]' and he saw himself as a friend to 'plain dealing and common justice'. In reality L'Estrange was more of a hired hack.[54]

L'Estrange eagerly undertook to investigate both the plot and the murder of Godfrey on behalf of James II. He used his new-found authority to examine parliamentary journals, council papers, public depositions, printed trials and narratives. Only the coroner's report and evidence eluded him, until in March 1687 he obtained a warrant from Secretary of State Sunderland ordering the Coroner of Middlesex, John Cooper, to deliver up to him the information taken in October 1678. L'Estrange then began his *A Brief History of the Times*, which he eventually published in three parts beginning in August 1687.[55] In this work he claimed that he had taken great care to 'lay open the matter of Fact on the one side, as on the other; for where should any man look for the true and reasonable grounds of a verdict, but in the words and Import of the evidence?'[56] In fact, although L'Estrange somewhat muddied the waters, and permanently removed some evidence from circulation, he underwrote his work by collecting valuable information from some forty witnesses whose statements he then cut and pasted in his book in such a way as to prove that Godfrey had committed suicide.

L'Estrange's main thesis was simple enough. He claimed that the Godfrey brothers had covered up the crime of suicide, or *felo de se*, in conjunction with the advice of the Whig Earl of Shaftesbury, in order to save their estate and damage the regime. For L'Estrange, Edmund Godfrey's melancholia was the main element of this drama and he was keen to uncover further evidence relating to the magistrate's state of mind prior to his demise. So he had Henry Moor, Godfrey's former clerk, hunted down and interrogated in his retirement in the Isle of Ely.[57] This and much of L'Estrange's other evidence gathered some years after the event was of course not above suspicion. There seems little doubt that L'Estrange manipulated some of his witnesses and they in turn feared his power. He rewrote some of the witness statements to make them into more suitable and fluid accounts; he may even have altered evidence to suit himself. Certainly few of the witnesses who now came forward with different stories from the ones they had told in 1678 were willing to stand up against the propagandist L'Estrange's robust methods of research. Yet, some of the evidence he found (and he had the advantage of being upon the scene much earlier that any subsequent historian) does ring true. Once his book was published the case for suicide rested, and although it was not generally well received it did convince the playwright Aphra Behn to write a poem praising L'Estrange's efforts. James II, however, fell from power in December 1688, after which it was not thought politic to raise the spectre of a suicidal Godfrey for the time being, now that the Protestant monarchs of William and Mary were on the throne and the former magistrate's nephew was giving financial assistance to King William's war.[58]

After the Revolution of 1688 the historians of the day mostly regurgitated evidence taken from the contemporary pamphlets. They had little new evidence to add to the case. Two exceptions were the former courtier and legal officer Roger North and the philosopher and part-time historian David Hume.[59] North was the most pertinent as he was actually in London at the time of the death and its aftermath. His book, *Examen*, was finally published in 1740.[60] In part of this work North presented his view of how Godfrey might have died. He claimed that the plot was in fact 'sinking' until Edward Coleman's dangerous letters emerged and that the idea that the murder proved the plot was simply wrongheaded. In fact, he thought the Roman Catholics were probably innocent of the crime but he doubted that Godfrey had killed himself. Instead North laid the blame upon those 'execrable villains, behind the curtain, who first gave life and birth to the plot, and inspired the wicked testimony of it'. He also claimed that he would not 'deal in Opinions, but in Things and make no Conclusions, but what flow irresistibly from them'. North's statement that the link between the plot and the murder was the men who contrived the scheme went little further. After a brief review of the evidence he obscurely hinted that the real culprit was either Oates himself, Danby or Oates's backers, by whom he presumably meant Shaftesbury and the other Whig leaders.[61]

David Hume, on the other hand, was the first to make the sensible suggestion that Godfrey's murder might not have been connected with the Popish Plot at all. After his review of the evidence, Hume commented that the Catholics had no reason to kill Godfrey, as he was friendly towards them, and it was too clumsy and absurd a crime for the Whigs to execute. Hume concluded by noting that:

> We must, therefore, be contented to remain forever ignorant of the actors in Godfrey's murder; and only pronounce in general that that event, in all likelihood, had no connection one way or the other, with the Popish Plot. Any man, especially so active a magistrate as Godfrey, might, in such a city as London, have many enemies, of whom his friends and family had no suspicion. He was a melancholy man; and there is some reason, notwithstanding the pretended appearances to the contrary to suspect that he fell by his own hands. The affair was never examined with tranquillity, nor even with common sense during the times; and it is impossible for us, at this distance, certainly to account for it.[62]

During the nineteenth century, the strange death of Edmund Godfrey was occasionally mentioned but little new evidence came to light. Various candidates were put forward as killers, ranging from a group of rogue Catholics, to the Whigs and Republicans or Titus Oates. In the early 1900s, however, the case once more erupted into debate. Andrew Lang, in another guise from his authorship of fairy stories, wrote a most sensible account of the affair, but in 1903 John Pollock, a pupil, if not disciple, of the great liberal historian Lord Acton, wrote a book entitled *The Popish Plot*. Pollock's solution to the puzzle pleased some and outraged others.[63] His thesis was that there really was a Popish Plot. While the details were obscure, the plot was an attempt by Roman Catholics to gain power and bring the nation back under the control of Rome. According to Pollock, Edmund Godfrey had revealed the Oates depositions to Coleman and during their conversations the latter told him that there had in fact been a secret consult of Jesuits on 24 April in St James Palace, and that Charles II and James, Duke of York, both knew of this. It is true that

James at a later date did claim that if this event had become known to Oates and his friends, then it would have led to serious trouble. Pollock's view was that at the time, to save the Duke of York, the innocent Godfrey had to die. In this view, therefore, we have a motive for Godfrey's death in that he was to be eliminated to cover up a 'great secret'. Pollock's theory then identified the murderers. He claimed that although Prance brought false evidence against a trio of innocent men, he did in fact relate the real facts of the crime. Moreover, even after he admitted his perjury in the mid-1680s Prance remained a friend of the Jesuits to the extent that he eventually left the country in 1688 in the company of a fleeing Jesuit. The evidence against Green, Berry and Hill was, therefore, used to screen other more important and still-guiltier persons: the men accused by William Bedloe.[64]

Pollock's theory was ingenious rather than convincing and it rested the reason for Godfrey's death on the magistrate's knowledge of the secret meeting. However, it is not that clear whether Coleman did actually know of this matter, and if he did, being a loyal son of the Catholic church, why would he blurt it out to Edmund Godfrey? Moreover, there was also no reason to believe, until Coleman was arrested and his papers were read, that the plot would develop in the way it did. Further, we also need to believe that having revealed to Godfrey the real plot, such as it was (and it was not that much of a plot, merely secret meetings), Coleman then went on to tell the Jesuits and his master that he had made such a blunder.

The famous secret consult described by Oates was in reality the provincial congregation usually held every third year by the Society of Jesus for the purposes of electing a proctor to be sent to Rome. Forty senior members of the district met in St James's Palace in a room placed at their disposal by the Duke of York. The question must be whether this meeting was as secret as some made out? In fact, if it was supposed to be a secret, it was not a terribly well-kept one, for a few years later, in 1681, it was well known that the meeting *had* taken place and *not* where Oates had claimed. It also seems that a meeting that was a regular part of the district affairs was hardly a significant reason to kill a Protestant magistrate at the beginning of an anti-

Catholic agitation. Finally, Pollock's thesis also rested upon the tales of two known liars and perjurers, each of whom came up with stories that did not match the other in particulars, both of whom used a palace which on any given day would be typically crowded with people, and both of whom would not have lasted very long in a modern court of law. Disregarding the latter point, in its favour the theory firmly places Miles Prance at the centre of the plot. In this respect Prance, if he really was lying (as we must suppose he was), was either a fortuitous choice for Bedloe to make or he really did know something of the crime.

In Catholic journals and elsewhere Pollock's version of the events that led to Godfrey's death was either roundly attacked or dismissed in the early twentieth century.[65] Undaunted, he defended his position in vigorous terms, particularly in light of a pro-Catholic work that came out in answer to his claims, namely, Alfred Marks's book *Who killed Sir Edmund Berry Godfrey?*[66] Marks returned to the suicide theory. Prance and Bedloe were dismissed as liars and the Somerset House theory fell by the wayside. Instead Marks turned to the melancholic Godfrey who committed suicide on Primrose Hill by using his own sword. We shall return to this theory in the next chapter, but needless to say it has its own set of problems.

It was J.G. Muddiman who in 1924 introduced a new and more melodramatic figure into the plot. His theory was based on an ingenious link between the man who killed Godfrey and a mad aristocrat with an apparently similar *modus operandi.* [67] This theory takes us in part back to the mysterious butcher Edward Linnet and his dog mentioned by William Griffith in a 1678 newsletter. Linnet was a St Giles butcher whom Muddiman was to claim had really dumped the corpse in the ditch and was to 'find' it sometime later. Not that Linnet was the killer. Rather, Muddiman claimed that Roger North knew the killer but had been afraid to speak out for fear of the murderer's friends. His theory was that the killing was actually committed by the rather ill-tempered and 'half-mad' Philip Herbert, Earl of Pembroke. Pembroke was a violent, drunken, 'Whiggish' aristocrat, who, when not attacking his enemies, or his supposed friends, had contacts with the opposition groups. In 1678 Edmund

Godfrey in his capacity as foreman of a jury had found Pembroke guilty of the crime of murder. Unfortunately Pembroke, being a lord, had been able to appeal to the House of Lords for his trial and had subsequently been released. Godfrey had then left the country for a while, but Pembroke had not forgotten him and in the autumn of 1678 he had sought his revenge on the magistrate. According to this theory, a worried Godfrey received a mysterious note on the Friday inviting him to a rendezvous. Godfrey had turned up on the Saturday afternoon only to be faced by an irate Pembroke. There he had been attacked, beaten and strangled by the mad earl. Coming to his senses in the aftermath of this attack the earl, or his servants, or Pembroke's friends, had kept the body until it was safe to dispose of it. They relied upon an ingenious method to cloud the issue and had taken the body in the butcher's cart to Primrose Hill to dump it there. The real clue was divulged in Mr Adam Angus's story (see pp. 100–1) about being approached in the bookshop some hours before Godfrey's body was discovered. We may remember that a man in a grey suit had told Angus that Godfrey had been discovered with his own sword run through him near Leicester Fields, which was close to where Pembroke had his London home. Once more there are considerable problems with this ingenious solution and we will examine them in the next chapter.[68]

In the 1930s the detective story writer John Dickson Carr developed Muddiman's theory into a book.[69] His is a work of historical detection, with occasional lapses into outright fiction. Nevertheless, Carr clearly stated the possible suspects at the time and chose Pembroke as the most likely candidate. It was left to the historian J.P. Kenyon to take another route in his version of events, written in the 1970s.[70] He relegated Godfrey's killing to an appendix. This was not out of any lack of interest, but rather because he did not see it as part of his brief to go looking for suspects. In reality he thought that the easiest solution to the problem was that of the unknown footpad with a grievance. This unknown, and by now undiscoverable man, was as likely a candidate for the killing of Edmund Godfrey as anyone else. Perhaps the crime was in fact unconnected with the events of the plot in Godfrey's life and this murder was merely a coincidence. Godfrey could have been waylaid and strangled on the Saturday, only to have been hidden until at least Wednesday when the killer had finally managed to arrange transport in order to dump the body near Primrose Hill. The sword was merely added to mystify the discoverers of the body, with the possibility that it would not have been found until the body had decayed so much that any marks of strangulation could not have been detected in any case. So suicide by his own sword would be the verdict. This solution, however, does not really explain Godfrey's moods of depression prior to his demise. In addition, the solution was perhaps too clever for an allegedly uneducated footpad to think up. Moreover, once he had realised the reaction that he had set in motion, the murderer would have had to work out what to do with the corpse. This must inevitably have meant the involvement of others, both to store the body and to help him move it. Additionally, the body was not robbed. Given the £500 reward being offered for information, no common criminal, however ingenious, could have kept the affair quiet in the face of what was in contemporary terms an enormous amount of money.

The lack of an obvious answer led to the somewhat wild solution that the late Stephen Knight put forward in the 1980s.[71] A former journalist, Knight had previously investigated the Whitechapel murders of 1888 and in that case had ingeniously found not one lone killer but three, all backed by a government plot that involved the royal family.[72] Having solved this puzzle to his own, if no one else's satisfaction, Knight turned to this earlier mystery. In his version of the story Knight simply piled one theory on top of another, implicating everyone who could possibly have played any part in the killing. The 'mad' Earl of Pembroke was once more accused of the murder. In addition, Knight also introduced into his version of events the spy John Scott, about whom we will shortly learn more. However, this time Pembroke was egged on to kill Godfrey by his own private motives, that is Godfrey's part in his trial, as well as those of the betrayed members of Sir Robert Peyton's gang. Godfrey, a former member of this group, had betrayed them by his links with the Catholics and was in turn killed to make the Catholics look guilty and bolster the plot. He had been summoned to a meeting with the gang on the Friday by the mysterious note. On turning up at the venue on the Saturday, he was murdered and the body was kept until it could be arranged in such a way as to implicate his Catholic friends.

Knight's theories were rather too ingenious and more than a little unhistorical. His startling new evidence was also somewhat lame, being neither very new nor that revealing, and his exaggerated view of the so-called Peyton gang led the whole book to fall somewhat flat. Another obvious question must also be whether any sensible group of plotters would have relied upon an apparently dangerous lunatic such as the Earl of Pembroke to do its bidding. Thus Knight's reckless earl, Republican plotters and murdered magistrate all come confusedly together in the author's enthusiasm for multiple plots, which appears to derive from his previous book on the Whitechapel murderer.[73] Historical puzzles, of course, still require solutions and in a case such as this, as we have seen, the evidence first points one way and then the other. We must once more re-examine the evidence to see which solution presents itself as the most likely in this most mysterious of historical mysteries.

CHAPTER SIX

The Case of Ockham's Razor

Entia non sunt multiplicanda praeter necessitatem.
[No more things should be presumed to exist than are absolutely
necessary.]

William of Ockham

'The finest work of [murder in] the seventeenth century', wrote
Thomas de Quincey ironically, ' is, unquestionably the murder of Sir
Edmondbury Godfrey, which has my entire approbation. In the grand
feature of mystery, which in some shape or other ought to colour
every judicious attempt at murder, it is excellent; for the mystery is
not yet dispersed.'[1] In point of fact the case for the murder of
Edmund Godfrey rests upon three main pillars: the medical or
forensic evidence; witness statements (of which that of Miles Prance
was the most significant); and the general belief of contemporaries
that the magistrate had been murdered. An alternative to the verdict
of murder does exist – namely, that the magistrate committed suicide
while of unsound mind or in a state of acute depression, and that his
body was found, held, manipulated and dumped in the ditch near
Primrose Hill to give a boost to an otherwise flagging Popish Plot.
This verdict also rests on three main foundations: an assessment of
Edmund Godfrey's mental state; the forensic evidence; and the
witness statements and rumours at the time.

Inventing solutions to 'disperse' De Quincey's grand mystery has
been a pastime for historians since 1678, and there are solutions
aplenty to choose from: a rogue group of Roman Catholics; the Earl
of Danby; the mad Earl of Pembroke; Shaftesbury; a Republican gang;
Titus Oates; William Bedloe; the two Godfrey brothers and Henry
Moor; Green, Berry and Hill. Or even, as John Dickinson Carr and J.P.
Kenyon have speculated, 'X the unknown'; at least this is a satisfyingly

This sympathetic portrait of Edmund Godfrey by an unknown artist, c. 1678, was probably completed posthumously.

A rather unflattering portrait of the crown-stealer, adventurer, spy and plotter Thomas Blood by Gerard Soest in 1680. The question of what part, if any, the Irishman Thomas Blood played in the death of Edmund Godfrey remains an open one.

Contemporary illustrated playing cards were often used to convey propaganda. This pack (236), of 'The Horrid Popish Plot' gives a contemporary impression of the strange death of Edmund Godfrey. We see Edmund Godfrey taking the depositions of Oates at his house in Hartshorne Lane and the plotters meeting to plan his murder. The magistrate was allegedly dogged by his killers and then strangled and run through with his own sword at Somerset House. The body was then carried out of the palace in a sedan chair by the murderers. After the discovery of the body a mass funeral was arranged and following Miles Prance's revelations three men died on the scaffold.

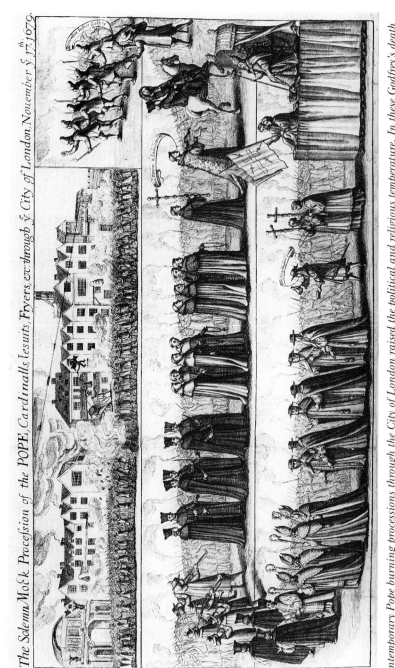

The Solemn Mock Procession of the POPE, Cardinalls, Iesuits, Fryers &c: through ye City of London, November ye 17:th:1679.

Contemporary Pope burning processions through the City of London raised the political and religious temperature. In these Godfrey's death played a prominent part. In this engraving he can be seen mounted in front of a Jesuit riding behind the crier who was hired to ring his bell and bellow 'Remember Justice Godfrey' to the massed citizens of London. Behind, rows of Roman Catholic Church figures and the Pope follow. The whole procession came to a halt near Temple Bar where the Pope was solemnly burnt to great cheering, while the devil, naturally enough, flew off to fight another day. The solemn mock procession of the Pope, Cardinals, Jesuits, Fryers &c through the City of London, November ye 17th 1679.

The happy instruments of England's preservation, *1681, is another piece of anti-Catholic propaganda. While the Pope and his Cardinals meet in an infernal conclave plotting yet more destruction, the Happy Instruments of England's preservation, including Titus Oates and William Bedloe, watch from above, under a Protestant God who will ensure the ultimate failure of Catholic plotting.*

THE DREADFUL
APARITION;
OR,
The POPE Haunted with Ghosts.

In Relation to Sir *Edmundbury-Godfrey's* Murther, and the Visitations of the late Sainted Traytors, who Suffered for The *Romish-Cause.*   The Figure being by the Verses at large Explained.

In The dreadful apparition: the pope haunted with ghosts in relation to Sir Edmundbury
Godfrey's murther and the visitations of the late sainted traytors, who suffered for the
Romish cause, *1680, the Pope is visited in bed by a series of ghosts who attempt to show him the
error of his ways. Edmund Godfrey is depicted with a number of swords thrust through his body.*

The Catholick gamesters of the dubble match of bowling, *1680, is a typical piece of enterprising coffee-house propaganda. Edmund Godfrey is shown valiantly dying in the gap of the fence which surrounds the king, parliament and English Protestant liberties as the protector of the country, while all around the rest of the image are shown other events and participants in the Popish Plot.*

The Godfrey family memorial in the cloisters of Westminster Abbey.

simple version, since it makes the culprit a man for whom the killing of Edmund Godfrey meant something personal, and the Popish Plot and Edmund's connections to it not very much at all. We have seen that Godfrey naturally created some enemies in the course of his life as a magistrate. However, far too often historians have arrived at their pet solutions by working back from the death and ignoring the man himself. Any real solution to the mystery should probably lie with who Edmund Godfrey was and how he died, his activities in London life and his part in the Popish Plot – about all these matters the reader will by now be arriving at his or her own conclusions.

The purpose of this chapter is to re-examine the forensic evidence, the usual suspects and the possible solutions to the mystery. I hesitate to say that any of the solutions put forward is the correct one because the evidence for each carries only a limited amount of weight. Until more evidence turns up, if it ever does, what follows has to remain an interesting set of theories; I would claim no more than this. As to the validity of these theories, the reader must be the judge. I will begin, however, as always, with the known and knowable hard facts about the death of Godfrey – the forensic evidence. Much attention has been devoted to this in the past and it still remains controversial.

STRANGULATION, WOUNDS AND SURGEONS: FORENSIC EVIDENCE

As with any crime of this nature, a description of the type of wounds found on the body is vital. The most important descriptions of the state of the corpse are to be found in the statements of the medical witnesses at the trial, who were, one must presume, the most expert of the witnesses there. Two surgeons were called to the inquest and the trial in 1679 to give evidence: Zachary Skillarne and Nicholas Cambridge. Both men appeared to give their information with some assurance and both were regarded as authorities, although there were some disagreements between them on certain matters and at the inquest they apparently confused the jury. Skillarne, who first saw the body at noon on Friday with Cambridge, said that he thought Godfrey's breast had been beaten with an obtuse weapon, fists or feet. He claimed that the neck was distorted, and that there were two wounds; the first had hit a rib and the second had penetrated the body through to the other side. Godfrey, he said, had not been killed by this second wound. Skillarne was clear that he thought that the neck had been broken and that, as he put it, more had been done to the neck than ordinary suffocation. Godfrey, he went on to say, had died four or five days earlier, which would put the time of death at sometime on Sunday or Saturday. Nicholas Cambridge, on the other hand, claimed that the neck was only dislocated, but he did agree that the breast looked as if it had been beaten. There were also two puncture wounds, both administered after death.

What were the credentials of these medical men? The élite English physicians were invariably Oxford or Cambridge trained although few began as medical students and in most cases Latin and books were the keys to success rather than clinical cases. Some anatomy was studied and many preferred to go to a good foreign medical school to undertake practical training in medicine. In general Skillarne and Cambridge, about whom we know little enough, would have been aware of the standards of their day, each skilled in his own way, but they were not exceptional physicians.[2]

There were other medical men who saw the corpse at the White House, in 1678 whose evidence only emerged later during the trials for libel in 1682. These men were the king's apothecaries, the Chases, father and son. One Mr Hobbs also came forward to say that the corpse's face appeared 'blotted', and although the eyes were bloody they were not 'fly blown'. Chase junior noted the two wounds and also a great contusion on the left ear. He also thought the face very bruised. His father saw the two wounds and a swelling on the left ear and that the dead man gave the appearance of having been beaten from neck to stomach. The last medical witness was Mr Lazinby, testifying four years after the death in 1682. He claimed that Godfrey had been strangled and a ligature kept about his neck until he was cold. The corpse's face was all bloody and the upper part of the neck, breast and stomach were discoloured, as was his mouth. Lazinby also observed that the collar was tight and there were two great creases both above and below the neck, the neck being swelled above the collar and below by the strangling with a cord or cloth. Godfrey's eyes had matter in them and were bloodshot. William Griffith, a newsletter writer who compiled his account of the death on 19 October 1678, noted that the magistrate had been strangled, his breast was bruised and blood had settled in a face that was in life rather sallow. There were impressions, he said, of cord marks around the neck with a 'cross broad wound in his breast'. It was supposed that Godfrey had been killed somewhere else and his sword wounds had been inflicted after death, but putrefaction had not set in.

To summarise this forensic evidence, therefore, contemporaries were faced with the corpse of a lean 56-year-old man, previously noted as being in poor health, possibly hard of hearing, and of a melancholy disposition. He had two puncture wounds, both of which appeared to have been inflicted after death with his own sword, and the second wound the sword had fully penetrated the body. There was little blood at the scene, 'bruising' on the breast and stomach, a bruise on the neck under the left ear, with marks around the neck below and above the collar. The neck was distorted, dislocated or even broken. The eyes were bloodshot and the face, in life noted as pale, was reddish in colour. The body was relatively malleable and did not appear to be yet subject to putrefaction until it was opened. Based on this evidence and other material, the coroner and jury, after some difficulty, came to a judgement of murder.[3]

What then are we to make of the forensic evidence as it has been reviewed in our own century? It has been the subject of many debates. In a 1952 radio programme on Godfrey, Professor Keith Simpson, a noted pathologist and a Reader in Forensic Medicine at the University of London, made some pertinent remarks about the forensic evidence.[4] He noted that the sword wounds on the body were not the cause of Godfrey's death and that the amount of blood involved, of which contemporaries made so much, threw little light on the mystery. It was clear, however, that Godfrey was dead when the sword was passed through him. Simpson also went on to say that the marks on the neck were indicative of strangulation with a cloth or band and were not compatible with hanging. He cited the fact that the jacket collar had to be undone to expose the neck marks in the first instance and they were also too low down to be consistent with hanging. He noted furthermore that those who die in such a way tend to have marks that lie under the lower jaw. It *was* possible, albeit rare, that the victim could have used a ligature to strangle himself by drawing it up so tightly that he lost consciousness and died of asphyxia. Of course, this would have required the removal of the ligature by a person or persons unknown. Simpson, of course, could not state whether this had occurred and he preferred the logical conclusion that the killer had removed it, but self-strangulation was not impossible.

Simpson easily dealt with the looseness of the neck, for he noted that it could well have become loose after the initial rigor mortis had passed. Rigor mortis begins in the muscles of the face and head. It then passes slowly and progressively downwards. Thus if the jaw was stiff and the arms mobile it was a good indication that death had occurred within a few hours. Unfortunately, Simpson thought, the surgeons were not pressed sufficiently about the nature of Godfrey's neck and only made some general comments concerning its looseness. Was it broken or not? The experts differed. The injuries to the chest and upper abdomen certainly required more thought. They were not, Simpson claimed, evidence of hypostasis, although he qualified this by noting that the contemporary descriptions were not detailed enough and so this still remained a possibility.

Hypostasis or post-mortem lividity sets in immediately following death. At the time of death the blood ceases to circulate around the body, and because of gravity it gradually sinks to the blood vessels in the lowest part of the corpse. The affected parts of the body then display a livid colour. After ten to twelve hours these purplish stains become fixed and resemble nothing so much as bruises. Lividity is used as a measure in that it can prove whether a corpse has been moved after death; in such a case the marks will differ on the body from the place where it has been laid. In fact, the resemblance of hypostasis to bruises has led to many a conflict between modern medical experts, hence Simpson's hesitation in making a judgement on a case some 300 or so years old. The point is significant, of course, for if the bruises on Godfrey's body were really only signs of post-mortem lividity then the case that Godfrey was beaten before he was murdered almost disappears, for a man face down in a ditch would have such lividity marks where the surgeons found 'bruises'.[5] In fact, Simpson inclined towards the opinion that Godfrey had been beaten by fists, boots, or both as he defended himself.

Unfortunately no examination was made of the victim's hands (an essential requirement of a modern inquest) to show whether there was any evidence of resistance. The bruise under the left ear was either a knot mark or else came from the strangler's fingers in the course of twisting or tying a ligature. Thus, in Simpson's view, the evidence pointed to strangulation. The face was livid and the eyes discoloured and this could only have occurred if the circulation had been intact, thus the sword must have been thrust through either at the point of death, as a *coup de grâce*, or after death. The timing of the injuries would be significant as it would take several minutes for the bruises to develop and they would only have appeared during life. Therefore, Simpson considered Godfrey's death to have resulted from a 'beating up' lasting several minutes and resulting in bruising, followed by strangulation by ligature lasting twenty to thirty seconds. Godfrey's body was then transfixed by his own sword, either before or after his death.[6]

The internal autopsy was poorly carried out. As we have seen, there appears to have been some argument as to whether or not the body should actually be opened. Once it was opened, if there really was little or no food in the stomach this could, Simpson claimed, be put down either to an incompetent post-mortem (quite likely given the conditions) or to Godfrey having eaten only certain easily digestible foods, such as eggs, milk, white bread, wine and so on. Alternatively Godfrey, who everyone agreed had been melancholic before his death, may not have been eating very much in any case. Simpson thought that Godfrey had died on or about Saturday. So in spite of a distinct lack of detail that a modern pathologist would certainly supply (crucially in the case of the hands), Simpson was willing to claim that there was clear evidence of three episodes in this death: bruising, asphyxia and stabbing. Other doctors also examined the evidence during the twentieth century, but their opinions need not detain us here. They were drawn upon to bolster or refute the argument between Pollock and Marks over whether Godfrey had taken the Roman way of death and fallen upon his own sword.[7]

THE MENTAL STATE OF EDMUND GODFREY

We have seen what sort of man Edmund Godfrey was and what sort of life he led. However, we must also try to assess his state of mind prior to his death. There are two possible conclusions. Either the evidence collected after his death was grossly exaggerated to fit the image of a careworn martyr torn by persecution, or the witnesses actually saw Edmund Godfrey in the throws of a breakdown or personality crisis. Although it is clear there was some exaggeration, not all of the witness statements can be easily dismissed. There were probably other witnesses who did not or would not come forward, or like Judith Pamphlin, appear to have been deliberately ignored, despite being able to offer reliable evidence as to the magistrate's state of mind. There is certainly information to support the view that at the very least Godfrey was subject to depressive tendencies throughout his life and that these tendencies had reached crisis point just before his death. Taken together, therefore, they point towards suicide as a possible cause of death.

The producers of the 1952 radio programme also called in a professor of psychological medicine at the University of Durham, Alexander Kennedy, to examine Godfrey's death.[8] His brief was to explore, from the evidence available, Godfrey's state of mind just prior to death. Like Keith Simpson's evidence, this makes interesting although inconclusive reading. Assessing the psychological condition of a man or woman long dead is a hazardous business for any practising doctor at the best of times, although historians of course do it constantly. None the less Kennedy clearly outlined the evidence for a state of morbid depression. Its effects, he claimed, would have made Godfrey a potential suicide. The extremities of depression would have brought gloomy ideas about the future, difficulties in sleeping, little or no appetite, and episodes of agitation and crisis. If such a crisis did strike Godfrey during the course of his duties, he might well have felt unable to cope.

Lewis Wolpert, in his illuminating book *Malignant Sadness: the Anatomy of Depression*, has outlined the distinguishing symptoms and characteristics of depression as he himself experienced it.[9] These are, he notes, overwhelming sadness, numbness, dullness and apathy.

Thoughts of suicide are common, alongside an inability to concentrate, fatigue, a lack of energy and general anxiety. Certain people are more prone to depression than others and episodes might last a day, a week, or years. Wolpert also gives a clinical description of the features of depression formulated by the German psychiatrist Emil Kraepelin in 1921 that is worth quoting in full. The depressive, he states:

> feels solitary, indescribably unhappy, as a creature disinherited of fate; he is sceptical about God, and with a certain dull submission, which shuts out every comfort and every gleam of light, he drags himself with difficulty from one day to another. Everything has become disagreeable to him; everything wearies him . . . Everywhere he sees only the dark side and difficulties. . . . Life appears to him to be aimless . . . the thought occurs to him to take his life without knowing why. He has a feeling as if something has cracked in him.[10]

In the seventeenth century the idea of melancholia was less clinically expressed. It was defined in two ways: both as an illness and a temperament.[11] Most medical knowledge was still based upon Galen's principles of the four humours (blood, yellow bile or choler, black bile and phlegm) governing the human condition. The ideal temperament held all four in balance, but this rarely occurred. In fact, to the medical men of the day most individuals were subject to one or two predominant humours which produced the sanguine, phlegmatic, choleric and melancholic personalities they saw around them. Melancholy was thought to be the result of an excess of one of the humours (black bile) over the others. In 1621 Robert Burton, who himself suffered from the illness, spent a great deal of time and energy dissecting the various conditions in his large book *The Anatomy of Melancholy*.[12] He concluded by stating: 'I can say no more, or give better advice to such as are any way distressed in this kind, than what I have given and said. Only take this for a corollary and conclusion, as thou tendrest thine own welfare in this, and all other melancholy, thy good health of body and mind, observe this short precept, give not way to solitariness and idleness. Be not solitary, be not idle.'[13]

At that time there would have been little more by way of treatment for this condition than letting blood to balance the humours, which we know Godfrey did indulge in, and the sufferer's reliance upon the support of a family. For a lonely bachelor this would have been difficult and this is possibly why Godfrey turned to Mrs Gibbon. Was this also why Godfrey was so anxious for the correspondence with his friend Valentine Greatrakes to be maintained, as it diverted him and made him less prone to thinking morbid thoughts? It seems possible. Another cure was to escape to the country to get over it all, a solution that we know Sir Robert Southwell had at first suspected the magistrate to have adopted in October 1678.[14] According to Burton and today's doctors the tendency to depression also runs in families. Burton called this an 'inward, inbred cause of Melancholy . . . the temperature, in whole or in part, which we receive from our parents'.[15] There is some evidence that such illness ran in Godfrey's family.[16] Contemporaries mention his father's alleged bouts and attacks. Godfrey himself even seems to have recognised the 'black dog' as hereditary and this may not have been the first attack he had suffered. We may also add as evidence of depression Godfrey's apparent lack of a degree at Oxford, the subsequent trip to Europe, the mysterious abandonment of his studies at the Inns of Court and his retreat thereafter into the countryside, as well as his visits to France in 1668 and 1678. Indeed, his physicians were allegedly responsible for sending him there the second time. Godfrey may well have returned still depressed and unable to sleep. He was noted as someone who wandered the streets at all hours of the night. His business, judicial, financial and personal activities seemed designed to keep him very busy at all times. The phrases noted by contemporaries are pertinent here; with their continual references to him being prone to 'sadness', being 'pensive', 'discontented', or in 'disorder', or 'very sad' and so on, they cannot all be discounted as exaggeration after the event. In a statement, admittedly given well after the death, William Church described how in 1677 the magistrate especially shunned the company of his own kind at Richmond. Instead he exercised on the bowling green with ordinary company, footmen and the man who helped to roll and make the ground for the game. When a shocked Church asked Godfrey why he acted in this way, the magistrate's reply was very revealing. He said: 'That company was very irksome to him; That he Bowl'd and exercise'd with those mean People, that he might run up[w]ard[s] and down, and do what he would to divert Melancholy, for he was so overpower'd with melancholy that his life was very uneasie and Burdomsom to him.'[17]

Alexander Kennedy also made an interesting diagnosis of Godfrey's frequently described habit of wiping his mouth and looking upon the ground: it could have been evidence of hardening of the arteries.[18] All of which may well have aggravated his depression still further and led to expressions of paranoia and fears for his life. At no point does it appear that Godfrey was of unsound mind, that is, in the throws of madness, but if we take this view the evidence does seem to point towards a man heading towards a breakdown. He could well have been already morbidly depressed when Oates and Tonge turned up on his doorstep. In that case fears that parliament, Danby or the king himself would extract vengeance for his part in the affair meant that Godfrey may well have seen suicide as a way out of his problems. The burning of his papers and settling of debts would reflect some sense of responsibility prior to his demise. In short, Kennedy's conclusion was that here was a man aged fifty-six, with a history of attacks of depression, and no immediate family, wife or children to rely upon, who in such a crisis was predisposed to suicide. That he committed suicide, therefore, Kennedy claimed to be not only a logical conclusion of the evidence but, given the state of his life, almost inevitable. However, if one does not accept that suicide is the easiest and most logical solution to the mystery of the strange death of Edmund Godfrey, then one must consider it murder by one man or by a group of men.

THE INFORMERS

The first suspect is obviously the man who apparently had most to gain from Godfrey's death in the sense that it might help to confirm the Popish Plot: Titus Oates.[19] It is possible to create a scenario whereby, in the midst of a failing plot, Oates tracked down and murdered Godfrey in a bizarre fashion in order to confirm the reality of the Roman Catholic threat. Yet several factors are against this. First, Oates was just not this type of villain. While he was certainly a rogue, had the intelligence to bring such a murder off had he chosen to do so, and, of course, had a motive, he was rather too much of a coward to resort to physical violence. We may recall, for example, his beating at the hands of no less than St Omers' schoolboys and yet another beating by his neighbour. His subsequent whines were not the reactions of a hardened killer. Instead he tended to resort to spiteful recriminations – when it was safe to do so. In the end Oates is ruled out, if only because for much of this period he was actually under guard in Whitehall. Although the king had given him rooms in the palace as a result of his revelations, Charles II had also insisted that guards were to be placed near him to prevent him being prompted in his revelations. How strict this guard was we do not know, but it is very unlikely that Oates could have slipped away for a few days, killed Godfrey in such an elaborate manner, moved the body and then returned. Moreover, knowing what we do of Titus's character, it is equally unlikely that having committed such a crime he would not have then given himself a more prominent part in the affair, hinting at revelations in the charged arena of the Commons and in his own pamphlets. In fact, he was relatively restrained at the trial of Green, Berry and Hill. If we are to believe his old teacher William Smith, Oates knew little enough about the killing of Godfrey except that it was very convenient, and his compatriots Bedloe and Prance apparently knew even less. Smith noted that:

Coming one evening to visit him [Oates] at Whitehall, I found Bedloe and Prance with him; among other discourses, they talkt of Sir Edmundbury Godfrey: Oates laught at the business, and said, Here is Bedloe, that knew no more of the Murder than you or I did. But he got the five hundred-pound, and that did his work, and give this blockhead [Prance] 30*l* of it. He pickt him up in the lobby of the House of Lords, and took him for a loggerhead fit for his purpose; at which Bedloe laught heartily and Prance look'd a little dull, as displeased. At this rate I have heard Oates and Bedloe discourse very often, who used always themselves to make the business of Godfrey a ridiculous story and entertain'd themselves when private with the jest on't.[20]

However, another version of this story is possible. In it we find Oates, who had been dogging Godfrey, coming across the dead body of the magistrate who had committed suicide. Seizing this opportunity to bolster the flagging Popish Plot, he and his colleagues manipulated the body to make it look as though the Catholics had killed Godfrey. Yet all of this theory in the end remains rather tenuous. The same reservations about Oates's involvement remain. Once more we must take his own words, as witnessed by William Smith. Smith alleged that: 'This business happen'd well for Oates, as he afterwards often told me. He would usually say, "I believe not a word on't; but my plot had come to nothing without it; it [was] made well for me; I believe the Council would have never taken any farther notice of me else, if he had not been found".'[21]

The other suspects around Oates are even less likely to have had a hand in any murder. Israel Tonge was both too old and half-mad. Christopher Kirkby, after his prominence during the early days of the Popish Plot, dropped from sight. Although we do know that Kirkby was occasionally mistaken for Oates and was disappointed that he was not reaping enough attention and rewards, there is little to suggest he would have had a hand in a killing.[22] A timid man at the best of times, although he knew of some of Godfrey's part in the affair, would he have tried to engineer a bigger role for himself by murder? It is unlikely. If he had, then why did he not subsequently come forward with real evidence in the matter and take the substantial reward and credit for the discovery? With Oates, Kirkby and Tonge unlikely suspects, this leaves William Bedloe and Miles Prance. To these two gentlemen we will return later.

COURT POLITICS

A number of Restoration statesmen had been involved in murderous schemes or were aware of government assassination plots in the early 1660s.[23] With this in mind a number of reasons can be put forward for

Lord Treasurer Danby as a potential prime suspect in the killing of Godfrey. We may first note that Danby apparently had a motive. His ministry was in the political doldrums and with Charles II forming new alliances with Louis XIV his chances of survival at court were diminishing by the day. The 'Church and King' policy was just not delivering the necessary political alliances and funds that he required. The Popish Plot, therefore, was something of godsend to Danby. If it could be manipulated correctly, he would find favour with parliament, bolster 'Church and King', find scapegoats among the Roman Catholics, check the Yorkist faction at court and even suspend the king's need for a French alliance. Or so it might seem to a worried statesman. Danby was never a popular minister but he was very shrewd, and if, by appealing to the nation's baser instincts, a suitable Roman Catholic agitation could bring benefits in its wake, he would have been willing to use it.

It was unfortunate for Danby that things went seriously wrong, for Edmund Godfrey interfered with his schemes. Brought into the affair by Oates, Tonge and Kirkby, Godfrey was not content merely to play the part devised for him in taking the depositions and thus making the plot more public. He not only read the documents but also told his friend Edward Coleman about the scheme. In turn Coleman told the Duke of York who made a fuss about the matter at court and so brought the plot into the open. Danby would doubtless have been furious at the magistrate's interference. As we have seen, it was said that he summoned Godfrey and threatened him. There seems little doubt that Danby was one of the great men whom Godfrey mentioned as being upset with him. They already disliked one another. But why have Godfrey killed?

We can speculate that Godfrey may have been murdered at Danby's behest in order to make the plot look as convincing as possible and allow the first minister to recapture the initiative. Alternatively, it could be surmised that Danby was so angry that, in the manner of Henry II and Beckett, the incensed minister blurted out in the company of his servants and hangers-on: 'Will no-one rid me of this troublesome magistrate?' Danby was surrounded by men who might well have stooped low enough to do this deed on his behalf, whether he really wished it or not. One of the more significant men in this respect, for example, was to act for him in 1680 in another scheme designed to damage the Duke of Buckingham: Edward Christian.[24]

Edward Christian had served the Royalist cause in the Civil War, and from 1660 he had acted as a rent-collector for George Villiers, Duke of Buckingham, on his estates. Before long his abilities had seen him promoted to the position of the duke's chamberlain and financial secretary. There seems little doubt that Christian was corrupt above the ordinary sense of the word in the seventeenth century. He embezzled large sums of money from Buckingham's estate before his dismissal in 1673. By 1676 he had approached Danby for employment and, despite his reputation, Danby had made him his steward. Accusations that Danby had been involved in the killing of Godfrey were made by his opponents soon after the event. Christian's staunch defence of the earl at the time proves the trust between them. Christian also defended Danby in print and was subsequently accused of having a part in the affair himself, although he claimed to have been in Stamford, Lincolnshire, at the time. Later on in 1680 we can find other evidence of Danby and Christian working together.[25]

The political whirlwind that was the Popish Plot ruined Danby, like so many others. Revelations over his secret dealings with France led to calls for his impeachment and the king was forced to place his minister in the Tower of London in 1679 to save him. This was a low point in Danby's life; he was to spend the next few years there.[26] None the less he still retained some authority and continued to dabble in political scheming. Attempts were made in 1680, possibly at Danby's behest, to destroy the reputation of the Duke of Buckingham, then prominent as a leader of the Whig opposition. Edward Christian was by now also eager to damage his old master, against whom he retained a grudge, and seems to have provided money to suborn witnesses to accuse the duke of sodomy, a crime of grave significance.[27] Two Irishmen, Philomen Coddan and John Ryther, were to swear that Buckingham had committed sodomy on one Sarah Harwood and then sent her into France. Further witnesses were to emerge in the shape of Philip Le Mar and his mother Frances Loveland. The former was a not very bright young man who had fallen into the hands of sponsors cruder and more dangerous than himself. His mother joined him in the accusations in what seems to have been an unusual show of maternal affection. As the mud flew in all directions, the various parties attempted to make political capital out of the affair. Robert Spencer, Earl of Sunderland, the Secretary of State, was incriminated in the affair and insisted that Le Mar be rigorously examined. During this interrogation Le Mar revealed the names of the Earl and Countess of Danby. It was alleged that Le Mar had been offered £300 by the couple to swear the crime of sodomy against Buckingham.

Coddan and Ryther's design was laid along different lines. Coddan knew another Irishman by the name of Maurice Hickey, alias Higgins, or Higges. According to his own version of events, he and Hickey had come down to London in 1679 and settled in Long Acre, near Westminster, where they raised some suspicion by their frequent loud talk and conversations in Gaelic. The target of their scheme was Samuel Ryther, whom they intended to use to swear against Buckingham in exchange for copious amounts of drink and money. As soon as Ryther had signed a paper to the effect that he knew that Buckingham had committed sodomy on Sarah Harwood, he was to be kept close in case he should change his mind. Ryther, as it turned out, was a man given to changing his mind quite frequently. Coddan was to play the role of the second witness and was willing to swear anything as long as he was well paid. Hickey was the brains behind the group, although he was also being told what to say and do by his sponsors. As Ryther proved increasingly fearful and uncooperative, one Thomas Curtis entered the plot. Curtis's involvement leads us to the real object of our inquiry: Thomas Blood.[28]

As a former soldier, intriguer, crown stealer and double agent, the Irishman Thomas Blood was talented at this sort of plotting.[29] By the mid-1670s he was associated with many at the Court. He had settled down there into a position of special agent and 'gun for hire'. In the course of a long career on both sides of the law, Blood had been used by Danby, the Duke of York, Buckingham and the secretary of state's office. Born in Sarney, County Meath, around 1618 as the son of a blacksmith and ironworker, he lost his lands during the civil wars in

Ireland, served in England as a Royalist soldier then deserted the king's cause in 1650 and joined that of parliament. During the Restoration, affairs in Ireland did not go well for him and he resorted to the usual course for the discontented: plotting against the regime. The collapse of the Dublin plot of 1663, in which Blood had been heavily involved, forced him to go on the run. He spent much of the later 1660s involved in plotting and espionage activities of one sort or another on both sides of the political divide.

He may well have been working for the government at one point as a double agent, but in July 1667 he made a genuine name for himself in a successful ambush to rescue his friend and fellow plotter Captain John Mason from a group of soldiers who were escorting Mason to York. In 1670 Blood engaged in a second spectacular venture by ambushing and launching a failed kidnap attempt upon the prominent royal minister James Butler, Duke of Ormonde, in the streets of London, probably at the behest of Ormonde's great enemy Buckingham. Most famously, of course, in 1671 Blood, heavily disguised as a parson, had attempted another spectacular coup by trying to steal the crown jewels from the Tower of London. Having been caught, he managed to talk his way out of this act of treason and even made a profit into the bargain.[30]

Given this background, Blood seems a potential candidate for engineering the killing of Edmund Godfrey. He had just the right amount of wit to make the more bizarre elements of the murder work. He knew of the magistrate's connection with Peyton's gang, for he had apparently investigated that gang on behalf of the government. Blood also knew Oates later on, and according to one source had planned to upset the informer's credibility by planting treasonable letters in Oates's papers. Nor was Blood sympathetic to crazy old Israel Tonge, especially as the latter was fond of blaming him for starting the Great Fire of London.

Blood was also involved in the plot in 1680 against Buckingham, where he seems to have acted as a go-between for the Irish plotters Coddan and Ryther and Christian. And Christian, of course, was Danby's servant. In the game of double bluff that followed, Coddan and Ryther soon changed sides and betrayed the scheme to

Buckingham's lawyer Mr Whitaker, whereupon Hickey fled and Blood and Christian were arrested. After a series of engineered delays on both sides, with disappearing witnesses and other mysterious events, Christian, Blood, Le Mar, Curtis, Hickey and three others were tried at the King's Bench. It was this case that brought a premature end to Blood's career, for in prison the 62-year-old adventurer caught a fever, and, even though he was eventually released, he died on 24 August 1680.[31]

What part, if any, did Thomas Blood play in the Godfrey affair? Both Blood and Christian were certainly capable of murder and were thus a logical choice to resolve the Lord Treasurer Danby's little problem. As we have seen, Danby was one of the men most accused at the time of involvement in Godfrey's death. Unfortunately, these accusations were mixed up with political mudslinging from a number of very dubious Irish informers imported on to the English scene by Shaftesbury. But, in reality, Danby had no real need to have the magistrate killed. In fact, he had plenty of reasons to keep Godfrey alive. Godfrey's part in the plot could have been used to prove just how far the design had proceeded in the corruption of a Protestant magistrate. Godfrey could also have been useful at a witness in any future trials. In the end this solution to the mystery remains far too complicated. Not only does Godfrey have to have been in the right place but also the right men have to have been hired. It would have needed more than one man to do the job, and presumably Danby was not going to kill Godfrey himself. This would certainly mean the involvement of still more untrustworthy individuals who would undoubtedly have revealed the scheme when Danby fell from power. We have already seen how the plan to damage Buckingham's reputation fell apart in a welter of betrayal, and this was merely libel! So although Danby did have the contacts to do the job there is no real evidence against him. In any case even if Danby did order it, or if it was done on his behalf, why the elaboration on the body? Surely it would have been simpler to merely kill Godfrey, dump him in the Thames, and blame the Catholics? Moreover, it is one thing to have been angry at Godfrey's interference and quite another to have him murdered in a fit of pique. Finally, it was altogether too dangerous for

Danby to allow an act such as this to be committed. It would have been a huge gamble that would have been quite out of character for the Lord Treasurer and this in the end rules him out.

However, about Thomas Blood we are entitled to some further speculation. In fact the nature of the death and some of its more *outré* aspects do smack of Blood's previous *modus operandi*. The problem here is that although he is a striking and previously unused candidate for the killing no evidence actually exists of him having had any part in the scheme whatsoever. In order to blame Blood for the murder we would need to discover who his sponsors were, for he would not have done it for his own purposes. This, given his penchant for obscuring his trail in these years, is virtually impossible at this late date. Besides no contemporary linked him with the crime, which is surprising given his past, although his name was mentioned in some of Oates's writings. On a more positive note we do know that at this time Blood was being drawn further than ever before into the squalid and unstable London world that informers such as Oates and Bedloe inhabited.[32] In the down-at-heel gin shops, taverns and low gambling dens of this world a shrewd man like Blood could pick up much intelligence. In a part of London inhabited by rather unsavoury thugs, pimps, prostitutes and weak-willed liars, such quarrelling criminal folk occasionally came across a little bit of the truth which Blood, with his connections, was able to sell on elsewhere. We also know that from 1678 to 1680 he was either at the centre or on the periphery of a number of sham plots that emerged and during this part of his career we can find him working for the king, Sir Joseph Williamson, the Secretary of State, his old master, the Duke of York and even Danby. It remains entirely speculation but if anyone could have perpetrated such a crime as Godfrey's killing in such a bizarre manner then it probably *was* Thomas Blood. Conversely if anyone could have solved such a crime then it was probably the same man.

THE WHIG CAUSE

One of the many theories that have surfaced over the years was that Godfrey was murdered to make the Popish Plot look more successful than it really was. According to this scheme, Godfrey was a convenient corpse to be manipulated. Panic would set in at the death of a Protestant magistrate and this could have been used by the murderer's sponsors for their own designs. The Roman Catholics would take up the theme of suicide when the actual evidence pointed another way, and this in turn would make them look even guiltier of trying to cover up the murder. This idea is, of course, applicable to many interested parties. Among them was Shaftesbury, who intended to use the plot for his own purposes before anyone else could do so. However, Shaftesbury only came up to London in time for parliament and after Godfrey's death, and in the end he seems as unlikely a candidate as his opponent Danby. Both men, in fact, sought to exploit the situation but did not cause it. It is possible of course, but equally unlikely, that Shaftesbury provided the backing for the killers. Ultimately, however, Shaftesbury was a cool and calculating politician who merely seized the opportunities given to him.[33]

The late Stephen Knight put forward a different proposition for this 'Whig' side of the affair. He concentrated on the so-called Peyton gang.[34] We have met this group before. Its leader was Sir Robert Peyton and Godfrey had at one time been associated with it. It was made up of pseudo-Republican opposition members with links to the City of London. That they were hostile to Danby, his regime and French influence is clear, but in his version of the plot Knight has them assisting Oates and Tonge in nursing along the latters' scheme. Knight claimed that the gang was indeed the mysterious 'honourable friends' who pointed the pair in the direction of Godfrey as a suitable magistrate to read their evidence. Knight's interpretation failed in certain respects. First of all, why choose Edmund Godfrey when there were other more rabid anti-Catholic magistrates available, such as Sir William Waller?[35] Knight also saw Godfrey baulking at the scheme laid out by the 'gang' and then going on to betray them all to Edward Coleman, and thus the Duke of York. For that, naturally, he had to die, for he also knew too much about the group. He knew not only of their plotting but also that they had also taken bribes from the French ambassador. Thus Godfrey was doubly damned. He had not only betrayed the Peyton gang, but also the plot itself. Knight's speculation then led him to suppose that, strangely enough for a group of men only recently planning the overthrow of a government, they were unwilling to kill their former friend themselves. Instead they decided to hire a professional man to arrange Godfrey's murder in such a way as to lay the blame on the Catholics. Knight claimed that Peyton and friends hired none other than John Scott to do the deed.[36]

John Scott, a double agent, informer and *bête noir* of Samuel Pepys, has attracted speculation over the years about his involvement in the killing of Godfrey. Sir John Pollock was to use Scott's ramblings to bolster his theory that the Popish Plot had a basis in fact. Under the name of John Johnson, Scott was arrested in April 1679, and on interrogation he revealed that in Paris the late Roman Catholic Earl of Berkshire had made a substantial deathbed confession to him of a plot much like that revealed by Oates. Moreover, he had implicated Coleman, Bellasis and others. Unfortunately Pollock knew little enough of Scott's background when he used him as a reliable witness. In fact, Scott was something of a dual personality. He could be charming when he wished; he was a writer of poetry and a gentleman of wit. On the other hand, there was a darker side to this man. He was a foul-mouthed, drunken misanthrope, a rogue, liar and a coward, a man whom few, if any, could trust, and those who did were often singularly disappointed.

Scott's career began inauspiciously enough in the Americas[37] to where he had been transported as a child. In his adult life Scott acquired a bad reputation in the colonies; he deserted his wife and ended up in gaol. He reappeared on the English scene in 1660 when he returned home on behalf of some respectable New Englanders. While Scott was in England he was introduced to Sir Joseph Williamson; the latter took a keen interest in colonial matters. One of Scott's more legitimate talents was as a cartographer, and one of Williamson's interests was maps, so their acquaintance prospered. Scott then returned to America, but not before he had perpetrated a confidence trick on a Quaker couple and gained possession of their son, whom he then rather imprudently sold to a New Haven innkeeper. After various adventures, Scott left for the West Indies where he took a commission in Sir Thomas Bridges' regiment. There he saw some action in the disastrous English military expedition to St Kitts to fight the French. When in action he was accused of cowardice, having apparently left his men in the lurch and hid behind some rocks: they were captured and he was court-martialled. In the event Scott was soon back in England once more. Over the next few years he remained close to the regime's secretariat, despite spending some time in the Gatehouse prison, and in 1669 he re-emerged within the Republican exile community in the Netherlands as a spy. He remained a soldier and eventually became a colonel in the Dutch army. None the less Scott's main activity for the next few years was espionage. He served as a professional agent for a number of masters and regimes. He acted as a spy for the Stuarts, as well as for the Dutch Republic and the French government of Louis XIV. He spent much of 1678 going back and forth across the Channel to haunt the entourage of the Duke of Buckingham and other groups opposed to Danby.[38] He was also gathering intelligence for Louis XIV's government. It was while he was thus engaged that Thomas Blood, acting on behalf of the government at this point, picked up some intelligence about Scott's associates. One of Blood's sources was a tobacconist by the name of John Harrison. According to him, Scott had many friends among Buckingham's minions and the London-based extremists. This may also have been linked to another alleged plot that combined three extreme groups: the Fifth Monarchists, the 'atheists' and Sir Robert Peyton and his 'gang', one of whom, of course, had been Edmund Godfrey.

Beyond this connection there is little else to link Scott with Godfrey.[39] We do know that Scott had made Godfrey's acquaintance in the late 1660s. This was not surprising, as both men had been within the precincts of the court. We also know that Scott was behaving very oddly in the week of Godfrey's death – in fact he abruptly left London two days before the body was discovered. He later claimed that he had fled the city because he had heard he was to be 'clapped up and starved'. Although there was little reason for him to believe this according to the public statements issued by the two secretaries of state, we know that in private both Sir Joseph Williamson and Henry Coventry, his partner in the secretariat, were having Scott watched. Scott later admitted that he had been travelling the coasts of Sussex and Kent gathering intelligence that summer and had stayed with Sir Francis Rolle, a Member of Parliament who had previously taken money from the French government. So while there was reason enough for Scott to leave at that time, the Stuart regime was already on his trail, and there was little reason for him to depart in such a dramatic fashion especially while using the surprising alias of 'Godfrey'. It is also true that Scott's espionage activities were sufficiently interesting for Samuel Pepys to become involved in attempts to capture him. Pepys mistakenly believed that Scott was a Jesuit priest, and was later to suffer from Scott's malice because of this when the latter accused him of selling naval secrets to the French. More than this, there is little real evidence to link Godfrey with Scott – a secret agent with interests far beyond that of a troubled magistrate from St Martin's-in-the-Fields.[40]

In Knight's version of events, of course, Scott cuts a much more prepossessing figure. Indeed, Knight believed that having been hired by Peyton to get rid of Godfrey, Scott did not take the more logical route of hiring a professional killer from the criminal classes. While such men could be relatively easily found in some parts of London, this would have been too obvious. Instead, Knight believed that he used the mad Earl of Pembroke, who although he bore Godfrey a grudge, as we shall see, tended to attract attention to himself. Pembroke having killed Godfrey, Scott arranged for the body to be dumped on Primrose Hill and fled the scene. Where does this leave us? To answer that question, we must now examine the next suspect: Philip Herbert, Earl of Pembroke and Montgomery.[41]

THE EARL OF PEMBROKE

The mad Philip Herbert, Earl of Pembroke and Montgomery, has long been a suspect in the killing of Godfrey. His name first entered the lists in an article written in 1924 by J.G. Muddiman.[42] Other historians have subsequently elaborated Muddiman's views, most notably Stephen Knight. In reality the crucial aspect of Pembroke's candidacy as a murderer, as we shall see, rests not with his character, which was bad enough, but with whether *contemporaries* ever linked him with the strange death of Edmund Godfrey. The answer, unfortunately for some theorists, appears to be negative. Indeed, no one at the time ever seems to have linked Pembroke with the deed. Those who favour his candidacy, however, claim that the burden of truth rests not so much upon positive as negative evidence. Indeed, the argument put forward is that no one named Pembroke because they were too frightened to do so on account of what he, a man with a penchant for violence, might do to them. This argument is somewhat fallacious, especially given Pembroke's death in December 1683. We are meant to believe that even after his death at the height of the Tory reaction and the persecution of the Whigs (with whom he was closely associated), no one dared come forward with his name when an awful lot of old scores were being settled. Surely some hint would have been made at this time? Yet there is only silence. So Muddiman's likely suspect is ruled out for that reason alone. But there are other reasons to eliminate Pembroke, as we shall see.

Even at first glance Pembroke does seem a well-qualified suspect. Philip Herbert, 7th Earl of Pembroke, was a child of the disrupted 1650s. He was born in January 1653 as the son of the fifth earl and his second wife. For much of his short life, Pembroke managed to get into one scrape after another, being at various times imprisoned for murder and for blasphemy. He was also the subject of a number of revealing pamphlets of the day. Although these were anonymous, the fact that they came out in print when Pembroke was still alive gives the lie to the view that people were too frightened to write about him at the time. Indeed, quite often it seems that Pembroke went out of his way to court notoriety. He was certainly guilty of an excessive passion for life and was probably an abuser of his wife into the bargain. He was also most likely an alcoholic. His massive drinking bouts appear to have brought out his violent streak and involved him in numerous duels and at least two killings – in 1678 and 1681. As far as we know, he was also a somewhat ill-educated young man. He was to spend his later days, after a life of aristocratic dissipation, mad and under lock and key at Wilton House in Wiltshire, the family seat.[43]

He succeeded to the family title in July 1674. Within days he was involved in a duel and had been twice run through. The poet Rochester labelled him 'Boorish Pembroke brave', and as the new earl followed a wild career, his fearsome reputation began to proceed him.[44] In December 1674 he decided to marry. His choice was an unusual one. Henriette Mauricette was the sister of the king's mistress Louise de Kéroualle, Duchess of Portsmouth, a figure of some importance at court. Philip and Henriette were not a happy couple and what she saw in the earl is unclear. Pembroke had to wait until he had recovered from his wounds after a duel before the marriage could actually take place and thereafter he seems to have neglected his wife as much as possible, no doubt to her great relief. Indeed, he pointedly refused to lay out any expenses for her lying in on her pregnancy and when the Duchess of Portsmouth threatened to inform the king of the matter he crudely replied that 'if she did so he would put her upon her head, and show his family the grievance of the nation'.[45] Those who sought the repayment of debt from the young earl did not fair much better; they were threatened with violence. So Pembroke's life settled into a round of drunkenness, duels, and hunting on his estates. His political ambitions were consequently limited. He was Lord Lieutenant for his country and thus had some authority, which he was later to use for the Whig cause, but beyond this his influence was restricted.

Very few people were at ease in his company; although one author claimed that he was in reality full of virtue and treated with 'Respect and Honour by all that know him, and reputed ill by only such as are not worthy [of] his Acquaintance'.[46] Despite these words in Pembroke's defence it is clear that when he was drunk, or even sober, he was a dangerous man to be around. Pembroke was a notorious duellist, although it must be said not a very accomplished one. He lost quite a few duels in this time and was run through on a number of occasions. After one such contest in 1676 he treated the jury that acquitted him to a drink, but no one dared sit near him until Sir Francis Vincent did so. The two men promptly got into a quarrel and Pembroke smashed a bottle of wine over Vincent's head. As Vincent staggered out Pembroke drew his sword and Vincent roaring that he was 'never afraid of a naked sword in his life', drew his own weapon in return. In the ensuing fight Pembroke's sword broke and the two men resorted to fisticuffs in which the earl was badly beaten. One of Pembroke's servants ended up in the River Thames into which a maddened Vincent had thrown him.[47]

In fact, in an era when aristocratic violence was common enough, young Pembroke, who was still only twenty-three, had much in common with his peers. To the Restoration aristocrat of his generation violence was fairly commonplace and was linked to the code of honour. This aristocratic code had emerged over a number of years. A series of unwritten rules, it revolved around individual self-esteem and reputation. Men such as Pembroke were unusually sensitive to the least slight as a result, the more so as they were also desirous of as much praise as possible. Naturally the gentleman aristocrat was bound to show courage, fortitude, and familiarity with his equals, but of necessity he was to receive in return respect, praise and even esteem. Indeed, to lose one's reputation was to lose the immortal part of a gentleman's soul. Thus affronts were frequently looked on unfavourably and were usually settled by the code of honour on the duelling field. Giving someone the lie, as contemporaries put it, was also looked upon as a dangerous business. The moral code that most aristocrats lived by was exemplified by their willingness to fight those of equal status. Indeed, to be 'challengable' was desirable in any gentleman. This private system of law regulated life between men of honour, for a gentleman's word was his bond. Conversely mere violence was to be offered to those unfortunate souls who lurked below the code of honour. Pembroke was guilty on both counts. He fought those who were his social equals and he beat to a pulp those whom he thought beneath him. Occasionally, of course, he went too far as in the case of Nathaniel Cony.[48]

On Sunday 3 February 1678 Pembroke was drinking with his friends in Long's House in the Haymarket when Nathaniel Cony and his friend Goring came into the tavern.[49] As Pembroke knew Cony, he invited the pair to drink at his table. At first the wary Cony refused, but he and Goring were eventually persuaded. Towards midnight, after some heavy drinking, Pembroke and Goring quarrelled.

Pembroke threw wine into the man's face and a scuffle broke out. As the two were forcibly separated, Goring threatened to draw his sword and he was bustled out of the room. Pembroke then turned on Cony in a fit of rage, kicking and punching him severely. Having satisfied his honour, he then left with his friends. Cony was soon pushed out of the tavern, taken home and put to bed. He died of his injuries a week later. Goring later remembered that the quarrel was over 'families and play', but he remembered little else, being, like the others, already befuddled with drink. One Captain Savage in Pembroke's company said that Goring told Pembroke that 'he was as good, or a better gentleman then he was'[50] and got wine in his face as a result. A gentleman called Shelly was also there. He claimed that the fight broke out over gambling. Goring asked Pembroke to play, but when the earl was about to send for £500 he backed out. A peeved Pembroke said: 'you are an idle fellow that you propose these things and [do] not pursue them. Upon that Mr. Goring tells my Lord, his name was a better name than his Lordships, and he a better gentleman then my Lord'[51] and so they set too. Cony only got involved when Goring had been hustled out of the room. Pembroke apparently told him to go and join his friend. Cony replied somewhat insolently that he did not know why Goring had been taken out in the first place, and so Pembroke knocked him to the ground and brutally kicked and stamped on him. Captain Fitzpatrick, another witness, told another tale. He later claimed that Goring, who was drunk, said 'I will drink, I will play, I will fight any with man'.

'Who is this gentleman,' said Pembroke, 'that I should never hear of him.'

''s Blood,' said Goring, 'not hear of me? My name is Goring, a name and family as good as any gentleman in England.'

'There is nobody doubts it,' said Pembroke.

'Your betters', said Goring and then Pembroke threw the wine in his face.[52] Pembroke was subsequently arrested and sent for trial.

It is at this point that Edmund Godfrey briefly enters the story. Godfrey was the foreman of the grand jury that brought in a verdict of murder and necessitated further action. The grand jury having found Pembroke guilty, as they were bound to do given the evidence against him, he pleaded his status as peer of the realm and was sent up to the House of Lords to stand trial before his peers. Fortunately for him, they only found him guilty of manslaughter and, having paid a fine, he was set free.[53]

What is one to make of this case, for upon it rests the argument that the 'psychotic' Pembroke subsequently sought revenge (or was encouraged by Scott to seek revenge), on the foreman of the grand jury, Edmund Godfrey. In fact, Pembroke emerges not as a psychotic, but as a drunken boor of man, certainly prone to violence, but not given to premeditated murder. Rather he was a man who acted upon impulse. If he even remembered the foreman of the grand jury, it is unlikely that he cared very much about him, for after all he was ultimately acquitted and released to continue his merry way with other deeds of drink and violence. Moreover, why single out the foreman of the jury? What of the other men involved and those who gave their evidence in his trial? The connection between the pair is thus tenuous and full of supposition. The idea that Godfrey subsequently scurried across the Channel when Pembroke was liberated is also fallacious. Nor was the magistrate who had stood up to the king and a number of assaults in the street likely to be frightened away by a drunken lout such as Pembroke, for all of his aristocratic airs and graces. In addition, although Pembroke was a violent man, as we have seen within his code of honour and given the way in which he lived, he will undoubtedly have thought himself cleared of Cony's death: he was proved right by his peers, having been found guilty of manslaughter. Cony was not important – he was not a gentleman. Nor in Pembroke's eyes were the members of the jury. Moreover, as K.H.D. Haley long ago pointed out, Pembroke may not have even been in London in September and October 1678. He was irregular in his habits at the best of times and his attendance in the House of Lords mirrored his life. In fact, he seems not to have been there in person until at least 5 December 1678.[54]

Pembroke is ultimately an unlikely suspect, however violent he was in his life, and his candidacy smacks of certain historians looking too hard for a suspect and ignoring the full facts of the case. In the end he continued to live life to the full as he saw it. A further killing followed in 1681, after which the king intervened to pardon him. Pembroke having eventually been removed to his estates for his own, and others' safety, he finally burnt out and died aged thirty in 1683.[55] The case against him, therefore, remains purely circumstantial. It is true that Pembroke had inflicted injuries on one of his victims that in a number of ways resembled those found upon Godfrey, but in the end the answer must be that he had little real motive to kill the magistrate.

MURDERED FOR THE CAUSE: THE ROMAN CATHOLICS, PRANCE AND BEDLOE

On 18 September 1680 the Roman Catholic midwife Mrs Elizabeth Cellier was nearly another victim of the Popish Plot crisis. She was standing in the pillory having been found guilty of libel, with stones and other rubbish thrown at her head by the howling Protestant mob of London. Cellier's crime was that earlier in 1680 she had published pamphlets that called the Popish Plot witnesses liars and blamed the king for allowing them to make a profit out of their perjuries. Her other charges were that both Miles Prance and Francis Corrall, a somewhat garrulous hackney coachman, had been tortured in Newgate prison to make them inform upon the Catholics, from which Cellier had suggested that Protestantism itself was basically anti-royalist. These were formidable charges and her presence in the pillory that day suggests that the authorities took them seriously enough to ensure her punishment. Yet her presence there was also the result of a series of sham plots in which she, with the help of other minor Roman Catholics, had tried to engineer a shift in responsibility for the crisis from the Roman Catholic community to the Whig opposition. Cellier and her cronies thus provide an interesting entrance to the next, and most popular, group of suspects in the strange death of Edmund Godfrey: the members of the Roman Catholic community of London themselves.[56]

It is generally accepted by most modern historians that the Catholics had no real reason to kill Edmund Godfrey, and that the three men who were executed for his murder, Robert Green, Henry

Berry and Lawrence Hill, were entirely innocent. Indeed, the case against the Roman Catholics rests largely upon the evidence given at the trials of 1679–80, the literature written by men such as Titus Oates, William Bedloe and Miles Prance, and the popular belief at the time that, whatever the reality of the plot, one element of suspicion above all others was at least justified: that the Catholics had murdered Edmund Godfrey. However, a number of questions need to be explored: were Prance and Bedloe really telling the truth about the murder at Somerset House? Or, as Pollock suggested in 1903, was Prance actually telling the truth but disguising the names of those involved in order to protect the real culprits? Why would the Catholics want Godfrey to die in any case? Was the strange death of Edmund Godfrey in reality a mistake, a serious error of judgement on the part of a rogue group within the Catholic community? Or had the Jesuits and other Catholics killed Godfrey for their own reasons? We must begin to answer such questions by examining the basis for the belief that the Catholics killed Godfrey – the evidence of Bedloe and Prance, and their claim that this crime had taken place in Somerset House in the Strand.

Edward Seymour, Duke of Somerset and Lord Protector of Edward VI constructed Somerset House in 1549.[57] Located in the Strand, next door to the older and by the 1670s largely decayed, Savoy Palace, Somerset House became the abode of the Roman Catholic queen consorts of the realm in the seventeenth century. It had a respectably large establishment of Catholic servants, priests, confessors, laymen and even the odd discreet Jesuit inhabiting the precincts of the queen's court and home. Under Queen Catherine of Braganza, who was the royal occupant in 1678, the palace had a notable Roman Catholic chapel mainly for royal use but also available to the numerous Catholics who lived about the palace in the crowded streets off the Strand. In a sense, therefore, by 1678 Somerset House had become something of an island of Catholicism in Restoration London and was naturally suspect. As such, the palace also provided a suitable setting for the theory that one of the most heinous crimes of the century, the murder of Edmund Godfrey, was committed by Roman Catholics.

The English belief in the cunning of Catholics in general and of the Jesuits in particular has already been noted. The Jesuits themselves were seen in English eyes as containing in their ranks the most cunning Catholics of all, who were given to going about in disguise and, being more fanatical than most in their devotion to the 'anti-Christ', that is the Pope in Rome, were ever eager to create mayhem in Protestant countries. They were also believed to obey a creed that did not rule out the elimination of the opposition by political violence where necessity and the Lord willed it. Indeed, it was claimed that the Jesuit order even possessed a philosophical justification for the assassination of monarch, minister, or subject in the doctrines laid down by Juan de Mariana.[58] The Spanish Jesuit Mariana's view that 'anyone who [was] inclined to heed the prayers of the people may attempt to destroy a tyrant' was seen by some as evidence of the basic immorality of the order, which had been established in the 1530s by Ignatius Loyola. Thus the plethora of images in Oates's and Tonge's imaginings of secret groups of Jesuit assassins stalking the king and his land pandered to a tenacious set of beliefs among good Protestant folk in general. Yet few appear to have questioned Oates's account of the incompetent Irish assassins, Grove and Pickering, dropping flints and silver bullets from guns behind bushes, and hired by the Roman church to murder a monarch who was inclined to their religion and who had done his best to bring relief to Catholics where he could. Indeed, if elements of the the Catholic church really had wished to kill Charles II, they could have hired hands far more competent than Oates's 'fantasticks', as there were professional assassins aplenty available for hire in Europe. Nevertheless, Oates had set the scene with his revelations of murdering papists, and it only remained for his fellow informants to provide tales of men who had actually murdered a Protestant magistrate.[59]

We must begin with the information of William Bedloe.[60] Bedloe's accusations about the murder were significant mainly because he was the first to come forward to the authorities with any evidence of how Godfrey died. It was also Bedloe who first singled out Somerset House as the scene of the crime. Despite being a large rambling place it was, unfortunately for him, a poor choice. Like most seventeenth-century palaces, Somerset House was liable to be crowded with people at all times of the day and night. Nevertheless Bedloe had lived in London and undoubtedly knew his way about the place; he was able, for example, when taken back there after his revelations to the Privy Council, to locate the very room in which he had seen the body of Godfrey by the light of a lantern. It was a 'lobby or place for servants to attend in'. It was not the best of choices in retrospect, but at least there were Catholics in the vicinity. Of course the servants of the queen and other inhabitants of the palace who both saw Bedloe and heard his tale made much of the fact that this was a public room, claiming that his whole story was a 'falsehood and an impossible thing'. Moreover, they also appear to have had some previous dealings with Bedloe and knew him for a 'notorious robber and highwayman'.[61] Bedloe even admitted he had occasionally been on the wrong side of the law.

If his setting for the crime was improbable Bedloe's account of the deed was still more so. The men he accused, as we have seen, were named as Le Phaire or Le Fèvre, Walsh, Samuel Atkins (until Atkins' alibi was proved), Pritchard (a waiter in the queen's chapel) and other vague individuals, including Miles Prance, when Bedloe finally recognised him. He said that they had met Godfrey in the King's Inn in the Strand and persuaded him that they had evidence of the plot in Somerset House. But once he had been lured into a small room, the magistrate had been threatened with a pistol, had refused to submit and had thus been stifled between two pillows as well as strangled. His corpse had been lugged behind a suitable arras, or the high altar in the queen's chapel (William was not quite sure which) and concealed there for a few days. Thereafter by sedan chair and coach the conspirators had moved the corpse to Primrose Hill. Various sums, from 2,000 to 4,000 guineas, had been offered to Bedloe to join in but he had refused them all and fled precipitously back to the West Country. He said the murder had taken place sometime between 2 and 5 o'clock on the Saturday.

There were many improbabilities within Bedloe's tale and he was deliberately vague. So much so that we must question his evidence, for few seem to have dared do so at the time. The improbabilities of

Bedloe's story mount with each reading. Why had no one else seen this crime? It was carried out in a royal palace bustling with people in mid-afternoon. How had no one prevented this group of men leaving a guarded royal palace with a corpse? This aside, it must have soon become clear that Bedloe not only had a history of European-wide fraud and criminality behind him, but also his past could not be completely covered up, and so his word was hardly trustworthy. In fact he had been languishing in jail just a few weeks before the killing.

If his evidence was untrustworthy, was he himself a candidate for the murderer? This is possible. Bedloe knew of Oates and may well have got wind of his schemes either in Spain or in London. But once more we are faced with insurmountable problems. If Bedloe was guilty, where was the deed carried out? Where was the body hidden for at least five nights? Bedloe seems an unlikely murderer in the end for Oates himself admitted that William had never even seen the magistrate before and knew nothing of the crime, but was only involved for the £500 reward. In general those involved were willing to accept any answer they could find to solve the puzzle, however improbable, and William Bedloe, of course, pointed out Miles Prance as being central to the case.

Titus Oates called Prance a blockhead. He was not such a rogue as Oates, but he was a self-confessed perjurer and eventually proved rather a worthless man all round. Yet Miles Prance was crucial to the official version of how Godfrey met his end. It was Prance who confirmed Somerset House as being the scene of the crime, and it was Prance who provided the authorities with some culprits who had not vanished: Green, Berry and Hill. They had all been arrested by 24 December 1678. Naturally, as we have seen, all three men denied having anything to do with the crime, but were ignored. Even after Prance had recanted his first confession and changed his mind under pressure, only to be persuaded to return to his first story, he was a prime witness, and a desperate regime, anxious to placate parliament with some culprits, was not willing to give up on him. How was it possible then for Prance to create his version of events?

We may first remember that Prance would have been well aware of Godfrey's actual injuries.[62] Unlike Bedloe, he had connections among the crowd at the White House. The club of which Prance was a member met on the Sunday after the inquest had closed. Also the nature of Godfrey's injuries was published soon after the inquest, certainly before Prance's arrest. Prance also knew his way around Somerset House: he had not only worked there, but was also a familiar figure to the residents. He may also have known that Bedloe had used the palace as his setting for the murder. After Bedloe's revelations the government had sent troops to surround the palace and seize any suspicious-looking papers. Bedloe himself had been taken down to the building and caused something of stir there. It would not have taken much to put together what exactly the authorities had been looking for in the palace. But unfortunately Prance's tale differed considerably from that of William Bedloe. While Prance named Fathers Girald and Kelly, who had fled, he also picked on his acquaintances Green, Berry and Hill, but he left out the men whom Bedloe had named. Moreover, Prance's relation of the crime and his statements were not only more detailed than those of Bedloe, they also differed from Bedloe's account. The motive for the killing now became that Godfrey had been overly busy in the persecution of Catholics, as one might expect from a man with the reputation of a staunch and worthy upholder of the law. This, said Prance, was why the priests wanted him eliminated. Prance apparently did not know, or simply ignored the fact, that the magistrate was in reality liberal to Roman Catholics. Moreover, in Prance's version of the murder Godfrey was dogged, drawn into the yard at Somerset House and there beaten and strangled near the stables with a twisted handkerchief. The body was then put in a room in Dr Goddin's lodgings. In Prance's version the murder took place between 9 and 10 o'clock at night, with the body subsequently stored in various places before the comical moves by sedan chair and horse to a place Prance knew very well – Primrose Hill.[63]

Although Prance's tale differed considerably from Bedloe's, both were used in the trial. In the trial Prance performed well, but there the king's counsel and the judge protected him. Later on Prance supported some of Oates's statements in a number of other trials. By 1686, however, Prance had finally admitted his perjury. He said that he had been lying all along and as a result he was punished by a fine of £100, and sentenced to be pilloried and whipped. Strangely enough, the latter part of the sentence was not carried out. Indeed, the next time Prance appeared was as an escapee in the company of some Jesuits in December 1688. Captured off Gravesend, he was sent up for further examination, but it is probable that he ultimately found his way into Europe and lived there until his death.

Prance's tale is full of improbabilities. Pollock saw him as the shrewd man trying to protect his fellow killers by placing the blame for the crime on innocent men.[64] But once again we must remember that here we have an account of a crime taking place in a royal palace. Indeed Prance set his murder in an open yard, where even at 9 o'clock at night there would have still have been lot of comings and goings by grooms and stable folk about their business. In addition, the king himself later remembered that both he and his court had actually been at the palace that night. This appears to ruin the whole tale completely. Charles II's court, though lax at times, was still heavily guarded. Nor does Prance's tale really explain away the presence of guards at the palace gate, whom he largely ignored. Moreover, the amateurish activities of the murderers seem to have been created merely to explain why the body did not appear in the ditch before Thursday. In addition, Somerset House was next door to the Savoy, a place that had already been the focus for Oates and his guards. They had already made a number of arrests of people who lived there. It is entirely possible that Somerset House was itself already under observation. In any case it would have been extremely risky for the killers to take the body out of the palace's most minor doors. An over-officious guard or a tipsy reveller could have spelled disaster. Prance's tale *was* believed, however, or was used simply because the government had no one else at hand except the dubious Bedloe and wanted to placate a disaffected parliament and country. Not for the first time was the regime of Charles II willing to sacrifice innocent men to calm a troublesome nation.

If Prance and Bedloe were lying, are there any alternative scenarios to implicate the Catholic community and Jesuits in London? It has been suggested that a group of worried Roman Catholics, hearing of

Edmund Godfrey's part in the affair, decided to eliminate him from the scene. Yet why kill a man, a magistrate indeed, just at the point when rumours of a Popish Plot were flying about London and when his death would bring down the wrath of the Protestant nation on the head of the Roman Catholic community? It could, of course, have been a simple miscalculation – history is full of mistakes and miscalculations of this sort. Yet, on the other hand, although there is no extant evidence that Godfrey was making inquires of his own among the Catholics after the visit of Oates and Tonge to his home, he may well have taken (as was his custom in other cases) to probing just a little too deeply into the Popish Plot. Fearful that Godfrey might uncover still more incriminating evidence, or even manufacture some, a group of overzealous Catholics may well have miscalculated: they may have had him murdered. Some were to make just such a miscalculation when fed the Meal Tub fiasco in 1679 by the informer Thomas Dangerfield. This scheme to bring discredit upon the Whigs and blame the origin of the Popish Plot upon them misfired spectacularly.[65] An alternative, of course, is that Edmund Godfrey really did have access to a great secret and therefore had to be killed. Was this, as some have claimed, Coleman's information about the secret meeting of the Jesuits at St James's Palace or other evidence that a plot existed? As we have seen, it is unlikely. Alternatively, did the Catholics wish to kill Godfrey because in their minds he had become associated with Oates and Tonge? This version of events could perhaps explain his death. It is always possible that a group of foolish men, fuelled by scare stories, arrests and alarms, who thought they were doing the right thing in removing an officious troublesome enemy of the church, killed him and made a clumsy attempt to make the whole affair look like suicide by his own sword. They would only have discovered their mistake after his death. This is a plausible tale. But there is yet another simpler and more logical alternative.

'OH THIS IS MY BROTHER GODFREY!': MICHAEL AND BENJAMIN GODFREY

To most mysteries there is a simple – and logical – solution if one knows where to look. This is medieval philosopher William of

Ockham's razor: 'No more things should be presumed to exist than are absolutely necessary'.[66] We know that Godfrey's involvement in the Popish Plot was to cost him dearly, but it is in his personal life that the real solution to the mystery of his death may well lie. For here we find the magistrate already subject to bouts of melancholy, with Tonge and Oates on his doorstep informing him of tales of a serious plot. Edmund Godfrey's actions thereafter smack of someone in a state of acute depression. His subsequent errors in dealing with their evidence soon piled up against him: Godfrey's keeping the whole affair secret, when it would have been much more sensible to go to the secretary of state and lay any evidence before higher authorities; his urgent discussions with Edward Coleman; his appearing gloomy at Lady Pratt's house and elsewhere; his fears of persecution by some 'great persons'; his fears of being punished for his alleged wrong doing; his fears of being the 'first martyr'. The alleged burning of his papers on the Friday evening and his actions on the Saturday morning until he left the yard at Hartshorne Lane at around 9 o'clock were the actions of a worried man. After asking directions to Primrose Hill that Saturday morning, wandering around in a state of distress for some hours unable to decide what he wished to do, he finally arrived at a solution: Edmund Godfrey committed suicide by self-strangulation near Primrose Hill. The forensic evidence showed the wounds to his breast as having been inflicted after his death and thus he could not, as Alfred Marks once argued, have fallen upon his own sword. The 'bruises' on the body could just be explained by post-mortem lividity. The answer to the mystery that supplies itself, then, is that of self-strangulation. This at least has the merit of fitting the forensic evidence in some way. It must be agreed that it remains an odd method of death, but it does, of course, place the demise of Godfrey where it was always most likely to lie: with the man himself.

Suicidal strangulation could be effected by the victim tying and tightening a ligature, often in a double knot, or with the ligature wound around the neck more than once. The ligature would need to be tied at one end to ensure that the pressure on the neck was maintained even when the victim had passed into unconsciousness. A convenient tree would seem most suitable for this purpose. The investigators of a Victorian murder case at Chelmsford Assizes in 1851, however, made a number of illuminating judgements on this matter. In the course of that nineteenth-century affair they found that in some cases the two ends of a suitably coiled and knotted cord, with both of the ends held tight or coiled around the hands, could enable a person to commit suicide. A ligature placed tightly around the neck would produce almost immediate insensibility, and also a loss of muscular power. A.S. Taylor cited the case of two men who *had* succeeded in committing suicide in such a manner and also the self-experiments of one Dr Fleischman as to the most suitable places to put the actual ligature. Fleischman's final horrifying description of the effects of this form of death form a coda to the strange death of Edmund Godfrey: 'The face becomes red, and the eyes congested, and protruding; the head feels hot, there is a sense of weight followed by vertigo, and there is a sudden hissing noise in the ears. This last is a symptom of impending danger, and unless the experiment be discontinued at this time, the result will be fatal.'[67]

So suicidal strangulation can occur in exceptional circumstances. The puzzle in the Godfrey case could only have been resolved by a minute examination of the victim's hands and neck. The investigating surgeons appear to have done their best in trying circumstances, but of course Godfrey's body, while it had marks around the neck that could possibly agree with such a death, had no actual ligature in place when it was discovered. Indeed, both his band and cravat were also missing. In addition his sword had been passed though his body. How do we resolve this final problem? The only way forward is that someone removed the ligature and someone pushed the sword into him after his death.[68]

At which point we must of necessity speculate still further. Our first speculation is that Henry Moor, Godfrey's clerk, did indeed find his master's body on the Sunday. What would he do? Given what we now know of his character and actions in the course of this crisis, there seems little doubt that he would have tried to cover the crime up. Moreover, he would have immediately contacted Godfrey's two brothers. This was a family matter; the shame of suicide should not be underestimated and his master's estate would probably have been forfeited because of it. With Michael and Benjamin in charge, however, the body could be shifted to a safe place while the Godfrey brothers and Moor decided what to do next. The two prominent businessmen could easily have found the opportunity and means to shift their brother's body in secret had they set their mind to it. Did they consult with others on the matter? This seems unlikely. Michael was a strong and independent character; it was more logical that the affair would have been kept in the family, much as it seems their own father's serious illnesses may have been. The brothers' subsequent haste in visiting the Privy Council and their fervent accusations against the Roman Catholics are therefore explained as a device to allow them time to cover up a suicide. It was not until Wednesday that they dared to move the body back to Primrose Hill, and lay it there in such a way that implications of suicide would soon be discounted and blame laid upon the Roman Catholics. It had to be made to look like a clumsy killing. Hence the sword that was nervously pushed through the body not once but twice. The body was then pushed into the ditch with its face covered, almost as if they could not bear to see Edmund's accusing eyes. It may also have been placed there with the hope that perhaps by the time it was found putrefaction would have set in and any traces of suicide would consequently have disappeared. Once the body was found, it was also essential that the conclusion be reached that Edmund must have been murdered. Hence the brothers' interference with the coroner and the arguments about the opening of the body. A surgeon, Dr Skillarne, was brought in by Michael Godfrey to do the work and was used to sway a rather confused jury.

If this had been merely a family affair, then little would have come of it in the end. Many a time coroner's juries had brought in a verdict of misadventure to save the family and estate from shame.[69] But here there were political overtones, and Michael knew this. His connections with the City opposition and Shaftesbury would have swiftly informed him of the dangers and opportunities in his brother's death. He also knew of the problems facing such men in this crisis. His foolish brother Edmund was to be the sacrifice to a greater cause and to be honoured as a Whig martyr rather than a damned suicide. Edmund Godfrey could not just be allowed to have killed himself because those who had most to gain from his death wanted to have him as a martyr to their greater cause, whatever that was: Shaftesbury, and his client Oates, to keep up the plot; Bedloe to collect the reward; and Prance because he had no choice. The government had a murdered magistrate foisted upon it because it had no choice; the courts needed a murdered magistrate because three men had to die to solve the riddle of the Popish Plot. Thus a death in the family became a national crisis and proof of a plot; the real reason for the melancholic Godfrey's death became ignored.

This scenario of Godfrey's demise has the merit of at least being relatively simple. But is it plausible? The Godfrey brothers, serious businessmen who were prominent in London, would not wish to see the estate forfeited and the family disgraced because of their brother's suicide. Certainly Henry Moor could have been kept quiet. If we believe Mrs Gibbon, who claimed to know Godfrey better than most, she also was asked to keep quiet about Edmund's state of mind prior to his death by the Godfrey family. Moreover, the Godfrey brothers had the necessary connections and the apparent motives to perform the deed. We do know that Moor appears to have lied throughout this escapade, that he was searching near Primrose Hill on the Sunday or Monday, that Judith Pamphlin thought he knew something more than he told her. Nor was Moor called to the trial, although he was at the coroner's inquest to give the slightest possible evidence as to when his master left the house. Naturally he was at the hearing in the company of Michael and Benjamin Godfrey. That the coroner's inquest lasted far longer than it should have done given a supposedly obvious case of murder was also unusual. As we have seen, in reality it was a chaotic affair which began in a crowd and then adjourned to another venue where a group of rather bemused jurors had to be persuaded and even cajoled (if we are to believe some sources) to bringing a verdict of murder.

But to follow this line of argument we must really explain the Godfrey brothers' actions and motives. Would they have really undertaken such extreme measures to obscure the real cause of death just to save the estate and the family's reputation, and then knowingly send three innocent men to the gallows? Or did the events all too soon escape their control because they were at first unaware of the recent important political aspects of their brother's dealings? Certainly Michael Godfrey had the toughness and connections to carry out this cover-up. In the 1670s and 1680s he was very much the City politician. He had entered into opposition circles and continued to be active throughout the Exclusion Crisis. He was certainly more ambitious, more successful and better connected than his brother Edmund. Indeed, Michael had always shown the correct proportions of gravity, attention to detail and will that made the successful businessman. In 1643 as a young man he had openly stated his ambitions to his great friend Thomas Papillon. Michael promised that if he ever became Mayor of London his friend would be his swordbearer with £200 a year for his pains.[70] This was no mere musing for the ambitious young man; he had the Godfrey drive and ambition to achieve many things. Active in the mid-1670s against the government, this pattern to his career continued in the period after his brother's death. He was a hard-edged merchant politician benefiting from being the brother of the martyr. He was there at all of the major events in the City. He sat on the grand jury that brought in an ignoramus or not-proven verdict in 1681 when the government tried to find treason charges against Shaftesbury. Michael's movements and attitudes were thus suspicious. He was not called at the trial or inquest to give evidence about his brother, but he was always there in the background. He swiftly took control of his brother's papers; he was at the inquest, at Mrs Gibbon's home, at the funeral, at the Lords Committee, at the trials, always, or so it seems, pushing for the solution that the Roman Catholics had murdered his brother. Finally, what would be his motivation for such an action? Ambition and power perhaps, shame, as well as fearing the loss of his brother Edmund's property, much of which eventually passed to him. Did Moor and Edmund's brothers find him dead and use his death for their own cause? Was the mystery of Edmund Godfrey ultimately not really a mystery at all, but merely an unfortunate death in the family?

Epilogue: Memorials

On the wall of the east cloister of Westminster Abbey, ignored by the many tourists who daily pass through and who only occasionally glance at it, lies a memorial to Edmund Godfrey. In 1696 Edmund's brother Benjamin decided to make an addition to the family memorial already in place there. This addition is in Latin, which no doubt accounts for the general lack of interest shown by modern tourists. But since there is no known grave for the magistrate whose death sparked off such a crisis in London in the autumn of 1678, it makes interesting reading:

EDMUNDUS BERRY GODFREY, equestri dignitate ob merita sua in Regem et Patriam ornatus, Justitiarii munere singulari fide et diligentia functus, demum ab oculis suorum ereptus, iv, idus Octobris MDCLXXVIII. Post quintum diem repertus est morete affectus nefaria et atroci; caetera Historia loquetur. Hoc monumentum vetustate attritum reparavit, addito fratris Edmundi elogio, Benjaminus ex filiis Thomae Godfrey predicti natu mimimus et nunc solus superstes, iv Aprilis MDCXCVI.

[Edmund Berry Godfrey made knight on account of his loyal service to king and country. He discharged [the] office of magistrate with notable trustworthiness and diligence, was finally snatched from the eyes of his family, 4 days before [the] ides of October 1678. Five days later he was discovered murdered in a shocking and criminal manner and of the other details let History speak. This monument was repaired having been eroded by time, with an addition of a eulogy of his brother Edmund, by Benjamin, the youngest son of Thomas Godfrey and the rest of his line, 4 April 1696.]

Epilogue: Memorials

In the end only one man could really have explained the strange death of Edmund Godrey and that was Godfrey himself. By 3 o'clock on Saturday 12 October 1678, however, he had disappeared into oblivion. We can follow him that far but no further. For the rest we must observe the words written on his memorial: *caetera Historia loquetur*, 'let History speak'.

Notes

All volumes were published in London unless otherwise stated.

INTRODUCTION: A DEATH IN THE FAMILY

1. R. L'Estrange, *A Brief History of the Times* (1688), III, pp. 212–13. N. Thompson, *A true and perfect narrative of the late terrible and bloody Murther of Sir Edmund Berry Godfrey who was found murthered on Thursday the 17th of this instant October in a field near Primrose Hill with a full accompt of the manner in which he was found also the full proceedings of the Coroner who sat upon the inquest &c* (1678). *Sir Edmundbury Godfrey's ghost or an answer to Nathaniel Thompson's second letter from Cambridge to Mr Miles Prance in relation to the murder of Sir Edmundbury Godfrey* (second edn, 1682). T.B. Howell (ed.), *State Trials* (21 vols, 1816), VII, pp. 187–5. W. Thornbury and E. Walford, *Old and new London, a narrative of its history, its people and its places* (6 vols, 1873–8), V, pp. 287–90. G. Burnet, *A history of my own time* (2 vols, Oxford, 1897–1900), II, pp. 162–4. A.D. Webster, *The Regent's Park and Primrose Hill, history and antiquaries* (1911), pp. 56–87.

2. Previous work upon this subject includes L'Estrange, *Times*, III,

pp. 168–299. R. North, *Examen* (1740), pp. 203–5. J. Pollock, *The Popish Plot, a study in the history of the reign of Charles II* (Cambridge, 1903). A. Marks, *Who killed Sir Edmund Berry Godfrey?* (1905). J. Dickson Carr, *The Murder of Sir Edmund Berry Godfrey* (1936). S. Knight, *The Killing of Justice Godfrey* (1986). J.G. Muddiman, 'The mystery of Sir Edmund Bury Godfrey', *The National Review* (1924), 138–45. A. Marshall, 'The Westminster magistrate and the Irish stroker: Sir Edmund Godfrey and Valentine Greatrakes, some unpublished correspondence', *Historical Journal,* XL (1997), 499–505.

3. *The bloody murtherer, or, the unnatural son (Henry Jones) his just condemnation . . . for the murther of his mother Mrs Grace Jones &c* (1672), p. 2.

4. A. Conan Doyle, 'Silver Blaze', *The Memoirs of Sherlock Holmes* (Oxford, 1994), p. 4.

1 FAMILY AND EARLY LIFE

1. P. Laslett, ' The gentry of Kent in 1640', *Cambridge Historical Journal,* IX (1948), 148–64. P. Clarke,

English Provincial Society from the Reformation to the Revolution: Religion, Politics and Society in Kent, 1500–1640 (1977). S. Robertson, 'Churches in Romney Marsh: Lydd', *Archaeologia Cantiana*, XIII (1880), 440–1. E. Halstead, *History of Kent* (12 vols, 1897), VIII, p. 311. 'The family of Godfrey', *Gentleman's Magazine*, CXXIII (1848), 483–90. F. Heal and C. Holmes, *The Gentry in England and Wales, 1500–1700* (1994).

2. 'Family of Godfrey', pp. 483–90. 'The Visitation of the county of Kent', *Archaeologia Cantiana*, VI (1866), p. 260. J. Nichols, *Topographer and Genealogist* (3 vols, 1853), II, pp. 450–67.

3. See C.W. Chalkin, *Seventeenth-century Kent, a social and economic history* (1965), p. 3.

4. Ibid.

5. 'Visitation', p. 264.

6. Ibid., p. 265. British Library, Lansdowne MSS 235, 'The domestic chronicle of Thomas Godfrey'. 'Family of Godfrey', pp. 483–90. 'Visitation', p. 260. Nichols, *Topographer*, II, pp. 450–67. Robertson, 'Churches in Romney Marsh', pp. 440–1. Halstead, *History*, VIII, p. 311. R.H. D'Elboux, 'An armorial Lambeth Delf plate', *Archaeologia Cantiana*, LX (1947), 121–2.

7. BL, Lansdowne MSS 235, 'The domestic chronicle of Thomas Godfrey'. 'Family of Godfrey', pp. 483–90 Nichols, *Topographer*, II, pp. 450–67.

8. Ibid.

9. Ibid.

10. Ibid. L.L. Peck, *Northampton: Patronage and Policy at the Court of James I* (1982), pp. 8–9.

11. BL, Lansdowne MSS 235, 'The domestic chronicle of Thomas Godfrey'. 'Family of Godfrey', pp. 483–90. Nichols, *Topographer*, II, pp. 450–67. R.M. Warnicke, *William Lambarde, Elizabethan antiquary 1536–1661* (1973), p.138. Lambarde was also a historian of Kent.

12. Peck, *Northampton*, pp. 60–3, 172, 174. *Calendar of State Papers Domestic, (CPSD) 1619–1623*, p. 351.

13. D'Elboux, 'Armorial', pp. 121–2. BL, Lansdowne MSS 235, 'The domestic chronicle of Thomas Godfrey'. 'Family of Godfrey', pp. 483–90. Nichols, *Topographer*, II, pp. 450–67. A.N. Harrison, *The family of Godfrey of Woodford, Essex and East Bergholt, Suffolk* (Transactions of the Woodford and District Historical Society, pt. XII, 1966).

14. 'Family of Godfrey', pp. 487–8. *Godfrey of Woodford*, pp. 5–12. The Godfrey children from the marriage of Thomas and Margaret Godfrey were: Lambard, Thomas (i). The second marriage of Thomas Godfrey, to Sarah Isles, resulted in eighteen children, the most notable being: unnamed twins, Jane, Thomas (ii), Peter, Richard, John, Edmund Berry, Elizabeth, Michael, Thomas (iii), Edward, Catherine, Benjamin, Sarah.

15. BL, Lansdowne MSS 235, 'The domestic chronicle of Thomas Godfrey'. 'Family of Godfrey',

pp. 483–90.' Nichols, *Topographer*, II, pp. 450–67. Peck, *Northampton*, p. 61. *CSPD, 1619–1623*, pp. 104, 111, 115, 121, 124, 136, 155, 249, 351.

16. BL, Lansdowne MSS 235, 'The domestic chronicle of Thomas Godfrey'. Nichols, *Topographer*, II, pp. 450–67. Dom. A. Bellenger *English and Welsh Priests 1558–1800, a working list* (Downside Abbey, Bath, 1984), p. 38.

17. As we shall see below in chapter three. Also see J. Stoye, *English travellers abroad, 1604–1667* (revised edn, 1989), p. 183.

18. BL, Lansdowne MSS 235, 'The domestic chronicle of Thomas Godfrey'. 'Family of Godfrey', pp. 483–90. Nichols, *Topographer*, II, pp. 450–67. Clarke, *English Provincial Society*, p. 313. A. Everitt, *The Community of Kent and the Great Rebellion, 1640–1660* (Leicester, 1966), pp. 22, 74, 151, 152, 181. C.H. Firth, *The Last Years of the Protectorate* (2 vols, 1909), I, pp. 76.

19. L. Stone, *The Family, Sex and Marriage in England 1500–1800* (1979 edn). P. Earle, *A City Full of People, Men and Women of London, 1650–1750* (1994). K. Wrightson, *English Society, 1580–1680* (1986), pp. 60–120. Heal and Holmes, *Gentry*, pp. 48–96.

20. BL, Lansdowne MSS 235, 'The domestic chronicle of Thomas Godfrey'. 'Family of Godfrey', pp. 483–90. Nichols, *Topographer*, II, pp. 450–67.

21. Nichols, *Topographer*, II, pp. 450–67.

22. Ibid. Everitt, *Community of Kent*, pp. 7–9. S.R. Gardiner, *The History*

of England (10 vols, 1900), IX, pp. 84–118, 218,

23. BL, Lansdowne MSS 235, 'The domestic chronicle of Thomas Godfrey'. 'Family of Godfrey', pp. 483–90. Nichols, *Topographer*, II, pp. 450–67. W. Lloyd, *A sermon at the funeral of Sir Edmund Bury Godfrey* (1678), p. 24 claimed that Thomas was 'sometimes afflicted with Melancholy, almost to Distractions, but it was before he was fifty years old, [and] he soon recovered of it'.

24. BL, Lansdowne MSS 235, 'The domestic chronicle of Thomas Godfrey'. 'Family of Godfrey', pp. 483–90. Nichols, *Topographer*, II, pp. 450–67.

25. Nichols, *Topographer*, II, pp. 450–67. Also G.F. Russell Barker and A.H. Stenning, *The Records of Old Westminster* (2 vols, 1928), I, p. 378. R. Tuke, *Memoires of the life and death of Sir Edmund Berry Godfrey* (1682), pp. 5–6.

26. *Dictionary of National Biography* (*DNB*), Lambert Osbaldeston.

27. J.A. Winn, *John Dryden and his World* (Yale, 1987), p. 38. Gardiner, *History*, VIII, p. 390.

28. Winn, *Dryden*, p. 37.

29. Ibid., pp. 39–41.

30. Tuke, *Memoires*, p. 8–9.

31. BL, Royal MSS 12 A, XII, 'Viola Martia', f.16.

32. Ibid.

33. J. Aubrey, *Brief lives, chiefly of contemporaries, set down by John Aubrey, between the years 1669 and 1696*, ed. A. Clark (2 vols, Oxford, 1898), I, p. 269. *Alumni Oxonienses,*

the members of the university of
Oxford, 1500–1714 (8 vols, 1891),
II, p. 576.

34. Tuke, *Memoires*, pp. 2–3. Aubrey,
Brief Lives, I, p. 269. Lloyd, *Sermon*,
p. 13.

35. Tuke, *Memoires*, p. 8.

36. Ibid. Aubrey, *Brief Lives*, I, p. 269.
Marshall 'The Westminster
Magistrate', pp. 499–505.

37. Tuke, *Memoires*, p. 8. Lloyd,
Sermon, p. 14, calls it 'wanting
health'. W.R. Prest, *The Rise of the
Barristers, a Social History of the
English bar, 1590–1640* (Oxford,
1991).

38. North, *Examen*, p. 199. L'Estrange,
Times, III, pp. 174–5.

39. L'Estrange, *Times*, III, pp. 174–5,
182. Lloyd, *Sermon*, p. 17–21.

40. Stone, *Family, Sex and Marriage*,
p. 242.

41. For Godfrey's opinions on women
see National Library of Ireland,
MSS 4728, ff. 8–9, 13. See also for
more on gender relations in the
period T. Henderson, *Disorderly
Women in Eighteenth-century London
Prostitution and Control in the
Metropolis 1730–1830* (1999).
E.A Foyster, *Manhood in early
modern England honour, sex and
marriage* (1999).

42. Tuke, *Memoires*, p. 9, Howell (ed.)
State Trials, VII, p. 164. Thomas
Robinson, a former schoolfriend
of Godfrey's, noted his absence
from London during the civil war
years.

43. BL, Add. MSS 33578, f.33.

44. BL, Add. Charters, 19471, 'Will of
Michael Godfrey (1689)'.

J.R. Woodhead, *The Rulers of
London 1660–1689, a biographical
record of the aldermen and common
councilmen of the city of London*
(London and Middlesex
Archeological Society, 1965), p.
77. A.F.W. Papillon, *Memoirs of
Thomas Papillon of London, merchant
(1623–1702)* (Reading, 1887), pp.
13, 18. *CSPD, 1652–3*, p. 68. I.
Scouludi, 'Thomas Papillon,
merchant and Whig, 1623–1702',
*Proceedings of the Huguenot Society of
London*, XVIII (1947), 49–72.
Harrison, *Godfrey of Woodford*, p. 6.
For Benjamin Godfrey see
'Visitation', p. 267.

2 THE LONDON WOODMONGER

1. Tuke, *Memoires*, pp. 11, 23. Lloyd,
Sermon, p. 15.

2. Tuke, *Memoires*, p. 20.

3. See D. Piper, *Catalogue of
Seventeenth-century Portraits in the
National Portrait Gallery,
1625–1714* (Cambridge, 1963), p.
141.

4. See F. Sheppard, *London, a history*
(Oxford, 1998), chapter 10. L.
Beier and R. Findlay (eds),
*London, 1500–1700, the making of
the metropolis* (1986). N.G. Brett
James, *The Growth of Stuart London*
(1935). W.G. Bell, *The Great Fire of
London in 1666* (1920). S.
Rappaport, *Worlds within Worlds,
Structures of Life in Sixteenth-century
London* (Cambridge, 1989). M.D.
George, *London Life in the*

Eighteenth Century (1985 edn)
S. Porter, *The Great Fire of London*
(Stroud, 1996). R.M. Smuts, 'The
Court and its neighbourhood,
royal policy and urban growth in
the early Stuart West End', *Journal
of British Studies*, XXX (1991),
117–49. J. Stow, *The survey of
London* (1987 edn). J. Schlör,
*Nights in the Big City: Paris, Berlin,
London 1840–1930* (1998).
B. Weinreb and C. Hibbert, *The
London Encyclopedia* (1983).

5. Brett James, *Growth of Stuart
   London* pp. 67–125, 126–82.

6. See *Boswell's London Journal
   1762–1763* ed. F.A. Pottle (1950),
   pp. 68–9.

7. J. Evelyn, *Fumifugium: or the
   Inconvenience of the Aer and Smoak
   of London Dissipated* (1661)

8. H. Peacham, 'The art of living in
   London' (1642) in X. Baron
   (ed.), *London, 1066–1914, literary
   sources and documents* (3 vols,
   Moorfield, 1997), I, p. 438.

9. J. Gay, 'Trivia; or the art of
   walking the streets of London'
   (1716) in Baron, *London*, I,
   pp. 610–30. See also P. Hyland,
   Ned Ward, The London Spy
   (Lansing, Michigan, 1993).

10. Gay, 'Trivia', in Baron, *London*, I,
    p. 611, lines 21–4.

11. Ibid., I, pp. 616, 623, lines 227–30,
    523–38. R. Ashton, 'Samuel Pepys'
    London', *The London Journal*, XI
    (1985), 76.

12. Gay, 'Trivia', in Baron, *London*, I,
    p. 621, lines 428–32.

13. Gay, 'Trivia', in Baron, *London*, I,
    p. 617, lines 275–84.

14. Ibid., pp. 627–8, lines 111–30.

15. P. Earle, *City Full of People, Men and
    Women in London, 1650–1750*
    (1994), pp. 217–21, 240–6. L.O.
    Pike, *A history of crime in England* (2
    vols, 1876). J.A. Sharpe, *Crime in
    seventeenth-century England: a county
    study* (Cambridge, 1983). L.B.
    Faller, *Turned to Account, the Forms
    and Functions of Criminal Biography
    in Later Seventeenth and Early
    Eighteenth century England*
    (Cambridge 1987). R. Bryne,
    Prisons and Punishments of London
    (1992). C. Hibbert, *The Road to
    Tyburn, the Story of Jack Sheppard and
    the Eighteenth-century Underworld*
    (1957), pp. 19–20. K.M. Brown,
    'Gentlemen and thugs in
    seventeenth-century Britain',
    History Today, XL (1990), 27–32.

16. Westminster City Archives, F1096,
    Parish Archives of St Martin's-in-
    the-Fields, Poor Rate Ledger,
    High Street, 1661, f. 7. F4533,
    Parish Archives of St Martin's-in-
    the Fields, William Doddington,
    Constable's Account, *c.* 1664, f.39.
    G.H. Galer and E.P. Wheeler, *The
    survey of London, the Strand* (1937),
    XVIII, p. 24. G.H. Galer and E.P.
    Wheeler, *The Survey of London,
    Charing Cross, St Martin's-in-the-
    Fields* (1935) XVI, p. 261n. H.P.
    Wheatley and P. Lunnington,
    London Past and Present (3 vols,
    1891), II, p. 151. A. Cowper Coles,
    '"A place much clogged and
    pestered with carts", Hartshorne
    Lane and Angel Court, *c.* 1614–*c.*
    1720', *London Topographical Record*,
    XXVII (1995), 149–77.

17. A. Stapleton, *London Lanes* (1930), pp. 97–8. Galer and Wheeler, *The Strand*, p.24. R. Seymour, *A survey of the cities of London and Westminster, borough of Southwark and parts adjacent* (2 vols, 1735), II, p. 654. Cowper Coles, 'Hartshorne Lane and Angel Court', pp. 149–77.

18. Gay, 'Trivia', in Baron, *London*, I, p. 625, lines 25–8.

19. Cowper Coles, 'Hartshorne Lane and Angel Court', pp. 149–77. Seymour, *Survey of the cities*, II, p. 654. M.B. Honeybourne, 'Charing Cross Riverside', *London Topographical Record*, XXI (1958), 44–78. E. Beresford Chamberlain, *The Annals of the Strand, topographical and historical* (1912), pp. 87–8, 194, 248.

20. Westminster City Archives, F1100, Parish records of St Martin's-in-the-Fields, Poor rate ledger, 1662, ff.7–8. F1093, Poor rate ledger 1660, ff.9–10. Cowper Coles, 'Hartshorne Lane and Angel Court', pp. 152, 156.

21. Cowper Coles, 'Hartshorne Lane and Angel Court', p. 149.

22. Galer and Wheeler, *The Strand*, pp. 24, 43. Wheatley and Lunnington, *London Past and Present*, II, p.151. 'Family of Godfrey', p. 490.

23. *List of the merchants of London* (1677). Woodhead, *Rulers of London*, p. 77.

24. Cowper Coles, 'Hartshorne Lane and Angel Court', p. 159.

25. Ibid., pp. 160, 166, 167.

26. P. Earle, *The Making of the English Middle-class: Business, Society and Family Life in London, 1660–1730* (1989), pp. 212–18.

27. R.B. Westerfield, *Middlemen in English Business, particularly between 1660–1760* (Yale, 1915), pp. 218–413. R. Grassby, 'The personal wealth of the business community in seventeenth century England', *Economic History Review*, XXIII (1970), 220–34. J.U. Nef, *The Rise of the British Coal Industry* (2 vols, 1966 edn) I, pp. 394–400, 406–7, 408–10; II, pp. 84–9, 96–7, 100–1, 103, 105, 107, 300–15. J.U. Nef,'Dominance of trade in the English coal industry in the seventeenth century', *Journal of Economic and Business History*, I (1929), 423–33. H.G. Roseveare, 'The damned combination, the port of London and the wharfingers cartel of 1695', *The London Journal*, XXI (1996), 97–111.

28. *The grand concern of England explained* (1673), pp. 59–60.

29. H.B. Dale, *The Fellowship of the Woodmongers, Six Centuries of London Coal Trade* (1923), pp. 48–55. E. Bennett, *The Worshipful Company of Carmen of London* (1952), pp. 56–7. H.B. Dale, 'The worshipful company of Woodmongers and the coal trade in London', *Royal Society of Arts Journal* (1922), 817–19.

30. H.B. Dale, *The Fellowship of the Woodmongers, Six Centuries of the London Coal Trade* (1923), pp. 48–55. Bodleian Library, Rawlinson MSS D, 725 B are the

only remaining records of the
company dating from before the
Great Fire.

31. *House of Commons Journal*, VIII,
pp. 676, 18 January 1667. E.A.
McArthur, 'Sir Edmund Bury
Godfrey Woodmonger', *English
Historical Review*, XLIII (1928), 78.

32. 'The case of the woodmongers
within this City in relation to
Carrs' (1673) in Dale, *Fellowship of
the Woodmongers*, p. 62.

33. For this incident see *The Diary of
Samuel Pepys*, edited by R. Latham
and W. Matthews (11 vols,
1970–83), IX, p. 561. W.
Westergaard, *The First Triple
Alliance, the letters of Christopher
Lindenov, Danish envoy to London,
1668–1672* (New Haven, 1947),
pp. 121, 127. *The Bulstrode Papers,
1667–1675* (1897), pp. 101–3.

34. BL, Add. MSS 28053, f.24. *CSPD,
1667–68*, p. 426.

35. NLI, MSS 4728, ff. 7, 24–5.

36. Ibid., ff.7, 24–5. Beaven, *Aldermen
of the City of London*, pp. 52, 162.

37. NLI, MSS 4728, ff. 7, 24.

38. Ibid., ff. 2, 25–8, 28–9, 33.

39. Prerogative Court of Canterbury
Wills, PROB 11, 359, 46, ff. 357–9.
Greater London Record Office,
Accession 1376, nos. 205, 206, 207,
208, 210, 212. BL, Add. Charters,
19471, 'Will of Michael Godfrey,
1689'.D. Lysons, *Historical account
of those parishes in the counties of
Middlesex which are not described in
the environs of London* (1800),
pp. 249–67. J. Thorne, *Handbook of
the Environs of London* (2 vols,
1876), II, p. 568. C.J. Feret, *Fulham

Old and New* (3 vols, 1900), III,
pp. 214–5. L'Estrange, *Times*, III,
p.195. *The case of Thomas Critchely
esquire, Doctor William Denton,
Edward Diggs, William Hammond,
Robert Henley, Edmund Berry Godfrey
. . . &c* (1670). BL, Add. MSS,
33578, f.33.

40. L'Estrange, *Times*, III, p. 195.

41. NLI, MSS 4728, ff. 4–5, 8, 12, 21,
29–30, 31–3, B.D. Henning (ed.),
*The History of Parliament, the House
of Commons, 1660–1690* (3 vols,
1983), III, p. 445.

42. Smuts, 'Court and its
neighbourhood', pp. 117–49.

43. *The Diary of John Evelyn*, ed. E.S. de
Beer (7 vols, 1955), IV, p. 599.
T. Delaune, *Angliae Metropolis or the
Present state of London* (1690 edn),
p. 175. J. McMaster, *A short history
of the royal parish of St Martin's-in-
the-Fields* (1916). S. and B. Webb,
*English Local Government, the Parish
and the County* (1906), p. 11. M.J.
Power, 'The social topography of
Restoration London' in Beier and
Findlay (eds), *Making of the
Metropolis*, pp. 202, 206. V. Pearl,
'Change and stability in
seventeenth-century London', *The
London Journal*, V (1979), 3–34.
I. Archer, *The Pursuit of Stability:
Social Relations in Elizabethan
London* (Cambridge, 1991).

44. E.G. Rupp, *Religion in England,
1688–1791* (Oxford, 1986), pp. 40–2.

45. See N.G. Brett-Jones, *The Growth
of Stuart London* (1953),
pp. 127–86.

46. L. Picard, *Restoration London*
(1997), p. 6–7, 46–9.

47. P. Seaward, 'Gilbert Sheldon, the London vestries and the defence of the Church' in T. Harris, P. Seaward and M. Goldie (eds), *The Politics of Religion in Restoration England* (1990), p. 589. A. McCampbell, 'The London parish and the London precinct, 1640–1660', *Guildhall Studies in London History*, II (1976), 107–24. A. Whiteman, *The Compton census of 1676: a critical edition* (Oxford, 1986), p. 57. S. and B. Webb, *English Local Government, the Parish and the County*, pp. 173–236.

48. Seward, 'Gilbert Sheldon', p. 589.

49. George, *London Life*, p. 91.

50. Ibid., p. 92.

51. Greater London Record Office, Calendar of Session Books 302–361, May 1677–April 1679, September 1677, p. 154 (bk. no. 346).

52. Galer and Wheeler, *The Strand*, p. 113. *CSPD 1665–6*, p. 107.

53. E. Bohun, *The Justice of the Peace his calling, a moral essay* (1684), p. 14. M. Dalton, *The Country Justice* (1633), pp. 22–3. E. Wingate, *Justice revived being the whole office of a country Justice of the Peace* (1661 edn). W. Sheppard, *A sure guide for his majesty's Justices of Peace plainly showing their duty* (1669 edn), p. 5. S. and B. Webb, *English Local Government, the Parish and the County*, pp. 337–8. D. J. Johnson, *Southwark and the City* (Oxford, 1969), p. 221.

54. Bohun, *Justice*, p.1. S. and B. Webb, *English Local Government, the Parish and the County*, pp. 326–8.

55. Tuke, *Memoires*, pp. 4–5.

56. S. and B. Webb, *English Local Government, the Parish and the County*, pp. 337–8. Sir John Reresby also held this post in 1681, see ibid. p.338. Also R. Shoemaker, *Prosecution and Punishment: Petty Crime and the Law in London and rural Middlesex, c. 1660–1725* (Cambridge, 1991), p. 230.

57. Greater London Record Office, Calendar of Session Books 302–61, May 1677–April 1679, pp. 15, 73 (bks 305, 323).

58. For the plague see W.G, Bell, *The Great Plague in London in 1665* (1951 edn). Also Lloyd, *Sermon*, pp. 23–4.

59. Ibid., pp. 68, 41, 55, 214, 242.

60. *CSPD, 1665–6*, p. 107.

61. Tuke, *Memoires*, p. 49. Lloyd, *Sermon*, pp. 23–4. See also *Historical Manuscripts Commission Report (HMC)*, 7, p. 485. *London Gazette*, 18 September 1666. Bell, *Great Fire*, pp. 176, 353. Bell, *Great Plague*, pp. 70. Porter, *Great Fire of London*, p. 80.

62. Tuke, *Memoires*, pp. 27, 49. North, *Examen*, pp. 199–200. L'Estrange, *Times*, III, pp. 168–9.

63. Marshall, 'Westminster Magistrate', pp. 499–509.

64. For Greatrakes see *A brief account of Mr. Valentine Greatrak's & divers of the strange cures by him lately performed written by himself* (1666). E. Duffy, 'Valentine Greatrakes, the Irish stroker: miracles, science and orthodoxy in Restoration England' in K. Robbins (ed.), *Religion and*

Humanism, Studies in church history, XVII (1981) pp. 251–73. J. Buckley, 'Selections from a general account book of Valentine Greatrakes, A.D. 1663–1679', *Journal of the Waterford and South East of Ireland Archeological Society*, XI (1908), 211–24. P.C. Power, *History of Waterford, city and county* (Dublin, 1990), pp. 307–9. *Notes and Queries*, third series, 11 June 1864, 489. *Notes and Queries*, fifth series, 18 October 1879, 311–2. *Notes and Queries*, sixth series, 7 June 1884, 458. BL, Add. MSS, 25692.

65. *The Correspondence of Henry Oldenburg*, edited by A.R. Hall and M.B. Hall (13 vols, Madison Wisconsin/ London, 1965–86), II, p. 496. Also *CSP Ireland, 1663–5*, pp. 615–16. *The Conway letters, the correspondence of Anne, Viscountess Conway, Henry More and their friends, 1642–1684*, ed. M. Hope Nicolson (Oxford, 1992).

66. Greatrakes, *Brief account*, pp. 43–94. *Notes and Queries*, third series, 11 June 1864, 489; sixth series, 26 January 1884, 61–3; 7 June 1884, 458. *The Correspondence of Henry Oldenberg*, II, pp.496, 512–13, 556, 561; III, p. 59.

67. NLI, MSS 4728, f. 3

68. bid., ff. 4–5, 8. Henning (ed.), *History of Parliament*, III, pp. 445–6.

69. NLI, MSS 4728, f.13

70. Ibid., f.11.

71. Ibid., ff. 8–9, 13

72. See below chapter three and J.P. Kenyon, *The Popish Plot*,

(Harmondsworth, 1974), pp. 48–9.

73. NLI, MSS 4728, f.33.

74. Ibid., f. 22.

75. Ibid., f. 23.

76. 'A scheme of trade as it is at present carried on between England and France (1674)' in *The Somers Tracts*, ed. W. Scott (second edn 13 vols, 1809–15), VIII, pp. 30–1. For Michael Godfrey see BL, Add. Charters 19471, 'Will of Michael Godfrey' (1689). Papillon, *Memoirs of Thomas Papillon. List of merchants of London* (1677). N. Thompson, *True Domestick Intelligence*, no. 68 (24 February 1680), p. 179. Woodhead, *Rulers of London*, p. 77.

77. Thompson, *True Domestick Intelligence*, p. 179.

78. NLI, MSS 4728, f. 22.

79. *CSPD, 1676–7*, pp. 11–12. *CSPD, 1677–8*, pp. 388, 617–18. *CSPD Addenda, 1660–85*, p. 466. For a similar use of the word see BL, Add. MSS 34362, ff.4–15, 'The City Painter'.

80. *HMC*, Finch, II, pp. 44–46. J.R. Jones, 'The Green Ribbon Club', *Durham University Journal* NS, XVIII (1956–7), pp. 17–20. Magdalene College, Pepys Library, PL2875 'Journal of the Green Ribbon Club'. Umpherville was also a juror on the trial of Godfrey's supposed murderers. See *State Trials*, VII, pp. 159–250. PRO 31/3/ 141, Barillon to Louis XIV, 31 October 1678. J.S. Clarke, *The Life of James II* (2 vols, 1816), I, p. 526. Henning (ed.), *History of*

Parliament, II, pp. 232–4. *DNB
Missing Persons*: Robert Peyton. For
Mrs Cellier and her lot see p. 173.

81. *The poems and letters of Andrew
    Marvell*, ed. H.M. Margoliouth
    (third edn, 2 vols, Oxford, 1971),
    II, pp. 345–6. *Selections from the
    correspondence of Arthur Capel, Earl of
    Essex 1675–77*, ed. C.E. Pike
    (Camden Society, third series,
    XXIV, 1913), pp. 63–4.
    Correspondence of the family of Hatton,
    ed. E.M. Thompson (2 vols, 1878),
    I, pp. 132–3. *CSPD, 1676–7*, pp.
    193–5. *State Trials*, VI, pp. 1190–208.
    J.R. Jones, *Charles II, Royal politician*
    (1987), pp. 120–1. M. Knights,
    Politics and opinion in crisis 1678–81
    (Cambridge, 1994). G. De Krey, *A
    Fractured Society, the Politics of London
    in the first Age of Party, 1689–1715*
    (1985). Scouludi, 'Thomas
    Papillon', pp. 49–72. M. Priestley,
    'London merchants and opposition
    politics in Charles II's reign',
    *Bulletin of the Institute of Historical
    Research*, XXIX (1956), 205–19.
82. BL, Add. MSS 63 057B, 'Burnet's
    MS History', f. 41. Godfrey had
    attempted election to the
    common council for the City
    wards in 1664 for Farringdon
    Ward Without and later for Bread
    Street Ward. There is little doubt
    that given his association with the
    woodmongers he also kept up
    other City connections. See
    Beaven, *Aldermen of the City of
    London*, pp. 52, 162.
83. See below Chapter Four.
84. NLI, MSS 4728, f. 8.
85. S. and B. Webb, *English Local
    Government, Standing Authority for
    Special Purposes* (1921), p. 71. Of
    Edmund's later relationship with
    Greatrakes nothing is known for
    certain. Valentine's reaction to his
    friend's death is also unknown.
    Greatrakes spent the rest of his
    life in Ireland as a country
    gentleman, who only occaionally
    practised his cures. Ruth, his wife,
    about whom Godfrey had been so
    concerned, died in 1675.
    Greatrakes married again. He
    died in November 1683.

3.   TITUS OATES AND THE POPISH PLOT

1. C. Kirkby, *A Compleat true narrative
    of the manner of the discovery of the
    Popish Plot to his majesty by Mr.
    Christopher Kirkby with a full answer
    to a late pamphlet entitled reflections
    upon the Earl of Danby relating to the
    murther of Sir Edmundbury Godfrey
    in a letter to a friend* (1679). I.
    Tonge, 'Journal of the Plot, 1678'
    in D.G. Greene, *Diaries of the
    Popish plot* (Delmar, New York,
    1977), pp. 7–12.
2. For attitudes to Roman Catholics
    in England at this time the
    standard work is J. Miller, *Popery
    and Politics in England, 1660–1688*
    (Cambridge, 1973)
3. For Danby the standard biography
    remains A. Browning, *Thomas
    Osborne, Earl of Danby and Duke of
    Leeds, 1632–1712* (3 vols, Glasgow,
    1951). See also J. Le Neve, *Lives
    and Characters of the Most Illustrious*

persons British and Foreign who died in the year 1712 (1713), pp. 145–6. A. Marshall, *The Age of Faction: Court Politics, 1660–1702* (Manchester, 1999), pp. 106–20.

4. Browning, *Danby*, I, p. 236.
5. Burnet, *History*, II, p. 15. For Danby and bribes see M.K. Geiter and W.A. Speck (eds), *Memoirs of Sir John Reresby* (second edn, 1991), p. 172.
6. O. Airey (ed.), *Essex Papers, 1672–1679* (Camden Society, 1890), I, pp. 258–9.
7. Marshall, *Age of Faction*, pp. 106–20.
8. Browning, *Danby*, II, p. 70
9. Miller, *Popery and Politics*, pp. 67–90. Kenyon, *Popish Plot*, pp. 1–36. K.H.D. Haley, 'No Popery in the reign of Charles II' in J.S. Bromley and E.H. Kossmann (eds), *Britain and the Netherlands, V, Some Political Mythologies* (Hague, 1975), pp. 102–19. A. Dures, *English Catholicism, 1558–1642* (1983). W.C. Abbott, 'The origin of Titus Oates' story', *English Historical Review* XXV (1910), 126–8. E. Tonge, *An exact account of Romish doctrines in the case of conspiracy and rebellion by pregnant observations collected out of the express dogmatical principles of the papists, priests and Jesuits* (1679). M.D., *A seasonable advice to all true Protestants in England in this present posture of affairs, discovering the present designs of the papists with other remarkable things to the peace of the church and the security of the Protestant religion* (1679). J. Aveling, *The Handle and the Axe* (1976). B. Basset, *The English Jesuits* (1967). J. Bossy, *The English Catholic Community 1570–1850* (1975). M.V. Hay, *The Jesuits and the Popish Plot* (1934).
10. Miller, *Popery*, pp. 9–12.
11. Ibid., pp. 16–17.
12. For an introduction to the court see Marshall, *Age of Faction*. Also Miller, *Popery*, pp. 25–7
13. Miller, *Popery*, p. 24.
14. A. Marvell, *An account of the growth of popery and arbitrary government in England* (1678), p. 3. See also Kenyon, *Popish Plot*, p. 24
15. H. Care, *Weekly Paquet*, 19 November 1680.
16. D. Cressy 'The fifth of November remembered' in R. Porter (ed.), *Myths of the English* (1994), pp. 68–85. R. Hutton, *Stations of the Sun, a History of the Ritual Year in Britain* (Oxford, 1997), pp. 393–7. On attitudes to France as a threat see J. Scott, *Algernon Sidney and the Restoration Crisis, 1677–1683* (Cambridge, 1991), pp. 38–43. Also P. Sonnino, *Loius XIV and the Origins of the Dutch War* (Cambridge, 1988), J.B. Wolf, *Louis XIV* (New York, 1968). J.A. Lynn, *The Wars of Louis XIV 1667–1714* (1999).
17. Marshall, *Age of Faction*, pp. 133–7. The standard biography of James remains J. Miller, *James II, A Study in Kingship* (1989).
18. Ibid., also F.C. Turner, *James II* (1948) and Burnet, *History*, III, pp. 2–8.
19. Burnet, *History*, III, p. 13.
20. Marshall, *Age of Faction*, pp. 133–7.

21. *HMC*, Downshire MSS, I (1892), pp. 45–6.
22. M. Halie, *Queen Mary of Modena, her life and letters* (1905), p. 44. *HMC*, Dartmouth MSS, p. 31.
23. A. Barclay, 'The rise of Edward Colman', *Historical Journal*, XLII (1999), 109–32 is now the standard text for the life of Coleman. See also J. Miller, 'The correspondence of Edward Coleman, 1674–78', *Recusant History*, XIV (1977–8), 261–75. Kenyon, *Popish Plot*, pp. 37–51. *State Trials*, VII, pp. 1–78.
24. Coleman quoted in Miller, 'Correspondence of Edward Coleman', p. 267.
25. Barclay, 'Colman', p. 128.
26. Marshall, *Age of Faction*, pp. 167–9.
27. There is a rather dated biography of Oates in J. Lane (E. Dakers), *Titus Oates* (1971 edn). See also Kenyon, *Popish Plot*, pp. 52–87 and the illuminating article by P. Hammond, 'Titus Oates and sodomy' in J. Black (ed.), *Culture and Society in Britain, 1600–1800* (Manchester, 1997), pp. 85–101. See also I. McCormick (ed.), *Secret sexualities: a source book of seventeenth and eighteenth century writing* (1997), pp. 64–71, 121–5, 131–4, 147–50. For contemporary views of Oates, most of which are hostile, see *The life of Titus Oats from his cradle to his first pillorying for infamous perjury with a true account of his birth and parentage; impartially set forth for the satisfaction of all persons* (1685). *A hue and cry after Dr T.O.* (1681).

The memoiries of Titus Oates (1685). *Oates's Manifesto: or the complaint of Titus Oates against the doctor of Salamanca and the same doctor against Titus Oates comprized in a dialogue between the said parties on occasion of some inconsistent evidence given about the horrid and damnable Popish Plot* (1683). T. Brown, *The Salamanca wedding or a true account of a swearing doctor's marriage with a Muggletonian widow in Bread street* (1693). W. Smith, *Intrigues of the Popish Plot laid open with deputations sworn before the Secretary of State* (1685), p.25. *The Salamanca doctor's farewel* (1685).
28. Smith, *Intrigues*, p. 22. *Life of Titus Oats*, p. 1.
29. Smith, *Intrigues*, p. 22.
30. Ibid., p. 22.
31. Lane, *Titus Oates*, pp. 21, 141, 225.
32. Smith, *Intrigues*, p. 22.
33. *Life of Titus Oats*, pp. 1–2.
34. See W. Smith, *Contrivances of the fanatical conspirators in carrying on their treasons under the umbrage of the Popish Plot, laid open* (1685). C.J. Robinson, *A register of the scholars admitted to Merchant Taylor's School from 1562–1874* (2 vols, 1888), I, p. 272. *HMC*, Report 2, appendix, p. 117.
35. Robinson, *Register*, I, p. 272. *Life of Titus Oats*, p. 2. *HMC*, Report 2, appendix, p.117.
36. A. Bray, *Homosexuality in Renaissance England* (New York, 1995 edn) remains a standard work on this matter. However, much can be gained from the significant work of T. Hitchcock,

English Sexualities, 1700–1800 (1997). See also T. Hitchcock and M. Cohen (eds), *English Masculinities, 1660–1680* (1999). R. Trumbach, 'Sodomitical subcultures: sodomitical roles, and the gender revolution of the eighteenth century; the recent historiography' in R.P. Maccubbin (ed.), *'Tis Nature's Fault, Unauthorized Sexuality during the Enlightenment* (Cambridge , 1987 edn), pp. 109–21. R. Trumbach, 'London's sodomites: Homosexual behaviour and western culture in the eighteenth century', *Journal of Social History*, XI (1977), 1–33. R. Norton, *Mother Clap's Molly House: Gay Subculture in England 1700–1830* (1992). S.O. Murray 'Homosexual acts and selves in early modern Europe', *Journal of Homosexuality*, XVI (1989), 457–77. Hammond, 'Titus Oates and Sodomy', pp. 85–101.

37. Brown, *Salamanca wedding*, pp. 2–3. *Oates's Manifesto*, pp. 2, 5–6, 16.

38. See Bray, *Homosexuality*, chapter three. Hitchcock, *English Sexualities*, chapter five.

39. North, *Examen*, p. 224.

40. Smith, *Intrigues*, pp. 3–4.

41. *Life of Oats*, p. 2. Lane, *Titus Oates*, pp. 26–9.

42. Lane, *Titus Oates*, pp. 31–4

43. Smith, *Intrigues*, pp. 3–4.

44. Ibid., pp. 3–4. *State Trials*, X, pp. 1183–4. See also E. Everard, *The depositions of Mr. E. Everard concerning the horrid Popish Plot* (1679). *A true narrative and manifesto set forth by Sir Robert Walsh, knight* (1679). For Medburne see P.H. Highfill, K.A. Burnim, E.A. Langhans (ed.), *A Biographical Dictionary of Actors, Actresses, Musicians, Dancers, Managers and other Stage Personnel in London, 1660–1800* (15 vols, Edwardsville, 1984), IX, pp.164–5. L. Hotson, *The Commonwealth and Restoration Stage* (New York, 1962), pp. 212–14. M. Summers, *The Playhouse of Pepys* (New York, 1964 edn), p. 108.

45. Hammond, 'Titus Oates and Sodomy', p. 100.

46. Kenyon, *Popish Plot*, p.54. Lane, *Titus Oates*, pp. 48–9, 238–9. Burnet, *History*, II, p. 156.

47. Tonge, 'Journal', pp. 3, 44–5. For some examples of Tonge's later writings, the titles alone that give a flavour of his eccentricities and fads, see E. Tonge, *The northern star: the British monarchy: or, the northern, the fourth universal monarchy: Charles II and his successors the founders of the northern, last, fourth and most happy monarchy, being a collection of many choice ancient and modern prophecies* (1680). E. Tonge, *Jesuits assassins, or the popish plot further declared and demonstrated in their murderous practices and principles, the first part* (1680).

48. Tonge, 'Journal', p. 2.

49. Kenyon, *Popish Plot*, pp. 54–5.

50. *A vindication of the English Catholicks from the pretended conspiracy against the life and government of his scared majesty discovering the chief lies and*

contradictions contained in the narrative of Titus Oates (second edn,1681), p. 85. Smith, *Intrigues*, pp. 5–6.

51. M.E. Williams, *St Alban's College, Valladolid* (1986), pp. 48–51. *Records of the English province of the society of Jesus* (7 vols, 1877–83), VII (1882), pp. xxi–xxiii.

52. Quoted in Williams, *St Alban's College*, p. 49. *Vindication*, pp. 73, 75, 77, 85.

53. Williams, *St Alban's College*, pp. 49–50, 53–4.

54. *The life and death of Captain William Bedloe, one of the chief discoverers of the horrid Popish plot* (1681) gives one, very romanticised, version of Bedloe's life. See also *Vindication of the English Catholicks*, pp. 93–4. *Life of Titus Oats*, p. 2. E.C., *A full and final proof of the plot from the revelations whereby the testimony of Dr Titus Oates and Mr. William Bedloe is demonstrated by Jure Divino* (1680). *The examination of William Bedlow deceased, relating to the Popish Plot taken in his late sickness by Sir Francis North* (1680). M. Petherick, *Restoration Rogues* (1951), pp. 40–102. Burnet, *History*, II, p. 158.

55. Longleat MSS, Coventry papers (Microfilm), XI, ff. 272–272v.

56. Ibid. R. Head and F. Kirkman, *The English rogue described in the life of Meriton Latroon, a witty extravagant comprehending the most eminent cheats of both sexes* (1680). Compare with *Life and Death*, pp. 46–56

57. Petherick, *Restoration Rogues*, pp. 40–102.

58. Ibid. Lane, *Titus Oates*, pp. 58–60. Kenyon, *Popish Plot*, p. 57.

59. *Vindication of English Catholicks*, pp. 81, 90–1. *Records of the English Province of the Society of Jesus*, VII, pp. xxxvi–xl. Longleat MSS, Coventry papers (Microfilm), XI, ff. 205–6

60. *Vindication of English Catholicks*, p. 81.

61. *State Trials*, X, pp. 1200–3.

62. Ibid. *Vindication of English Catholicks*, p. 81.

63. Tonge, 'Journal', p.34. Tuke, *Memoires*, pp. 52–3. According to William Smith he 'sculckt about the Town in a secular habit' and renewed his intimacy with Medburne: Smith, *Intrigues*, p. 6.

64. Browning, *Danby*, I, p. 291.

65. Ibid., I, pp. 493–95 and see below chapter six.

66. Kenyon, *Popish Plot*, p. 72.

67. Tonge, 'Journal', p. 35. For Williamson's career see A. Marshall, 'Sir Joseph Williamson and the conduct of Administration in Restoration England', *Historical Research*, LXIX (1996), 18–41.

68. For the Hastings affair see p. 162. Tonge, 'Journal', p. 35. PRO, SP29/ 409, f. 58.

4. THE LAST DAYS OF EDMUND GODFREY

1. Tonge, 'Journal', p. 35. PRO, SP 29/409, f.58.

2. Tonge, 'Journal', pp. 36–7.

3. *HMC*, Kenyon MSS (1894), p. 106.

4. Smith, *Contrivances*, p. 8.
5. Tonge, 'Journal', p. 37.
6. *HMC*, Kenyon MSS, p. 106.
7. North, *Examen*, p. 174.
8. *HMC*, Kenyon MSS, p. 107.
9. Ibid., p. 106. North, *Examen*, pp. 174, 200–1. L. Echard, *History of England* (3 vols, 1718), III, p. 467. BL, Add. MSS 63097B, 'Burnet's MS History', f.41. North, *Examen*, pp. 200–1. *An answer to the earl of Danby's papers touching the murther of Sir Edmundbury Godfrey* (1679), p. 2.
10. North, *Examen*, pp. 200–1.
11. Misprision of treason was a serious crime in itself. In such cases it meant knowing that another person had committed treason, and not giving the information to the authorities within a reasonable amount of time. In common law it was punishable by imprisonment and forfeiture of property. But in the era of the Popish Plot such a revelation might well have led to Godfrey's death. For a definition of the crime see D.M. Walker, *The Oxford Companion to Law* (Oxford, 1980), p. 844.
12. Tonge, 'Journal', p. 39. For the Yorkshire plot of 1663 see A. Marshall, *Intelligence and espionage in the reign of Charles II, 1660–1685* (Cambridge, 1994), pp. 98–115. This was the only real attempt by a group of minor Cromwellians and Republicans to raise the northern counties against the regime of Charles II. It failed and many of those involved were imprisoned or executed as a result. Among them

13. Ibid., p.41. Burnet, *History*, II, p. 156.
14. Burnet, *History*, II, p. 156.
15. Ibid. 'Sir Robert Southwell's diary of what I did about the business in the council chamber October 1678', in Greene, *Diaries*, pp. 51–4.
16. Tonge,' Journal', p. 45. PRO, PC2/66, f.392.
17. *HMC*, Kenyon MSS, p.106. Tonge, 'Journal', pp. 46–7. PRO, SP/409, ff. 14–36. Kirkby, *Compleat true narrative*, pp. 2–3.
18. PRO, SP 409, ff. 14–36. T. Oates, *A true narrative of the horrid Plot and conspiracy of the Popish party against the life of his scared majesty, the government and the protestant religion* (1679). See also Lane, *Titus Oates*, pp. 91–102. Kenyon, *Popish Plot*, pp. 63–7.
19. See Marshall, *Intelligence*, pp. 142–68. Abbott, 'Origin of Titus Oates', pp. 26–9.
20. *State Trials*, X, pp. 1183–4. Lane, *Titus Oates*, pp. 91–102, Kenyon, *Popish Plot*, pp. 63–7.
21. *HMC*, MSS of the House of Lords (Lords Committee on the Plot) (1887), p. 3 and also *The compendium or a short view of the late tryals in relation to the present plot* (1679), p. 69.
22. This evidence is in PRO, PC 2/66, ff.392–397. *CSPD, 1678*, pp. 425–8, 431–3, 434, 451–3, 544–5, 550–1, 622–3. *HMC*, Ormonde MSS, NS, IV, pp. 455–8
23. PRO, PC 2/66, f.392.
24. PRO, PC2/66, ff.393–5. *CSPD,*

1678, pp. 425–6. Longleat MS Coventry papers (Microfilm), LXXXVII, ff.106, 227–227v. *HMC, Ormonde MSS*, NS, IV, pp. 454–5.

25. PRO, PC2/66, ff. 394–5. PRO 31/3/141, Barrillon to Louis XIV, 10 October 1678. *HMC, Ormonde MSS*, NS, IV, pp. 207, 455–6. Secretary of State Coventry noted of Oates that 'if he be a liar, he is the greatest and adritest I ever saw'.
26. PRO, PC2/66, ff.396–7.
27. Ibid., f. 396.
28. Ibid., f.396.
29. Ibid., ff.398 *et passim*. PRO, 31/3/141, Barrillon to Louis XIV, 13 October 1678. *HMC, Ormonde MSS*, NS, IV, pp. 457–60.
30. *HMC, Ormonde MSS*, NS, IV, p.458. Also North, *Examen*, p. 196.
31. What follows is based on the evidence from a number of core sources: *State Trials*, VII, pp. 159–230; L'Estrange, *Times*, III, 171–236; North, *Examen*, pp. 198–205; *HMC, Lords*, pp. 1–3, 46–52; Thompson, *A true and perfect narrative*.
32. Or so she claimed see PRO, SP 29/423, f.7.
33. PRO, SP 29/423, ff.7–10. SP29/366, f.305.
34. *HMC, Lords*, p. 9.
35. PRO, SP29/423, f.67. Echard, *History*, pp. 502–3. Also PRO, SP29/366, f.305.
36. PRO, SP29/366, f.305.
37. *State Trials*, VII, p. 168.
38. Ibid., p. 168.
39. L'Estrange, *Times*, III, p. 180.
40. Ibid., p. 181.
41. PRO, SP 29/423, f.10 also L'Estrange, *Times*, III, p.181. L'Estrange seemingly tidied up Mrs Gibbon's statements for publication, as can be seen by comparing the two statements given here. This is significant for the other evidence given by L'Estrange in his book. He seems to have clarified the sense but not necessarily to have altered all the meaning. A comparison of the manuscript deposition by Gibbon with L'Estrange's published version is pertinent at this point. Unfortunately the original depositions he used seem to have disappeared, possibly in the wake of the 1688 Revolution.
42. PRO, SP 29/423, f.10.
43. Westminster City Archives, F2004 Vestry Minutes, 11 October 1678, fo.236.
44. *HMC, Lords*, p. 48.
45. PRO, SP 29/423, f. 8. L'Estrange, *Times*, III, pp. 178–9. *State Trials*, VII, p. 187.
46. BL, Add. MSS, 38015, f.317.
47. BL, Add. MSS, 38015, f.317. Or was she? In fact the author of *An answer to the Earl of Danby's papers touching the murther of Sir Edmundbury Godfrey* (1679), p. 2 later claimed that Godfrey had complained to 'divers people how he was fallen into Danby's displeasure . . . [and this] has not only been declared to the Privy Council by the Lady Prat, but has been attested by the King himself in open discourses, acknowledg'd by a great courtier, Danby's own relations, and

confess'd by himself.' There is little further evidence of Lady Pratt's part in this affair.

48. *State Trials*, VII, p. 186. L'Estrange, *Times*, III, pp. 171, 188. *Several affidavits lately taken upon oath by divers of his majesties Justices of the peace which further confirm the testimony given concerning the murther of Sir Edmund Bury Godfrey* (1683), pp. 4–5.

49. L'Estrange, *Times*, III, p. 188 see also Mrs Gibbon's evidence PRO, SP 29/423, f. 7–9.

50. PRO, SP 29/423, f.9. L'Estrange, *Times*, III, p. 172.

51. L'Estrange, *Times*, III, p. 208.

52. PRO, SP 29/366, ff. 305–305v.

53. L'Estrange, *Times*, III, pp. 172–3.

54. Ibid., pp. 174, 188–9.

55. Ibid., p. 196.

56. PRO, SP 29/366, f 305–305v.

57. Ibid. *HMC*, Lords, p. 47

58. L'Estrange, *Times*, III, pp. 175, 196, 201. *HMC*, Lords, p. 47. PRO, SP29/366, f.305v. Lloyd, *Sermon*, p. 20.

59. PRO, SP.29/423, f.9. North, *Examen*, p. 201. L'Estrange, *Times*, III, p. 203.

60. PRO, SP.29/423, ff. 7–8.

61. BL, Add. MSS 38015, f.317.

62. North, *Examen*, p. 201.

63. L'Estrange, *Times*, III, pp. 198–9. Thompson, *True and perfect narrative*, p. 7. *State Trials*, VIII, p. 1396.

64. L'Estrange, *Times*, III, p. 203.

65. Ibid., p. 210.

66. North, *Examen*, p. 201. BL, Add. MSS, 38015, f.317. See also *HMC*, Report 6, p. 388. The latter gives important contemporary and independent evidence that Godfrey was thought to be 'melancholy and much discomposed a day or two before' he died.

67. PRO, SP29/423, f. 9.

68. Ibid. L'Estange, *Times*, III, pp. 190–2, 194.

69. PRO, SP29/366, f. 305. L'Estrange, *Times*, III, p. 209.

70. Ibid., *State Trials*, VIII, pp. 1394–5. *HMC*, Lords, p. 47.

71. BL, Add. MSS, 38015, f.317. *HMC*, Report 6, p. 388; Report 7, p. 494b. Lloyd, *Sermon*, p. 17. Lloyd claimed that the killers themselves spread such rumours.

72. L'Estrange, *Times*, III, p. 197. *State Trials*, VIII, p. 1392. See also below chapter five.

73. L'Estrange, *Times*, III, pp. 88–9. Burnet, *History*, p. 164.

74. *HMC*, Lords, p. 47. Thompson, *True and perfect narrative*, pp. 4–5. G. Manley, 'A preliminary note on early meteorological observation in the London region 1680–1717, with estimates of the monthly mean temperatures, 1680–1706', *Meteorological Magazine*, XC (1961), 303–10. G. Manley, 'Seventeenth-century London temperatures: some further experiments', *Weather*, XVIII (1963), 98–105. J. Playford, *Vade mecum or the necessary companion* (second edn, 1680), pp. 11, 15. Playford gave the time for sunrise on 12 October as 7.05 a.m. and claimed it set at 5 p.m. The sunrise for 17 October he has at

7.10 a.m., and it set at 4.50 p.m.
For the moon at this time see
S. Morland, *The description and use
of true arithmetick instruments &c*
(1673).

75. For this newsletter see 'Family of
Godfrey', pp. 489–90. Also *State
Trials*, VIII, p. 1396.

76. Muddiman in particular was to
use this tale. See below chapter
five.

77. *HMC*, Lords, pp. 46, 51. PRO,
30/24/43/63, ff. 438–438v.
J. Timbs, *Curiosities of London*
(1876), p. 692. J. Richardson,
Camden Town and Primrose Hill Past
(1991).

78. Thompson, *True and perfect
narrative*, p. 5. *Sir Edmundbury
Godfrey's Ghost*, p. 2. L'Estrange,
Times, III, p. 212.

79. L'Estrange, *Times*, III, p. 213.
Thompson, *True and perfect
narrative*, p. 5. Timbs, *Curiosities*,
p. 692.

80. PRO, SP29/423, f.9. 'Family of
Godfrey', pp. 489–90.

81. Thompson, *True and perfect
narrative*, p. 5. *Sir Edmundbury
Godfrey's Ghost*, p. 2. *HMC*,
Ormonde MSS NS, IV, p. 219.
L'Estrange, *Times*, III, pp. 212–13.
PRO, SP29/366, f.305.

82. Thompson, *True and perfect
narrative*, p. 2. *HMC*, Lords,
pp. 46, 51. PRO 30/24/43/63,
ff. 438–438v. Timbs, *Curiosities*,
p. 692. Richardson, *Camden Town
and Primrose Hill.*

83. Thompson, *True and perfect
narrative*, p. 5. PRO SP.29/423, f.9.
The band was a collar or ruff worn

about the neck; the cravat a neck
tie, a bow with long flowing ends.
The latter could have made a
useful ligature for strangulation.

84. Thompson, *True and perfect
narrative*, p. 8. *Sir Edmundbury
Godfrey's Ghost*, p. 5. PRO, SP
29/366, f.305.

85. L'Estrange, *Times*, III, pp. 213–22.
CSPD, 1678, p. 466.

86. Thompson, *True and perfect
narrative*, pp. 6–7. *HMC*, Report 3,
p. 306. R.F. Hunnisett, *The
Medieval Coroner* (Cambridge,
1961). T.R. Forbes, 'Inquests into
London and Middlesex homicides
1673–1782', *Yale Journal of Biology
and Medicine*, L (1977), 207–20.
M. MacDonald and T.R. Murphy,
*Sleepless Souls, Suicide in Early
Modern England* (Oxford, 1990),
pp. 57–8, 74, 80, 100, 110–12, 222.
D. Harley, 'The scope of legal
medicine in Lancashire and
Cheshire, 1660–1760' in M. Clark
and C. Crawford (ed.), *Legal
Medicine in History* (Cambridge,
1994), pp. 45–63.

87. *Sir Edmundbury Godfrey's Ghost*,
p. 3. L'Estrange, *Times*, III, p. 224.

88. Ibid.

89. L'Estrange, *Times*, III, pp. 230–1,
244–6.

90. *State Trials*, VII, p. 184.

91. *Sir Edmundbury Godfrey's Ghost*,
p. 4. Thompson, *True and perfect
narrative*, pp .6–7.

92. *State Trials*, VIII, pp. 1384–5,
L'Estrange, *Times*, III, pp. 230–1.

93. *State Trials*, VIII, pp. 1380. Also
Marks, *Who Killed Edmund Berry
Godfrey*, pp. 86–8.

94. L'Estrange, *Times*, III, pp. 230–1, 249. *State Trials*, VII, pp. 185–6. PRO, SP 29/366, f.305.
95. PRO, SP 29/366, f.305. L'Estrange, *Times*, III, pp. 230–5. *State Trials*, VII, p. 186; VIII, pp. 1361, 1369, 1381–5. Thompson, *True and perfect narrative*, pp. 6–7. *Sir Edmundbury Godfrey's Ghost*, p. 3. *HMC*, Lords, p. 46.
96. *Sir Edmundbury Godfrey's Ghost*, p. 4.
97. L'Estrange, *Times*, III, pp. 243–4, 246.
98. Ibid., pp. 246–7.
99. PRO, SP 29/423, f.9. PRO, 31/3/ 141, Barrillon to Louis XIV, 31 October 1678. *CSPD, 1678*, p. 478. PRO, SP 29/366, f.305.

5. REACTION

1. North, *Examen*, p. 202. *Reflections upon the murder of Sir Edmund Bury Godfrey* (1682), pp. 17–18.
2. Burnet, *History*, II, pp. 164–5.
3. A. Marshall, 'To Make a Martyr: The Popish Plot and Protestant Propaganda', *History Today*, XLVII (1997), 39–45. T. Dawks, *The murder of Sir Edmund Bury Godfrey* (1678). See also D. Kunzle, *The History of the Comic Strip, the early comic strip narrative strips and picture stories in the European broadsheet, c. 1450–1825* (Berkeley, 1973), p.130. *The dreadful apparition* (1680). Anon, 'On the murder of Sir Edmund Berry Godfrey' in F. Mengel, *Poems on affairs of state, Augustan satirical verse, 1660–1714* (7 vols, Yale, 1965), II, pp. 5–7. *The proclamation promoted or a hue and cry and inquisition after treason and blood upon the inhumane and Horrid murder of that late noble knight, impartial justice of the peace and zealous protestant sir Edmund Berry Godfrey of Westminster, a hasty poem* (1678). See also *To the right honourable the lord mayor at the anniversary entertainment in Guildhall* (1680). K. Thomas, *Religion and the Decline of Magic: studies in popular beliefs in sixteenth- and seventeenth-century England* (1980 edn), pp. 711–19. T. Harris, *London Crowds in the Reign of Charles II: Propaganda and Politics from the Restoration until the Exclusion Crisis* (Cambridge, 1987), p.145. *An elergie sacred to the memory of Sir Edmund Bury Godfrey, knight, 30 October 1678* (1678). E. Hawkins, *Medallic Illustrations of the History of Great Britain and Ireland to the death of George II* (2 vols, 1969 edn), I, pp. 576, 577, 579. J.R.S. Whiting, *A Handful of History* (Dursley, 1978), pp. 50–63. 'Sir Edmund Berry Godfrey', *Gentleman's Magazine*, CXXIV (1848), 365–9. *The solemn mock procession of the Pope, Cardinals, Jesuits & Fryers &s through the city of London November 17th 1679* (1679). *London's drollery* (1680). O.W. Furley, 'The pope burning procession of the late seventeenth century', *History*, XLIV (1959), 16–23. M.D. George, *English Political Caricatures to 1792, a Study of Opposition and Propaganda* (Oxford, 1959). S. Williams, 'The

Pope burning processions of 1679, 1680 and 1681', *Journal of the Warburg and Courtauld Institutes*, XXI (1958), 104–18. This was not merely a London phenomenon, see *The Pope's downfall at Abergavenny or a true and perfect relation of his being carried through the fair on a solemn procession with very great ceremony* (1679), p. 3. *London's defiance to Rome, a perfect narrative of the magnificent procession and solemn burning of the pope at Temple-Bar November 17th 1679* (1679), p. 2. J. Dryden, *Prologue to the Royal Brother, a play* (1682).

4. Prerogative Court of Canterbury Wills, PROB 11/359/46, f.357.

5. *HMC*, Lords, p. 3.

6. J. Dryden, 'Absalom and Achitophel' (1681), line 159. The standard work on Shaftesbury remains K.H.D. Haley, *The first Earl of Shaftesbury* (Oxford, 1968).

7. Haley, *Shaftesbury*, pp. 459–60.

8. Shaftesbury quoted in ibid., p. 462.

9. Ibid., pp. 458–9, 473–6.

10. Ibid., p. 469.

11. Ibid., pp. 473–6. *HMC*, Lords, (1887), pp. 1, 46. *Journal of the House of Lords*, 23 October 1678, pp. 298–9, 310, 346.

12. Ibid. Also E. Carpenter, *The Protestant Bishop, being the life of Henry Compton, 1632–1713, Bishop of London* (1956), p. 43.

13. Haley, *Shaftesbury*, pp. 474–75. BL, Add. MSS 32095, f.123. Longleat MSS, Coventry Papers, Microfilm, IX, f.237–8.

14. *HMC*, Lords, p. 49.

15. PRO, 31/3/ 141, Barrillon to Louis XIV, 31 October 1678. J.S. Clarke, *The Life of James II* (2 vols, 1816), I, p.526. *CSPD, 1678*, p. 466.

16. Marshall, *To Make a Martyr*, pp. 39–45. Tuke, *Memoires*, pp. 101–2. North, *Examen*, pp. 204–5.

17. Tuke, *Memoires*, pp. 101–2. North, *Examen*, pp. 204–5. Echard, *History*, III, p. 474. Burnet, *History*, I, p. 337. Evelyn, *Diary*, IV, p. 107.

18. The sermon's text was 2 Samuel 3: 33–4. Lloyd, *Sermon*, pp. 1, 2, 13. For more on Lloyd see Evelyn, *Diary*, IV, p107. Burnet, *History*, I, p. 337.

19. Lloyd, *Sermon*, p. 17.

20. Marshall, *To Make a Martyr*, pp. 39–45.

21. *CSPD, 1678*, pp. 472, 480.

22. Longleat MSS, Coventry papers, Microfilm, XI, ff.272–4. Burnet, *History*, II, pp.168–9. *HMC*, Lords, p. 99. Haley, *Shaftesbury*, pp. 477–8. *CSPD, 1678*, pp. 495, 503, 505–6. John Warner, *The history of the English persecution of Catholics and the Presbyterian plot*, ed. T.A. Birrell and J. Blish (Catholic Record Society, 1953) XLVII, pt. 1, XLVIII, pt. 2.

23. *CPSD, 1678*, pp. 495, 503, 505–6.

24. Ibid. Huntingdon Library, Hastings Collection of MSS, 59, 55 HA, 12 November 1678.

25. Haley, *Shaftesbury*, pp. 476–7. J.H. Wilson, *The Ordeal of Mr. Pepys's Clerk* (Ohio, 1972). *HMC*, Ormonde MSS NS, IV, pp. 284, 289.

26. M. Prance, *The additional narrative*

of Miles Prance of Covent Garden goldsmith (1679), p. 9.

27. Ibid., p. 12.
28. W. Boys, *The narrative of William Boys, citizen of London* (1680), p. 2. *CSPD, 1678*, pp. 425–8, 431–3, 434, 451–3, 544–5, 550–1, 622–3. There was some debate about the methods used to extract Prance's confession. The Roman Catholics claimed that he was tortured. See *A letter from St Omers in farther confirmation of the truth of the plot upon a consideration of divers circumstances of the trials* (1679), pp. 5–6.
29. Ibid., p. 5. M. Prance, *A true narrative and discovery of several remarkable passages relating to the horrid Popish Plot as they fell within the knowledge of Mr Miles Prance* (1679).
30. For what follows see Prance, *True and perfect narrative*, p. 8.
31. Ibid., p. 11.
32. Ibid., p. 12.
33. Ibid., p. 13.
34. Ibid., p. 14.
35. Ibid., p. 14.
36. *State Trials*, VII, p. 205.
37. For Scroggs see Kenyon, *Popish Plot*, pp. 133–4.
38. North, *Examen*, pp. 567–8.
39. For the nature of trials in the period see Sharpe, *Crime in seventeenth-century England*, p. 23. J.A. Sharpe, *Crime in early modern England, 1550–1750* (second edn, 1999), pp. 29–58. V.A.C. Gatrell, *The hanging tree, execution and the English people, 1770–1868* (Oxford, 1994).

40. *State Trials*, VII, pp. 159–60.
41. Ibid., pp. 161–7.
42. Ibid., pp. 167–9. *Compendium*, p. 15.
43. *State Trials*, p. 174.
44. Ibid., p. 210.
45. Ibid., pp. 183–4.
46. Ibid., pp. 184–95.
47. Ibid., p. 207.
48. Ibid., pp. 207–9.
49. Ibid., pp. 210–11.
50. Ibid., pp. 212–13.
51. Ibid., pp. 213–23, 230. Also S. Smith, *An account of the behaviour of the fourteen late popish malefactors while in Newgate and their discourses with the ordinary* (1679), pp. 9–17. *HMC*, Ormonde MS NS, IV, pp. 117, 325. Coleman was asked whether he knew anything of Godfrey's death and is alleged to have said 'on the word of a dying man that he knew nothing of it' in *Compendium*, p. 9.
52. *State Trials*, VIII, pp. 1359–98.
53. *DNB*: Sir Roger L'Estrange. G. Kitchen, *Sir Roger L'Estrange, a contribution to the history of the press in the seventeenth century* (1971 edn), pp. 347–9.
54. For Oates's later life see Lane, *Titus Oates*, pp. 278–364 also G. Campbell, *Imposter at the Bar, William Fuller, 1670–1733* (1961), pp. 80–1, 217, 231–2. William Bedloe, the third great informer, died, still dishonest and unrepentant, in Bristol in 1680. See *Life and death*, pp. 120–3. *The examination of William Bedlow*. Also *The anti-protestant or Miles against Prance being a solemn protestation of Miles Prance concerning the murder of*

Sir Edmund Bury Godfrey, in direct opposition to a late protestation made by him on the same subject (1685). L'Estrange, *Times*, III, 'To posterity' (unpaginated).

55. L'Estrange, *Times*, III, 'To posterity' (unpaginated). *HMC, Downshire*, I, pt I, pp. 138–9, 259. BL, Add. MSS 32095, f.123.

56. L'Estrange, *Times*, III, 'To posterity' (unpaginated). *Several affidavits lately taken upon oath by divers of his majesties justices of the peace* (1683), p. 43.

57. L'Estrange, *Times*, III, 'To posterity' (unpaginated).

58. A. Behn, *A poem to Sir Roger L'Estrange on his third part of the history of the times relating to the death of Sir Edmund Bury Godfrey* (1688). BL, Add. MSS, 38015, f. 316–317v. Harrison, *Godfrey of Woodford*, p. 9. 'Family of Godfrey', p. 488.

59. D. Hume, *The history of England from the invasion of Julius Caesar to the revolution in 1688* (6 vols, [1778] 1983 edn) VI, chapter LXVII.

60. *DNB*: Roger North

61. North, *Examen*, pp. 196– 205.

62. Hume, *History*, VI, pp. 343–4.

63. J. Pollock, *The Popish Plot, a study in the history of the reign of Charles II* (Cambridge, 1903). A. Lang, *The Valet's Tragedy and other Studies* (1903), pp. 55–103.

64. See Pollock, *Popish Plot*, pp. 146–8.

65. The literature, while not extensive in the 1900s, was occasionally very bitter and tinged with religious prejudice. See R. Lodge, 'Review', *English Historical Review*, IXX (1904), 788–92. J. Gerard, 'History ex-hypothesis and the Popish Plot', *The Month*, CII (1912), 2–22. A. Gwynn, 'Lord Acton and the Popish Plot', *Studies*, XXXIII (1944), 451–64. J. Pollock, 'The case of Sir Edmund Berry Godfrey', *The Law Quarterly Review*, XXII (1906), 431–50. A. Marks, 'The case of Sir Edmund Berry Godfrey', *The Month*, CIX (1906), 36–54. A. Lang, 'Who killed Sir Edmund Berry Godfrey?' *Cornhill Magazine*, XV (1903), 174–84. Hay, *The Jesuits and the Popish Plot*.

66. A. Marks, *Who killed Sir Edmund Berry Godfrey?* (1905).

67. Muddiman, 'Mystery of Sir Edmund Bury Godfrey', pp. 138–45. Adaptations of the Muddiman thesis can be found in N. Pain, 'Who killed Sir Edmund Berry Godfrey?', BBC Home Service broadcast, transcript 16/9/ 1952. H.R. Williamson, *Historical Enigmas* (1974), pp. 255–68 and in M. Macklem, 'Dashed and brew'd with lies: the Popish Plot and the country party', in H. K. Miller, E. Rothstein and G.S. Rousseau (eds), *The Augustan Milieu* (Oxford, 1970), pp. 32–58.

68. See below chapter six.

69. J. Dickson Carr, *The Murder of Sir Edmund Berry Godfrey* (1936). Also D.G. Greene, *John Dickson Carr: the man who explained miracles* (New York, 1995), pp. 190–6. Greene's 1989 edition of Carr, *The Murder of Sir Edmund Berry Godfrey* (New York, 1989) also contains an

important foreword and afterword that debates the case, the suspects and Carr's interpretation.

70. Kenyon, *Popish Plot.*
71. S. Knight, *The Killing of Justice Godfrey* (1986). See also J. Miller, 'Review', *Times Literary Supplement,* 18 January 1985, 57.
72. S. Knight, *Jack the Ripper: the final solution* (1976).
73. Knight's views were conclusively undermined in P. Sugden, *The Complete History of Jack the Ripper* (1995 edn), pp. 7–8.

6. THE CASE OF OCKHAM'S RAZOR

1. T. de Quincey, 'Murder as one of the fine arts', in T. de Quincey, *The English mail-coach and other essays* (1933 edn), p. 65.
2. See H.J. Cook, *Trials of an Ordinary Doctor, Joannes Groenvelt in seventeenth-century London* (Baltimore, 1994). P. Allen, 'Medical education in seventeenth-century England', *Journal of the History of Medicine,* I (1946), 115–43. A.W. Sloan, *English Medicine in the Seventeenth Century* (Bishop Auckland, 1996), p. 2. A.G. Debus (ed.), *Medicine in Seventeenth-century England, a symposium held at UCLA in honour of C.D. O'Malley* (Los Angeles, 1974). T.R. Forbes, *Surgeons at the Bailey: English forensic medicine to 1878* (New Haven, 1985), pp. 47, 75, 83. T. Palmer, *The admirable secrets of physick and chyurgery* (1696).

3. See also chapter four and *State Trials,* VIII, pp. 1381–6. L'Estrange, *Times,* III, pp. 224–57. R. Christison, 'Murder by suffocation', *Edinburgh Medical and Surgical Journal,* XXXI (1829), 236–50. 'Family of Godfrey', pp. 489–90.
4. Pain, 'Who killed Sir Edmund Berry Godfrey?', pp. 37–42.
5. B. Lane, *The Encyclopaedia of Forensic Science* (1992), pp. 380–1.
6. K. Simpson in Pain, 'Who killed Sir Edmund Berry Godfrey?', pp. 37–42.
7. Pollock, *Case of Sir Edmund Berry Godfrey,* pp. 431–50. Marks, *Case of Sir Edmund Berry Godfrey,* pp. 36–54. Lang, 'Who killed Sir Edmund Berry Godfrey?', pp. 174–84.
8. Pain, 'Who killed Sir Edmund Berry Godfrey?', pp. 34–7.
9. L. Wolpert, *Malignant Sadness, the Anatomy of Depression* (1999). M.A. Screech, *Montaigne and Melancholy: The Wisdom of the Essays* (Harmondsworth, 1991), pp. 22–36. A. Storr, *Churchill's Black Dog and Other Phenomena of the Mind* (1994), pp. 3–51.
10. Kraepelin quoted in Wolpert, *Malignant Sadness,* p. 2.
11. Ibid., pp. 3–4.
12. R. Burton, *The anatomy of Melancholy* (3 vols, [1621] 1923 edn).
13. Ibid., III, pp. 493–4. See also Screech, *Montaigne,* pp. 26–7.
14. BL, Add. MSS, 38015, f.317.
15. Burton, *Melancholy,* I, p. 121.
16. From Mrs Gibbon in PRO, SP29, 423, f.7, 10. How much of her evidence was local gossip and hearsay it is, of course, difficult to

say. Lloyd does appear to confirm some of the rumours (Lloyd, *Sermon*, p. 86) and Gibbon did claim knowledge of the family when in Kent, her native county, and that she had lived near the family's residence. Of course, Godfrey's own letters in the 1660s to Valentine Greatrakes illuminate part of this problem. See chapter two.

17. L'Estrange, *Times*, III, p. 183. Lloyd, *Sermon*, p. 17.
18. Pain, 'Who killed Sir Edmund Berry Godfrey?', p. 36.
19. For Oates as a suspect see North, *Examen*, pp. 196–206, 221–4. Dickson Carr, *Murder*, pp. 162–4, 321–2.
20. Smith, *Contrivances*, p. 25.
21. Smith, *Intrigues*, p. 8.
22. Kirkby, *Compleat and true narrative* (1679). Dickson Carr, *Murder*, pp. 167–9, 324–6.
23. Marshall, *Intelligence*, chapter eight.
24. For Christian see ibid., pp. 217–18, 221–2.
25. Ibid.
26. Browning, *Danby*, I, pp. 333–51.
27. Bray, *Homosexuality*, Hitchcock, *English sexualities*. R. Trumbach, 'Sodomitical subcultures' in Maccubbin, *'Tis Nature's fault unauthorized sexuality during the enlightenment*, pp. 109–21. Trumbach, 'London's sodomites'. Norton, *Mother clap's Molly house*. Murray 'Homosexual acts and selves', pp. 457–77. Hammond, 'Titus Oates and Sodomy' in Black, *Culture and Society in Britain*, pp. 85–101.

28. For the details of Thomas Blood's career see Marshall, *Intelligence*, pp. 186–223.
29. Ibid.
30. Ibid.
31. Ibid.
32. Ibid.
33. Haley, *Shaftesbury*, pp. 458–60. Lloyd, *Sermon*, p. 21. See also W. D. Christie, *A life of Antony Ashley Cooper, First Earl of Shaftesbury, 1667–1683* (2 vols., 1871), II, pp. 286–93.
34. Knight, *Killing*, pp. 245–59.
35. Ibid., pp. 259–82. Waller, a justice of the peace and son of the parliamentary general of the Civil War came to prominence during the course of the crisis and was noted for his hostility to all things Catholic. See Kenyon, *Popish Plot*, pp. 217–18 and W. Waller, *The tragical history of Jetzer* (1679). *Sir William Waller's kindness to the cities of London and Westminster particularly exprest* (1679). *A tale of tubbs or Rome's masterpiece defeated* (1679). *An elegy on the much lamented Sir William Waller who valiantly hang'd himself at Rotterdam 21 August 1683* (1683). The latter piece, a satire for Waller did not hang himself, links both Waller and Godfrey: 'Thou who at Fox hall dids't inspire those sots,/ Tongue, Oats and Kirkby to continue their plots; Who dis't through wonderous Labarinths of Ill,/ Conduct sir Godfrey safe to Primrose Hill;/ And by Mysterious ways, and oaths most quaint,/ Of an old Faggot made us a young saint. . .'

36. For Scott's career see Marshall, *Intelligence*, pp. 223–43. See also J. Joyne, 'A Journal, 1679', in Greene, *Diaries*, pp. 55–84.

37. Marshall, *Intelligence*, p. 224.

38. Ibid., pp. 224–41.

39. Knight, *Killing*, pp. 259–70. *CSPD, 1667–8*, p. 361.

40. Marshall, *Intelligence*, p. 241. *HMC*, Ormonde MSS NS, IV, p. 515. Scott accused Pepys of treason and was subsequently investigated in detail by Pepys and his servants. If any evidence of Scott's part in the killing of Godfrey had existed in fact, there seems little doubt that Pepys would have found it.

41. For Pembroke see *DNB*: Philip Herbert, 7th Earl of Pembroke. G.E. Cockayne, *The Complete Peerage* (13 vols, second edn 1910–46), X, eds H.A. Doubleday, G.H. White and Lord Howard de Walden (1945), p. 422. *An impartial account of the misfortune that lately happened to the right honourable Philip Earl of Pembroke and Montgomery* (1680). *Great and bloody news from Turham Green or a relation of a sharp encounter between the Earl of Pembroke and his company and the constable and watch belonging to the parish of Chiswick on the 18th instant* (1680). B.R., *Great newes from Saxony, or a new and strange relation of the mighty giant, Koorbmep* (1680). Aubrey, *Brief Lives*, I, p. 317. *HMC*, Report 6, pp.384a, 493. *HMC*, Report 7, pp. 461–2, 466, 467, 491, 493. *HMC*, Report 9, p. 100. *HMC*, Finch II, p. 37. *HMC*, Hastings, II, p.170. *HMC*, Ormonde NS IV, pp.128, 361. *HMC*, Rutland, II, p. 28. Airey, *Essex Papers*, I, p. 282. Brown 'Gentlemen and thugs', p. 30. D.T. Archer, 'The code of Honour and its critics: the opposition to duelling in England 1700–1850' *Social History*, V (1980), 409–34. R. Shoemaker, 'Reforming Male manners: public insult and the decline of violence in London, 1660–1740' in Hitchcock and Cohen, *English Masculinities*, pp. 133–50. F. Dabhoiwala, 'The constraints of honour, reputation and status in late seventeenth and early eighteenth century England', *Transactions of the Royal Historical Society*, sixth series, VI (1996), 201–14.

42. Muddiman, 'Mystery', pp. 138–45.

43. Aubrey, *Brief Lives*, I, p. 317.

44. The poem was alleged to be by Rochester and can be found as, 'An imitation of the first satyr of Juvenal' in J. Hayward (ed.), *Collected works of John Wilmot, Earl of Rochester* (1926), p. 86.

45. *HMC*, Report 7, p. 466.

46. *Impartial account*, p. 1.

47. *HMC*, Report 7, p. 493.

48. *The tryal of Philip Herbert, Earl of Pembroke for the murder of Nathaniel Cony before his peers in Westminster Hall on Thursday 4th of April 1678* (1679).

49. Ibid., and *State Trials*, VI, pp. 1310–50.

50. *Tryal*, p. 9.

51. Ibid., p. 10.

52. Ibid., p.12.

53. *State Trials*, VI, pp. 1310–50.

54. Haley, *Shaftesbury*, p. 458.

55. *DNB*: Philip Herbert, 7th Earl of Pembroke.

56. Pollock, *Popish Plot*, is the clearest modern statement against the Catholics. See also Lloyd, *Sermon*, pp. 20–1.

57. Pepys, *Diary*, Companion volume, X, pp. 380–81. A. Audrey Locke, *The Seymour family: history and romance* (1911), pp. 359–363. W.H. Hinds, 'The Strand in the seventeenth century its river front', *London and Middlesex Archaeological Society Transactions*, IV (1918–22), 211–27.

58. Marshall, *Intelligence*, p. 288.

59. See above for Prance's tale, chapter five. For another important assassination of the era see E. Godley, *The Trial of Count Königsmarck* (1929).

60. Longleat MSS, Coventry papers, Microfilm, XI, f.272. PRO, 31/3/41, Barrillon to Louis XIV, 24 November 1678, 8 December 1678.

61. *HMC*, Ormonde, NS, IV, p. 268.

62. Nathaniel Thompson had published the details in October 1678, or Prance could have heard the gossip at the White House or elsewhere. We should also recall that he was a regular at the White House and could well have been among the crowd at the first day of the inquest. *A succinct narrative of the bloody murder of sir Edmund Bury Godfrey Octob: 12 1678* (1683).

63. It was, as we have seen, near the White House.

64. Pollock, *Popish Plot*, pp. 120–6, 127–31, 132–48.

65. For the Meal Tub plot see R. Mansell, *An exact and true narrative of the late popish intrigue to form a plot and then to cast the guilt and odium thereof upon the Protestants* (1680). *A just narrative of the hellish new counter plots of the papists to cast the odium of their horrid treasons upon the Presbyterians* (1679). Marshall, *Intelligence*, pp. 210–11, 212–14. *HMC* Ormonde MSS, NS, IV, pp. 553–57. *Several affidavits lately taken upon oath by divers of his Majesties justices of the peace which farther confirm the testimony given concerning the murther of sir Edmund Bury Godfrey* (1683), pp. 3–4.

66. *The Oxford Dictionary of Quotations* (1979 edn), p. 364.

67. A.S. Taylor, 'Remarks on death from strangulation', *The Edinburgh Medical and Surgical Journal*, LXXVII (1852), 94. Also A. Keiller, 'Medico-legal observations on manual strangulation and death by external violence with experiments and illustrative cases', *Edinburgh Medical Journal*, I, (1855–6), 527–34, 824–30.

68. Lane, *Encyclopedia of Forensic Science*, pp. 592–3.

69. See Macdonald and Murphy, *Sleepless Souls*, pp. 58–9, 112, 227–38, 244–7, 259–300. See also as an example of contemporary reportage of suicide *A sad and dreadful account of the self-murder of Robert Long, alias Baker* (1685).

70. Papillon, *Memoirs of Thomas Papillon*, pp. 13, 18. BL, Add. Charters 19471, 'Will of Michael Godfrey 1689'.

Select Bibliography

Manuscript Sources

Bodleian Library, Oxford

Carte MSS 31–9, 46, 69, 81
Rawlinson A 173–5, 183, 185, 188
Rawlinson D 725 B

British Library, London

Additional MSS	4291	
Additional MSS	5750	
Additional MSS	25692	
Additional MSS	28047	
Additional MSS	28053	
Additional MSS	28054	Danby correspondence
Additional MSS	28945	Miscellaneous correspondence
Additional MSS	32095	
Additional MSS	33578	
Additional MSS	34176	
Additional MSS	34362	
Additional MSS	38015	
Additional MSS	63097B	'Burnet's Ms History'
Additional Charters	19471	'Will of Michael Godfrey (1689)'
Egerton MSS		
Lansdowne MSS	235	'The domestic chronicle of Thomas Godfrey'
Royal MSS	12A, XII	'Viola Martia'

Greater London Record Office

Accession	1376	
Calendar of Session Books	302–361	

Bibliography

Huntingdon Library

Hastings Collection of MSS 59, 55 HA, 12

Longleat House MSS

Coventry Papers (Microfilm)LXXXVII

Magdalene College, Cambridge, Pepys Library

PL2875   'Journal of the Green Ribbon Club'

National Library of Ireland

MSS 4728	Letterbook
MSS 13014	Flowers papers

Public Record Office, London

PC 2/66	Privy Council registers
PRO 30/24/43/63	Shaftesbury papers
PRO 31/3	Transcripts of French Diplomatic Correspondence
PROB 11	Prerogative Court of Canterbury wills, 359, 46
SP 29	State Papers Charles II
SP 44	Entry Books

Westminster City Archive

Acc 72/68	Hartshorne Lane lease of 1764
F1093	Parish archives of St Martin's-in-the-Fields, Poor Rate ledger, 1660
F1096	Parish Archives of St Martin's-in-the-Fields, Poor rate ledger, High Street
F1100	Parish archives of St Martin's-in-the-Fields, Poor Rate ledger, 1662
F2003	Parish archives of St Martin's-in-the-Fields, Vestry minutes, 1660–7
F2004	Parish archives of St Martin's-in-the-Fields, Vestry minutes, 1667–83
F4518	Parish archives of St Martin's-in-the-Fields, miscellaneous
F4523	Parish archives of St Martin's-in-the-Fields, William Doddington, Constable's Record, *c.* 1664
F4533	Parish archives of St Martin's-in-the-Fields, Poll tax book

PRINTED PRIMARY SOURCES AND CONTEMPORARY PAMPHLET
LITERATURE

A collection of state tracts published during the reign of King William III (3 vols, 1706)

A faithful account of the sickness, death and burial of Captain William Bedlow who dyed August the 20th and was buried August the 22nd 1680 (1680)

A hue and cry after Dr T.O. (1681)

A just narrative of the hellish new counter plots of the papists to cast the odium of their horrid treasons upon the Presbyterians (1679)

A letter from St Omers in farther confirmation of the truth of the plot upon a consideration of divers circumstances of the trials (1679)

A new apparition of Sir Edmundbury Godfrey's ghost to the E of D— in the Tower (1681)

A present from an unknown friend to sir Edmund-bury Godfrey's brothers (1682)

A sad and dreadful account of the self-murder of Robert Long, alias Baker (1685)

A succinct narrative of the bloody murder of Sir Edmund Bury Godfrey Octob: 12 1678 (1683)

A tale of Tubbs or Rome's masterpiece defeated (1679)

A true narrative and manifesto set forth by Sir Robert Walsh, knight (1679)

A true relation of the late barbarous assault committed upon Robert Pye esq., one of his majesties Justices of the Peace for the county of Hereford who died thereof 30 Jan. 1680 by John Bodnan esq. a notorious papist (1681)

A vindication of the English Catholicks from the pretended conspiracy against the life and government of his sacred majesty discovering the chief lies and contradictions contained in the narrative of Titus Oates (1681, second edn)

An account at large of the right honourable the Earl of Danby's arguments at the court of the King's Bench at Westminster upon his lordship's motion for bail the 27th day of May, Term Pasch. 1682 (1682)

An account of the life and memorable actions of Father Petre the Jesuit (1689)

An answer to the Earl of Danby's papers touching the murther of Sir Edmundbury Godfrey (1679)

An elergie on the right honourable, Sir Edmund Bury Godfrey, knight (1678)

An elergie sacred to the memory of Sir Edmund Bury Godfrey, knight, 30 October 1678 (1678)

An elegy on the much lamented Sir William Waller who valiantly hang'd himself at Rotterdam 21 August 1683 (1683)

An impartial account of the misfortune that lately happened to the right honourable Philip Earl of Pembroke and Montgomery (1680)

An impartial state of the case of the Earl of Danby (1679)

Character of a town-gallant exposing the extravagant fopperies of some vain self-conceited pretenders to gentility and good breeding (1675)

Character of William the Third (1688)

Great and bloody news from Turham Green or a relation of a sharp encounter between the Earl of Pembroke and the constable and watch belonging to the parish of Chiswick on the 18th instant (1680)

Great newes from Saxony, or a new and strange relation of the mighty giant Koorbmep (1680)

Oates's manifesto: or the complaint of Titus Oates against the doctor of Salamanca and the same doctor against Titus Oates comprised in a dialogue between the said parties on occasion of some inconsistent evidence given about the horrid and damnable popish plot (1683)

Reflections upon a paper intitled, some reflections upon the Earl of Danby in relation to the murder of Sir Edmund bury Godfrey in a letter to Edward Christian (1679)

Reflections upon the murder of Sir Edmund Bury Godfrey (1682)

Several affidavits lately taken upon oath by divers of his majesties Justices of the Peace which further confirm the testimony given concerning the murther of sir Edmund Bury Godfrey (1683)

Sir Edmundbury Godfrey's ghost or an answer to Nathaniel Thompson's second letter from Cambridge to Mr. Miles Prance in relation to the murder of sir Edmundbury Godfrey (second edn, 1682)

Sir William Waller's kindness to the cities of London and Westminster particularly exprest (1679)

The anti-Protestant or Miles against Prance being a solemn protestation of Miles Prance concerning the murder of Sir Edmund Bury Godfrey, in direct opposition to a late protestation made by him on the same subject (1685)

The bloody murtherer, or, the unnatural son (Henry Jones) his just condemnation . . . for the murther of his mother, Mrs Grace Jones &c (1672)

The case of Thomas Critchely esquire, Doctor William Denton, Edward Diggs, William Hammond, Robert Henley, Edmund Berry Godfrey . . . &c (1670)

The character of a sham-plotter or man catcher (1681)

The compendium, or a short view of the late tryals in relation to the present plot (1679)

The court in mourning, being the life and worthy actions of Ralph, first Duke of Montague (1709)

The courtier's calling shewing the ways of making a fortune and the art of living at court according to the maxims of policy and morality (1675)

The dreadful apparition (1680)

The examination of William Bedlow, deceased relating to the Popish Plot taken in his late sickness by Sir Francis North (1680)

The grand concern of England explained (1673)

The information of Stephen Dugdale gent. delivered at the bar of the House of Commons (1680)

The intriguing coxcomb or the secret history of Sir Edmund Godfrey (2 vols, 1759)

The Irish evidence convicted by their own oaths, or their swearing and counter-swearing plainly demonstrated in several of their own affidavits (1682)

The life and death of Captain William Bedloe, one of the chief discoverers of the horrid Popish plot (1681)

The life of Titus Oats from his cradle to his first pillorying for infamous perjury with a true account of his birth and parentage; impartially set for the for the satisfaction of all persons (1685)

Bibliography

The memoires of Titus Oates (1685)

The Pope's downfall at Abergavenny or a true and perfect relation of his being carried through the fair on a solemn procession with very great ceremony (1679)

The proclamation promoted or a hue and cry and inquisition after treason and blood upon the inhumane and Horrid murder of that late noble knight, impartial justice of the peace and zealous Protestant Sir Edmund Berry Godfrey of Westminster, a hasty poem (1678)

The Salamanca doctor's farewel (1685)

The sentiments, a poem to the Earl of Danby in the Tower by a person of quality (1679)

The solemn mock procession of the Pope, Cardinals, Jesuits & Fryers through the city of London November 17th 1679 (1679)

The tryal of Philip Herbert, Earl of Pembroke for the murder of Nathaniel Cony before his peers in Westminster Hall on Thursday 4th of April 1678 (1679)

To the right honourable the lord mayor at the anniversary entertainment in Guildhall (1680)

Vox populi: or the people's claim to their parliaments sitting (1681)

Aubrey, J., *Brief Lives chiefly of contemporaries, set down by John Aubrey between the years 1669 and 1696*, ed. A. Clark (2 vols, Oxford, 1898)

Aulney, C. d', *Memoirs of the court of England in 1675* (1913)

Baron, X. (ed.), *London, 1066–1914, literary sources and documents* (3 vols, Moorfield, 1997)

Behn, A., *A poem to sir Roger L'Estrange on the third part of the history of the times relating to the death of Sir Edmund Bury Godfrey* (1688)

Bohun, E., *The Justice of the Peace, his calling, a moral essay* (1684)

Bold, S., *A sermon against persecution preached on March 26 1682* (1682)

Boswell's London Journal, 1762–1763, ed. F.A. Pottle (1950)

Boyer, A., *The history of King William the third* (3 vols, 1702)

Boys, W., *The narrative of William Boys, citizen of London* (1680)

Brown, T., *The Salamanca wedding, or a true account of a swearing doctor's marriage with a Muggletonian widow in Bread street* (1693)

Bruce, T, Earl of Ailesbury, *The memoirs of Thomas Bruce, Earl of Ailesbury* (2 vols, Roxburghe Club, Westminster, 1890)

The Bulstrode Papers, 1667–1675 (1897)

Burnet, G., *A history of my own Time* (6 vols, [1723–4] second edn, Oxford, 1833)

——, *A history of my own time, part I: the reign of Charles II* (2 vols, Oxford, 1897–1900)

Calendar of State Papers Domestic series of the reign of Charles II (1860–1938)

Calendar of State Papers Ireland (1907)

Care, H., *Weekly Paquet* (1680)

Cavelli, E. Marquise Campana de (ed.), *Les derniers Stuarts à Saint-Germain-en-laye: documents inédits et authentiques* (2 vols, Paris, 1871)

Christian, E., *Reflections upon a paper intituled some reflections upon the Earl of Danby in relation to the murder of Sir Edmund Bury Godfrey* (1679)

Christie, W.D. (ed.), *Letters addressed from London to Sir Joseph Williamson while plenipotentiary at the congress of Cologne in the years 1673 and 1674* (2 vols, Camden Society, 1874)

Clarke, J.S. (ed.), *The Life of James II, collected out of memoirs writ of his own hand* (2 vols, 1816)

The Conway letters, the correspondence of Anne, Viscountess Conway, Henry More and their friends, 1642–1684, ed. M. Hope Nicholson (Oxford, 1992)

Dalton, M., *The Country Justice* (1633)

Dangerfield, T., *More shams still or a further discovery of the designs of the Papists to impose upon the nation the belief of their feigned Protestant or Presbyterian plot* (1681)

Dawks, T., *The murder of Sir Edmund Bury Godfrey* (1678)

Delaune, T., *Angliae Metropolis, or the Present state of London* (1690 edn)

Dryden, J., *Prologue to the Royal Brother, a play* (1682)

John Dryden, the Oxford Authors, ed. K. Walker (Oxford, 1987)

E.C., *A full and final proof of the plot from the revelations whereby the testimony of Dr Titus Oates and Mr. William Bedloe is demonstrated by Jure Divino* (1680)

Ellis, G.A.E. (ed.), *The Ellis Correspondence* (2 vols., 1829)

Essex Papers, 1672–1679, ed. O. Airey (Camden Society, 1890)

Selections from the correspondence of Arthur Capel, Earl of Essex 1675–77, ed.C.E. Pike (Camden Society, third series, XXIV, 1913)

The Diary of John Evelyn, ed. E.S. de Beer (6 vols, Oxford, 1955)

——, *Fumifugium: or the inconvenience of the aer and smoak of London dissipated* (1661)

Everard, E., *The depositions of Mr. E. Everard concerning the horrid Popish Plot* (1679)

Florus Anglo-Bavaricus (Liège, 1685)

Foxcroft, H.C., *Supplement to Burnet's history of my own time* (Oxford, 1902)

Greatrakes, V., *A brief account of Mr. Valentine Greatrak's & divers of the strange cures by him lately performed written by himself* (1666)

Greene, D.G. (ed.), *Diaries of the Popish Plot* (New York, 1977)

The Correspondence of the family of Hatton, ed. E.M. Thompson (2 vols, 1878)

Historical Manuscripts Commission Reports

Howell, T.B. (ed.), *State Trials* (21 vols, 1816)

Hyland, P. (ed.), *Ned Ward, The London Spy* (Lansing, Michigan, 1993)

Journal of the House of Commons

Journal of the House of Lords

Kirkby, C., *A Compleat true narrative of the manner of the discovery of the Popish plot to his majesty by Mr. Christopher Kirkby with a full answer to a late pamphlet entitled reflections upon the earl of Danby relating to the murther of sir Edmundbury Godfrey in a letter to a friend* (1679)

Le Neve, J., *Lives and characters of the most illustrious persons British and foreign who died in the year 1712* (1713)

L'Estrange, R., *A brief history of the plot* (1679)

——, *A brief history of the times* (1688)

——, *The Observator in a dialogue, the third volume* (1687)

The Lexington Papers, ed. H. Manners-Sutton (1851)

List of the merchants of London (1677)

Lloyd, W., *A sermon at the funeral of Sir Edmund Bury Godfrey* (1678)

London Gazette (1678–85)

Lord, G.F. de (general ed.), *Poems on affairs of state, Augustan satirical verse, 1660–1714* (7 vols., 1963–75)

Lowther, J., *Memoirs of the reign of James II* (York, 1808)

MacCormick, C. (ed.) *The Secret History of the Court and Reign of Charles the Second by a member of his privy council,* (2 vols, 1792)

McCormick, I.(ed.), *Secret sexualities: a source book of seventeenth- and eighteenth-century writing* (1997)

M.D., *A seasonable advice to all true protestants in England in this present posture of affairs, discovering the present designs of the papists with other remarkable things to the peace of the church and the security of the Protestant religion* (1679)

Mansell, R., *An exact and true narrative of the late Popish intrigue to form a plot and then cast the guilt and odium thereof upon the Protestants* (1680)

The Poems and Letters of Andrew Marvell, ed. H.M Margoliouth (third edn, 2 vols, Oxford, 1971)

Marvell, A., *An account of the growth of Popery and arbitrary government in England* (1678)

Morland, S., *The description and use of true arithmetick instruments &c* (1673)

North, R., *Examen* (1740)

——, *Lives of the Norths* (3 vols, 1890)

Oates, T., *A true narrative of the horrid plot and conspiracy of the Popish party against the life of his sacred majesty, the government and the protestant religion* (1679)

Palmer, T., *The admirable secrets of physick and chyurgery* (1696)

The Diary of Samuel Pepys, eds R. Latham and W. Matthews (11 vols., 1970–83)

Playford, J., *Vade mecum, or the necessary companion* (1680 edn)

Poems on affairs of state from the reign of K. James the first to this present year 1703 written by the greatest wits of the age (2 vols, 1703)

Prance, M., *A true narrative and discovery of several remarkable passages relating to the horrid popish plot as they fell within the knowledge of Mr Miles Prance* (1679)

——, *The additional narrative of Miles Prance of Covent Garden goldsmith* (1679)

Rapin-Thoyrns, Paul de, *The History of England* (third edn, 5 vols, 1743–5)

Records of the English Province of the Society of Jesus (7 vols, 1877–83)

Memoirs of Sir John Reresby, ed. M.K. Geiter and W.A. Speck (second edn, 1991)

Collected Works of John Wilmot, Earl of Rochester, ed. J. Hayward (1926)

The Poems of John Wilmot, Earl of Rochester, ed. K. Walker (1984)

John Wilmot, Earl of Rochester, the Complete Works, ed. F.S. Ellis (Harmondsworth, 1994)

The Complete Works of Thomas Shadwell, ed. M. Summers (5 vols, 1927)

Bibliography

Shadwell, T., *The Lancashire witches or Teague O'Divelly, the Irish priest* (1682).

Sheppard, W., *A sure guide for his majesty's Justices of the Peace plainly showing their duty (1669 edn)*

The diary of the times of Charles the Second by Henry Sidney, ed. R.D. Blencowe (2 vols, 1843)

Smith, S., *An account of the behaviour of the fourteen late popish malefactors whilst in Newgate and their discourses with the ordinary* (1679)

Smith, W., *Contrivances of the fanatical conspirators in carrying on their treasons under the umbrage of the Popish Plot, laid open* (1685)

——, *Intrigues of the Popish Plot laid open with depositions sworn before the Secretary of State* (1685)

Somers Tracts, ed. W. Scott (second edn, 13 vols, 1809–15)

Stow, J., *Survey of London* ([1603] 1987 edn)

Thompson, N., *True Domestick Intelligence* (1679–80)

——, *A true and perfect narrative of the late terrible and bloody murder of Sir Edmund Berry Godfrey who was found murthered on Thursday the 17th of this instant October in a field near Primrose Hill with a full accompt of the manner in which he was found also the full proceedings of the Coroner who sat upon the inquest &c* (1678)

Tonge, E., *An exact account of Romish doctrines in the case of conspiracy and rebellion by pregnant observations collected out of the express dogmatical principles of the papists, priests and Jesuits* (1679)

——, *Jesuits assassins, or the Popish plot further declared and demonstrated in their murderous practices and principles, the first part* (1680)

——, *The northern star: the British monarchy: or, the northern, the fourth universal monarchy: Charles II and his successors the founders of the northern, last, fourth and most happy monarchy, being a collection of many choice ancient and modern prophecies* (1680)

Tuke, R., *Memoires of the life and death of Sir Edmund Berry Godfrey* (1682)

Verney Letters of the eighteenth century from the MSS at Claydon House, ed. M.M. Verney (2 vols, 1930)

Waller, W., *The tragical history of Jetzer* (1679)

Warner, J., *The history of the English persecution of Catholics and the Presbyterian Plot*, ed. T. A. Birrel and J. Blish (Catholic Record Society, 1953), XLVII–XLVIII

Westergaard, W., *The First Triple Alliance, the letters of Christopher Linenov Danish envoy to London, 1668–1672* (New Haven, 1947)

Whiteman, A., *The Compton census of 1676: a critical edition* (Oxford, 1986)

Williams, N., *Imago saeculi: the image of the age represented in four characters viz: the ambitious statesman, instatiable miser, aetheistical gallant, factious schismatick* (Oxford, 1676)

Wingate, E., *Justice revived being the whole office of a country Justice of the Peace* (1661 edn)

Wilson, J.H. (ed.), *Court Satires of the Restoration* (Ohio, 1975)

Bibliography

SELECTED SECONDARY SOURCES

Abbott, W.C., 'The origin of Titus Oates' story', *English Historical Review*, XXV (1910)

Allen, D., 'Bridget Hyde and Lord Treasurer Danby's alliance with Lord Mayor Vyner', *Guildhall Studies in London History*, II (1975)

——, 'The political function of Charles II's Chiffinch', *Huntingdon Library Quarterly*, XXXIX (1975–6)

Allen, P., 'Medical education in seventeenth-century England', *Journal of the History of Medicine*, I (1946)

Alumni Oxonienses, the members of the University of Oxford, 1500–1714 (8 vols, 1891)

Archer, D.T. 'The code of honour and its critics: the opposition to duelling in England 1700–1850', *Social History*, V (1980)

Archer, I., *The Pursuit of Stability: Social Relations in Elizabethan London* (Cambridge, 1991)

Ashton, R., 'Samuel Pepys' London', *The London Journal*, XI (1985)

Audrey Locke, A., *The Seymour Family: History and Romance* (1911)

Aveling, J., *The Handle and the Axe* (1976)

Barclay, A., 'The rise of Edward Colman', *Historical Journal*, XLII (1999)

Barnes, A.S., 'Catholic chapels royal under the Stuart kings: IV, The later years of Charles II and James II', *Downside Review*, XXI (1902)

Basset, B., *The English Jesuits* (1967)

Baxter, S.B., *William III* (1966)

Beaven, A.B., *The Aldermen of the City of London* (1908)

Beier, L., and Findlay, R.(eds), *London, 1500–1700, the making of the metropolis* (1986)

Bell, W.G., *The Great Fire of London in 1666* (1920)

——, *The Great Plague in London in 1665* (1951 edn)

Bellenger, Dom. A., *English and Welsh Priests 1558–1800, a working list* (Downside Abbey, Bath, 1984)

Bennett, E., *The Worshipful Company of Carmen of London* (1952)

Benson, D.R., 'Halifax and the trimmers', *Huntingdon Library Quarterly*, XXVII (1963–4)

Beresford Chamberlain, E., *The Annals of the Strand, topographical and historical* (1912)

Birrell, T.A., 'Roger North and political morality in the late Stuart period', *Scrutiny*, XVII (1951)

Black, J. (ed.), *Culture and Society in Britain, 1600–1800* (Manchester)

——, and Gregory, J. (eds), *Culture, Politics and Society in Britain, 1660–1800* (Manchester, 1991)

Bloch, M., *The Royal Touch, Sacred Monarchy and Scrofula in England and France* (1973)

Borgman, A.S., *Thomas Shadwell, his Life and Comedies* (New York, 1989)

Bibliography

Bossy, J., *The English Catholic Community 1570–1850* (1975)

Bray, A., *Homosexuality in Renaissance England* (New York, 1995 edn)

Brett-James, N.G., *The Growth of Stuart London* (1935)

Bromley, J.S., and Kossmann, E.H. (eds), *Britain and the Netherlands: V, Some Political Mythologies* (Hague, 1975)

Brown, K.M., 'Gentlemen and thugs in seventeenth-century Britain', *History Today*, XL (1990)

Browning, A., 'Parties and party organization in the reign of Charles II', *Transactions of the Royal Historical Society*, fourth series, XXX (1946)

——, *Thomas Osborne, Earl of Danby and Duke of Leeds, 1632–1712* (3 vols, Glasgow, 1951)

Buckley, J., 'Selections from a general account book of Valentine Greatrakes A.D. 1663–1679', *Journal of the Waterford and South East of Ireland Archaeological Society*, XI (1908)

Campbell, G., *Imposter at the Bar, William Fuller, 1670–1733* (1961)

Carpenter, E., *The Protestant Bishop, being the life of Henry Compton 1632–1713 bishop of London* (1956)

Chalkin, C.W., *Seventeenth-century Kent, a social and economic history* (1965)

Christie, W.D., *A Life of Antony Ashley Cooper, 1st Earl of Shaftesbury, 1667–1683* (2 vols, 1871)

Christison, R., 'Murder by suffocation', *Edinburgh Medical and Surgical Journal*, XXI (1829)

Clark, M., and Crawford, C. (eds), *Legal Medicine in History* (Cambridge, 1994)

Clarke, P., *English Provincial Society from the Reformation to the Revolution: Religion, Politics and Society in Kent, 1500–1640* (1977)

Colvin, H.M., *The History of the King's Works* (7 vols, 1976)

Cook, H.J., *Trials of an Ordinary Doctor, Joannnes Groenvelt in Seventeenth-century London* (Baltimore, 1994)

Cowper Coles, A., ' "A place much clogged and pestered with carts", Hartshorne Lane and Angel Court, *c.*1614–*c.*1720', *London Topographical Record*, XVII (1995)

Crawford, R., *The Last Days of Charles II* (Oxford, 1909)

Dabhoiwala, F., 'The constraints of honour, reputation and status in late seventeenth- and early eighteenth-century England', *Transactions of the Royal Historical Society*, sixth series, VI (1996)

Dale, H.B., *The Fellowship of the Woodmongers, Six Centuries of London Coal Trade* (1923)

——, 'The Worshipful Company of Woodmongers and the coal trade in London', *Royal Society of Arts Journal* (1922)

Debus, A.G. (ed.), *Medicine in Seventeenth-century England, a symposium held at UCLA in honour of C.D. O'Malley* (Los Angeles, 1974)

De Krey, G., *A Fractured Society, the Politics of London in the First Age of Party, 1689–1715* (1985)

Delaune, T., *Angliae metropolis or the present state of London* (1690 edn)

D'Elboux, R.H., 'An armorial Lambeth Delf plate', *Archaeologia Cantiana*, LX (1947)

De Quincey, T., *The English Mail-coach and other Essays* (1933 edn)

Dickson Carr, J., *The Murder of Sir Edmund Berry Godfrey* (1936)

Dolan, Dom. G., 'James II and the Benedictines in London', *Downside Review*, XVIII (1899)

Dugdale, G.S., *Whitehall Through the Centuries* (1950)

Dures, A., *English Catholicism, 1558–1642* (1983)

Earle, P., *A City Full of People, Men and Women of London 1650–1750* (1994)

——, *The Making of the English Middle-class: Business, Society and Family Life in London 1660–1730* (1989)

Echard, L., *History of England* (3 vols, 1718)

Evans, A.M., 'The imprisonment of lord Danby in the Tower, 1679–1684', *Transactions of the Royal Historical Society*, fourth series, XII (1929)

Everitt, A., *The Community of Kent and the Great Rebellion, 1640–1660* (Leicester, 1966)

Faller, L.B., *Turned to Account, the Forms and Functions of Criminal Biography in later Seventeenth- and Early Eighteenth-century England* (Cambridge, 1987)

'The family of Godfrey', *Gentleman's Magazine*, CXXIII (1848)

Feiling, K., *A History of the Tory Party, 1640–1714* (Oxford, 1959 edn)

Feret, C.J., *Fulham Old and New* (3 vols, 1900)

Firth, C.H., *The Last Years of the Protectorate* (2 vols, 1909)

Forbes, T.R., 'Inquests into London and Middlesex homicides 1673–1782', *Yale Journal of Biology and Medicine*, L (1977)

——, *Surgeons at the Bailey, English Forensic Medicine to 1878* (New Haven, 1985)

Forneron, H., *Louise de Kerouaille, Duchess of Portsmouth, 1649–1734* (second edn, 1887)

Foxcroft, H.C., *The Character of a Trimmer, being a short life of the first marquis of Halifax* (Cambridge, 1946)

——, *The Life and Letters of Sir George Savile, Bart., First Marquis of Halifax* (2 vols, 1898)

Foyster, E.A., *Manhood in Early Modern England, Honour, Sex and Marriage* (1999)

Fraser, A., *King Charles II* (1980 edn)

——, *The Weaker Vessel, Women's Lot in Seventeenth-century England* (1987 ed.)

Furley, O.W., 'The Pope-burning procession of the late seventeenth century', *History*, XLIV (1959)

Galer, G.H., and Wheeler, E.P., *The Survey of London, Charing Cross, St Martin's-in-the-Fields* (1935), XVI

——, *The Survey of London, the Strand* (1937), XVIII

Gardiner, S.R., *The History of England* (10 vols, 1900)

Gaskill, M., 'Reporting murder: fiction in the archives in early modern England', *Social History*, XXIII (1998)

Bibliography

Gatrell, V.A.C., *The Hanging Tree, Execution and the English people, 1770–1868* (Oxford, 1994)

George, M.D., *English Political Caricatures to 1792, a Study of Opposition and Propaganda* (Oxford, 1959)

——, *London Life in the Eighteenth Century* (1985 edn)

Gerard, J., 'History ex-hypothesis and the Popish Plot', *The Month*, CII (1912)

Godley, E., *The Trial of Count Königsmarck* (1929)

Grassby, R., 'The personal wealth of the business community in seventeenth-century England', *Economic History Review*, XXIII (1970)

Greene, D.G., *John Dickson Carr: the man who explained miracles* (New York, 1995)

Grose, C.L., 'Louis XIV's financial relations with Charles II and the English parliament', *Journal of Modern History*, I (1929)

Gwynn, A., 'Lord Acton and the Popish Plot', *Studies*, XXXIII (1944)

Haley, K.H.D., *The First Earl of Shaftesbury* (Oxford, 1968)

Halie, M., *Queen Mary of Modena, her life and letters* (1905)

Hall, A.R., and Hall, M.B., *The Correspondence of Henry Oldenburg* (13 vols, Madison, Wisconsin/London, 1965–86)

Hall, J., *Four Famous Mysteries* (1927)

Halstead, E., *History of Kent* (12 vols, 1897)

Harris, T., *London Crowds in the Reign of Charles II, Propaganda and Politics from the Restoration until the Exclusion Crisis* (Cambridge, 1987)

——, *Politics under the later Stuarts, Party Conflict in a Divided Society, 1660–1715* (1993)

——, Seaward, P., and Goldie, M. (eds), *The Politics of Religion in Restoration England* (1990)

Harrison, A.N., *The Family of Godfrey of Woodford, Essex and East Bergholt Suffolk* (Transactions of the Woodford and District Historical Society, pt. XII, 1966)

Hawkins, E., *Medallic Illustrations of the History of Great Britain and Ireland to the Death of George II* (2 vols, 1969 edn)

Hay, M.V., *The Jesuits and the Popish Plot* (1934)

Heal, F., and Holmes, C., *The Gentry of England and Wales, 1500–1700* (1994)

Henderson, T., *Disorderly Women in Eighteenth-century London, Prostitution and Control in the Metropolis 1730–1830* (1999)

Henning, B.D. (ed.), *The History of Parliament, the House of Commons, 1660–1690* (3 vols, 1983)

Hibbert, C., *The Road to Tyburn, the Story of Jack Sheppard and the Eighteenth-century Underworld* (1957)

Highfill, P.H., Burnim, K.A., Langhans, E.A.(eds), *A Biographical Dictionary of Actors, Actresses, Musicians, Dancers, Managers and other Stage Personnel in London, 1660–1800* (15 vols, Edwardsville, 1984)

Hinds, W.H., 'The Strand in the seventeenth century, its river front', *London and Middlesex Archaeological Society Transactions*, IV (1918–22)

Bibliography

Hitchcock, T., *English Sexualities, 1700–1800* (1997)
——, and Cohen, M.(eds), *English Masculinities, 1660–1680* (1999)
Holmes, G. (ed.), *Britain after the Glorious Revolution* (1969)
——, *The Making of a Great Power, late Stuart and early Georgian Britain 1660–1722* (1993)
Honeybourne, M.B., 'Charing Cross Riverside', *London Topographical Record*, XXI (1958)
Horwitz, H., *Revolution Politicks: the Career of Daniel Finch, second Earl of Nottingham, 1647–1730* (Cambridge, 1968)
Hotson, L., *The Commonwealth and Restoration Stage* (New York, 1962)
Hume, D., *The History of England from the Invasion of Julius Caesar to the Revolution in 1688* (6 vols, [1778] 1983 edn)
Hunnisett, R.F., *The Medieval Coroner* (Cambridge, 1961)
Hutton, R., *Stations of the Sun, a History of the Ritual Year in Britain* (Oxford, 1997)
——, *Charles II, King of England, Scotland and Ireland* (Oxford, 1989)
——, *The Restoration, a Political and Religious History of England and Wales, 1658–1667* (Oxford, 1985)
Israel, J. (ed.), *The Anglo-Dutch moment, essays in the Glorious Revolution and its world impact* (Cambridge, 1991)
Johnson, D.J., *Southwark and the City* (Oxford, 1969)
Jones, J.R., *Charles II, Royal Politician* (1987)
——, *The First Whigs, the Politics of the Exclusion Crisis, 1678–1683* (Oxford, 1961)
——, 'The Green Ribbon Club', *Durham University Journal NS*, XVIII (1956/7)
——, *The Revolution of 1688 in England* (1984)
Jusserand, J.J., *A French Ambassador at the court of Charles the Second* (1892)
Keiller, A., 'Medico-legal observations on manual strangulation and death by external violence with experiments and illustrative cases', *Edinburgh Medical Journal*, I (1855–6)
Kenyon, J.P., *The Popish Plot* (Harmondsworth, 1974)
——, *Robert Spencer, Earl of Sunderland, 1641–1702* (1958)
Kitchen, G., *Sir Roger L'Estrange, a contribution to the history of the press in the seventeenth century* (1971 edn)
Knight, S., *Jack the Ripper: the Final Solution* (1976)
Knights, M., *Politics and Opinion in Crisis, 1678–81* (Cambridge, 1994)
——, *The Killing of Justice Godfrey* (1986)
Kunzle, D., *The History of the Comic Strip, the early comic strip narrative strips and picture stories in the European broadsheet, c. 1450–1825* (Berkeley, 1973)
Lane, B., *The Encyclopaedia of Forensic Science* (1992)
Lane, J., *Titus Oates* (1971 edn)
Lang, A., *The Valet's Tragedy and Other Studies* (1903)
——, 'Who killed Sir Edmund Berry Godfrey?', *Cornhill Magazine*, XV (1903)
Laslett, P., 'The gentry of Kent', *Cambridge Historical Journal*, IX (1948)

Lee, M., *The Cabal* (Urbana, 1965)

Le Neve, J., *Lives and Characters of the Most Illustrious Persons British and Foreign who died in the year 1712* (1713)

Lodge, R., 'Review', *English Historical Review*, IXX (1904)

Lynn, J.A., *The Wars of Louis XIV, 1667–1714* (1999)

Lysons, D., *Historical account of those parishes in the counties of Middlesex which are not described in the environs of London* (1800)

McArthur, E.A., 'Sir Edmund Bury Godfrey Woodmonger', *English Historical Review*, XLIII (1928)

Macaulay, T.B., *The History of England from the Accession of James II* (4 vols, 1953 edn)

McCampbell, A., 'The London parish and the London precinct, 1640–1660', *Guildhall Studies in London History*, II (1976)

Maccubbin, R.P. (ed.), *'Tis Natures Fault, Unauthorized Sexuality during the Enlightenment* (Cambridge, 1987 edn)

MacDonald, M., and Murphy, T.R., *Sleepless Souls, Suicide in Early Modern England* (Oxford, 1990)

McMaster, J., *A short history of the royal parish of St Martin's-in-the-Fields* (1916)

Manley, G., 'A preliminary note on early meteorological observation in the London region 1690–1717, with estimates of the monthly mean temperatures, 1680–1706', *Meteorological Magazine*, XC (1961)

——, 'Seventeenth-century London temperatures: some further experiments', *Weather*, XVIII (1963)

Marks, A., 'The case of Sir Edmund Berry Godfrey', *The Month*, CIX (1906)

——, *Who killed Sir Edmund Berry Godfrey?* (1905)

Marshall, A., *The Age of Faction: Court Politics, 1660–1702* (Manchester, 1999)

——, *Intelligence and Espionage in the Reign of Charles II, 1660–1685* (Cambridge, 1994)

——, 'Sir Joseph Williamson and the conduct of administration in Restoration England', *Historical Research*, LXIX (1996)

——, 'To make a martyr: the Popish Plot and Protestant propaganda', *History Today*, XLVII (1997)

——, 'The Westminster magistrate and the Irish Stroker: Sir Edmund Godfrey and Valentine Greatrakes, some unpublished correspondence', *Historical Journal*, XL (1997)

Marshall, W.G., *The Restoration Mind* (Newark, 1997)

Metzger, E.C., *Ralph, First Duke of Montagu, 1636–1709* (New York, 1987)

Miller, H.K., Rothstein, E., and Rousseau, G.S. (eds), *The Augustan Milieu* (Oxford, 1970)

Miller, J., *Charles II* (1991)

——, 'The correspondence of Edward Coleman, 1674–78', *Recusant History*, XIV (1977–8)

——, *James II, A Study in Kingship* (1989 edn)

——, *Popery and Politics in England, 1660–1688* (Cambridge, 1973)

Muddiman, J.G., 'The mystery of Sir Edmund Bury Godfrey', *The National Review* (1924)

Murray, S.O., 'Homosexual acts and selves in early modern Europe', *Journal of Homosexuality*, XVI (1989)

Nef, J.U., 'Dominance of trade in the English coal industry in the seventeenth century', *Journal of Economic and Business History*, I (1929)

——, *The Rise of the British Coal Industry* (2 vols, 1966 edn)

Nichols, J., *Topographer and Genealogist* (3 vols, 1853)

Norton, R., *Mother Clap's Molly House: Gay Subculture in England 1700–1830* (1992)

Notes and Queries (1849–84)

Ogg, D., *England in the Reign of Charles II* (Oxford 1963 ed.)

——, *England in the Reigns of James II and William III* (Oxford, 1984 edn)

O'Neill, J.H., *George Villiers, Second Duke of Buckingham* (Boston, 1984)

Owen, S., *Restoration Theatre and Crisis* (Oxford, 1996)

Oxford Dictionary of Quotations (1979 edn)

Pain, N., 'Who killed Sir Edmund Berry Godfrey?', BBC Home Service, broadcast transcript, 16 September 1952

Papillon, A.F.W., *Memoirs of Thomas Papillon of London, Merchant (1623–1702)* (Reading, 1887)

Pearl, V., 'Change and stability in seventeenth-century London', *The London Journal*, V (1979)

Peck, L.L., *Northampton: Patronage and Policy at the Court of James I* (1982)

Petherick, M., *Restoration Rogues* (1951)

Picard, L., *Restoration London* (1997)

Pike, L.O., *A History of Crime in England* (2 vols, 1876)

Piper, D., *Catalogue of Seventeenth-century Portraits in the National Portrait Gallery 1625–1714* (Cambridge, 1963)

Pollock, J., 'The case of Sir Edmund Berry Godfrey', *The Law Quarterly Review*, XXII (1906)

——, *The Popish Plot, a study in the history of the reign of Charles II* (Cambridge, 1903)

Porter, R. (ed.), *Myths of the English* (1994)

Porter, S., *The Great Fire of London* (Stroud, 1996)

Power, P.C., *History of Waterford, City and County* (Dublin, 1990)

Prest, W., *The Rise of the Barristers, a Social History of the English Bar, 1590–1640* (Oxford, 1991)

Priestley, M., 'London merchants and opposition politics in Charles II's reign', *Bulletin of the Institute of Historical Research*, XXIX (1956)

Ralph, J., *The History of England during the reigns of King William and Queen Anne and King George I, with introductory review of the reigns of the royal brothers Charles and James* (2 vols, 1744–6)

Ranke, L. von, *A History of England, principally in the seventeenth century* (6 vols, Oxford, 1875)

Rappaport, S., *Worlds within Worlds, Structures of Life in Sixteenth-century London* (Cambridge, 1989)

Richardson, J., *Camden Town and Primrose Hill Past* (1991)

Robbins, K. (ed.), *Religion and Humanism, studies in church history*, XVII (1981)

Robertson, S., 'Churches in Romney Marsh: Lydd', *Archaeologia Cantiana*, XIII (1880)

Robinson, C.J. *A register of the scholars admitted to Merchant Taylor's school from 1562–1874* (2 vols, 1888)

Roseveare, H.G., 'The damned combination, the port of London and the wharfingers cartel of 1695', *The London Journal*, XXI (1996)

Rupp, G., *Religion in England, 1688–1791* (Oxford, 1986)

Scholei, P.A., 'The Chapel Royal', *Musical Times*, XLII (1902)

Schlör, J., *Nights in the Big City: Paris, Berlin, London 1840–1930* (1998)

Scott, Dom. G., *Sacredness of majesty: the English Benedictines and the Cult of James II* (Huntingdon, Royal Stuart Society, 1984)

Scott, J., *Algernon Sidney and the Restoration Crisis, 1677–1683* (Cambridge, 1991)

Scouludi, I. 'Thomas Papillon, merchant and Whig, 1623–1702', *Proceedings of the Huguenot Society of London*, XVIII (1947)

Screech, M.A., *Montaigne and Melancholy: The Wisdom of the Essays* (Harmondsworth, 1991)

Seymour, R., *A survey of the cities of London and Westminster, borough of Southwark and parts adjacent* (2 vols, 1735)

Sharpe, J.A., *Crime in Early Modern England, 1550–1750* (1999 edn)

——, *Crime in Seventeenth-century England, a county study* (Cambridge, 1983)

Sharpe, K., *The Personal Rule of Charles I* (Yale, 1992)

Sheppard, F., *London, a history* (Oxford, 1998)

'Sir Edmund Berry Godfrey', *Gentleman's Magazine*, CXXIV (1848)

Shoemaker, R., *Prosecution and Punishment, Petty Crime and the Law in London and rural Middlesex, c.1660–1725* (Cambridge, 1991)

Sloan, A.W., *English Medicine in the Seventeenth Century* (Bishop Auckland)

Smuts, R.M., 'The Court and its neighbourhood, royal policy and urban growth in the early West End', *Journal of British Studies*, XXX (1991)

Sonnino, P., *Louis XIV and the Origins of the Dutch War* (Cambridge, 1988)

Speck, W.A., *Reluctant Revolutionaries: Englishmen and the Revolution of 1688* (Oxford, 1988)

Spurr, J., *The Restoration Church of England 1646–1689* (1991)

Stapleton, A., *London Lanes* (1930)

Stone, L., *The Crisis of the Aristocracy, 1558–1646* (Oxford, 1967 edn)

——, *The Family, Sex and Marriage in England 1500–1800* (1979 edn)

Storr, A., *Churchill's Black Dog and Other Phenomena of the Mind* (1994)

Bibliography

Stoye, J., *English Travellers Abroad, 1604–1667* (1989 edn)

Sugden, P., *The Complete History of Jack the Ripper* (1995 edn)

Summers, M., *The Playhouse of Pepys* (New York, 1964 edn)

Sutch, V.D., *Gilbert Sheldon, Architect of Anglican Survival 1640–1675* (Hague, 1973)

Taylor, A.S., 'Remarks on death from strangulation', *The Edinburgh Medical and Surgical Journal*, LXXVII (1852)

Thomas, K., *Religion and the Decline of Magic, studies in popular beliefs in sixteenth- and seventeenth-century England* (1980 edn)

Thormählen, M., *Rochester, the poems in context* (Cambridge, 1995)

Thorne, J., *Handbook of the Environs of London* (2 vols., 1876)

Thornbury, W., and Walford, E., *Old and new London, a narrative of its history, its people and its places* (6 vols, 1873–8)

Timbs, J., *Curiosities of London* (1876)

Trumbach, R., 'London's sodomites: homosexual behaviour and western culture in the eighteenth century', *Journal of Social History*, XI (1977)

Turner, F.C., *James II* (1948)

'The Visitation of the county of Kent', *Archaeologia Cantiana*, VI (1866)

Walker, D.M., *The Oxford Companion to the Law* (Oxford, 1980)

Warnicke, R.M., *William Lambarde Elizabethan antiquary 1536–1661* (1973)

Webb, S. and B., *English Local Government, the Parish and the County* (1906)

——, *English Local Government, Standing Authority for Special Purposes* (1921)

Webb, S.S., 'Brave men and servants to his royal highness: the household of James Stuart in the evolution of English imperialism', *Perspectives in American History*, VIII (1974)

Weber, H., *The Restoration Rake-hero: transformations in sexual understanding in seventeenth-century England* (Madison, Wisconsin, 1986)

Webster, A.D., *The Regent's Park and Primrose Hill, history and antiquaries* (1911)

Weinreb, B. and Hibbert, C., *The London Encyclopaedia* (1983)

Westerfield, R.B., *Middlemen of English Business, particularly between 1660–1760* (Yale, 1915)

Wheatley, H.P., and Lunnington, P., *London Past and Present* (3 vols, 1891)

Whitaker-Wilson, C., *Whitehall Palace* (1934)

Whiting, J.R.S., *A Handful of History* (Dursley, 1978)

Williams, M.E., *St Alban's College, Valladolid* (1986)

Williams, S., 'The Pope burning processions of 1679, 1680 and 1681', *Journal of the Warburg and Courtauld Institutes*, XXI (1958)

Williamson, H.R., *Historical Enigmas* (1974)

Wilson, J.H., *The Ordeal of Mr Pepys's Clerk* (Ohio, 1972)

Winn, J.A., *John Dryden and his World* (Yale, 1987)

Wolf, J.B., *Louis XIV* (New York, 1968).

Wolpert, L., *Malignant Sadness: the Anatomy of Depression* (1999)

Bibliography

Woodhead, J.R., *The Rulers of London 1660–1689, a biographical record of the aldermen and common councilmen of the city of London* (London and Middlesex Archaeological Society, 1965)

Wrightson, K., *English Society, 1580–1680* (1986)

Index